# COUNTERPOINT

*A Translation of KONTRAPUNKT*
by HEINRICH SCHENKER

Volume II
of *New Musical Theories and Fantasies*

Book II
Counterpoint in Three and More Voices
Bridges to Free Composition

*Translated by John Rothgeb and Jürgen Thym*

EDITED BY JOHN ROTHGEB

SCHIRMER BOOKS
*A Division of Macmillan, Inc.* New York
*Collier Macmillan Publishers* London

Collier Macmillan Canada, Inc.

Library of Congress Catalog Card Number: 86-18645

Printed in the United States of America

printing number
1   2   3   4   5   6   7   8   9   10


**Library of Congress Cataloging-in-Publication Data**

Schenker, Heinrich, 1868–1935.
   Counterpoint: a translation of Kontrapunkt.

   "Volume II of New musical theories and fantasies."
   Bibliography: p.
   Contents: bk. 1. Cantus firmus and two-voice counter-
point—bk. 2. Counterpoint in three and more voices,
Bridges to free composition.
   1. Counterpoint.   I. Rothgeb, John.   II. Title.
MT55.S2413   1987        781.4'2        86-18645
ISBN 0-02-873220-0 (set)
ISBN 0-02-873221-9 (v. 1)
ISBN 0-02-873222-7 (v. 2)

*To the Memory of My Mother*

# Contents

# Author's Preface

How am I to teach my children to sort out
the useless and the harmful?
Tell me!
Tell them about heaven and earth
what they will never comprehend!—Goethe

The most insidious of all errors is when
good young minds think they will lose
their originality by recognizing as true
what has already been recognized as true
by others.—Goethe

Twelve years have passed since the publication of the first volume of *Counterpoint*. But during this protracted interval my activity has not ceased; on the contrary, I have occupied myself by design with works that had the function of amplifying the basic concepts of the [*Neue musikalische*] *Theorien und Phantasien*.[1] As I found it useful at the time—following the demands of necessity—to precede *Counterpoint* with *Harmony* as the first volume, and, as I felt compelled—again following demands of necessity—to juxtapose immediately with voice leading in two-voice counterpoint the prolongations of free composition, by the same logic it appeared useful to show the operation of the laws I presented in *Harmony* and *Counterpoint I* in living works of art of the highest rank, even before I clarified those laws in subsequent volumes revealing their higher manifestation. For, as I have said, exigencies of the present time have inexorably demanded this sacrifice. The works I refer to are *Beethoven's neunte Sinfonie* (1912); *Erläuterungsausgabe der letzten fünf Sonaten Beethovens:* op. 109 (1913), op. 110 (1914), op. 111 (1915), op. 101 (1920); the edition of all the piano sonatas by Beethoven (thus far, eighteen sonatas); and *Der Tonwille*, vol. I (1921).[2]

This work-plan had the advantage that in the present volume, I could refrain from such a detailed and extensive comparison of strict counterpoint and free composition as was necessary in the first. I considered it important, however, to maintain the encyclopedic method of presentation.

If my theories (like all my other works) have been imprinted from the outset with the character of a rescue-effort (since the task at hand was to protect music from centuries of misconceptions by theory and historicism), the need for such endeavor has increased proportionately as the intervening World War has loosed all forces of destruction that have utterly eradicated musical art in the West. Today the task before us is more to transmit the essence of music to more distant eras, since we cannot expect it to be restored in the near future.

How appalling the image of desperation and impotence presented by our time! What a contrast to a truly art-creating, or even just art-perceiving epoch!

The World War resulted in a Germany which, although unvanquished in battle, has been betrayed by the democratic parties—the parties of the average and the inferior, of half- and non-education, of the most flagrant individuals ("each," as Brahms liked to say, "a summit unto himself"—a summit of humanity); the parties of incapacity for synthesis, of "omnipotence" (that is: impotence), of the most irresponsible doctrinarism and the blood-thirstiest insatiability for experimentation, along with terrorism, genocide, forgery, the lie of "the people," worship and aping of the West, and all that goes with it. This Germany has taken over from the hostile nations of the West their lie of "liberty." Thus the last stronghold of aristocracy has fallen, and culture is sold out to democracy, which, fundamentally and organically, is hostile to it—for culture is selection, the most profound synthesis based on miraculous achievements of the genius.

Since that time the decay continues unabated. It surely is not politics to say in retrospect that the Roman nation has done more of harm to world culture through its insatiable appetite for lands and peoples than of service through its modest intellectual legacy; by the same token, it is no more political when we evaluate nations still active today, just as we would evaluate individuals, with respect to the relation between claims and achievements.[3] The peoples of the West, contaminated by deception and profiteering and barely touched by civilization, have, under a leadership even more cunning [than that of the Roman Empire]—in fact, a leadership more depraved than anything that sits confined under lock and key—subsequently feigned "victory" by continuing, against the letter and spirit of the treaty [of Versailles], the blockade of the German stomach; by waging an economic war on behalf of their own backwardness; by pillaging nations and lands (or having the "League of Nations"—a veritable academy of national theft—do the pillaging); and by invading the nations, as yet unvanquished by them, with commissions and occupation armies, and sucking them dry. Up to this hour they wallow in the filth of such cowardice against a disarmed Germany; yet they already verge on rivalry with each other for "hegemony": there are just so many cravings for hegemony as there are nations! We know the lie of democratic "equality," which in the end plays itself out in the act of repression!

If capitalism fights now as ever against capitalism, and democracy against democracy, rallying slogans such as "international capital" and "brotherhood of the people" are given the lie. The fact that during the war workers stood against workers has likewise sufficiently exposed the lie of the "international proletariat." The masses are told that they have won, and they believe it. But masses can never win. In all corners of the earth and at all times, masses have been nothing but an eternal slumberer, a humus that is colored differently in different places only for climatic reasons. True, the masses were given their right to vote (*circenses*), but that has not changed the fact that millions of Chinese, Indians, Germans, Englishmen, and Frenchmen as well as thousands

of panderers to the people are worth less than just one Chinese, Indian, German, Englishman, or Frenchman. For masses become a suitable tool—be the cause noble or evil—only in the hands of an individual (for example, Gandhi or Kemal-Pascha). Alas, those people-panderers! More wretched and miserable than all the court-panderers, they themselves do not know the truth and only deceive the masses. (Isaiah: "My dear people, those who praise and esteem you, deceive you.") At best, they revel in the fruits of their "leadership" like musical directors performing hack-works: whatever boredom or repulsion may torture the listener, the conductor beats time and, thus, feels himself occupied, even pleasantly entertained. But in view of such unsuitability of the masses and the people-panderers, is it not certain that secret diplomacy will be conducted, the parliament deceived, and, finally, the masses lied to—worse than could ever have happened under monarchs?

But democracy stubbornly resists recognizing its own misconceptions and lies, its violations of nature and culture. If Nature herself decreed evolution for humankind from its cradle onward, the people-panderers have proclaimed evolution to be unnecessary for a democratic man: as he is, so he remains—perfect, faultless, even without synthesis an art-work of creation. If, according to the teaching of one of its greatest spokesmen—the teaching of a Goethe—, culture characterizes the meaning of life with the words *Stirb und werde!* [Die and become!],[4] the people-panderers teach instead that man arrives on earth in perfect and unalterable condition, provided only—in keeping with the democratic belief taught in school and in the world—that he avoid any ties, any connections with his ancestors. The democrat will not comprehend that there truly exist more divine miracles than Western skepticism and relativism can ever imagine. He has long since lost that wonderful astonishment, such as the Bible proclaims in its own way when commemorating the miracles of creation. He always sees only himself and the work of his hands as well as his calculations; he cares little for God, the "manufacturer" (to use his own language) of so many enigmas. In the worthless school of the West, the modern democrat has learned to be silent about God just as he prefers to be silent about any particular human genius. What is left to him is a kind of talcum of the soul (but ask not how attractive the soul is when the talcum has been blown away), commerce, and manual labor.

If universal intelligence, using Goethe—to cite again this most illustrious chief witness of culture—as a medium, praises "activity" [in general], the people-panderer associates this virtue only with manual labor, as, allegedly, the only activity that yields value. Where Goethe leads his Wilhelm Meister from noble dilettantisms to a useful occupation, democracy on the contrary guides its followers away from occupations (which would perhaps better suit them, or would at least be honorable) to activities and pursuits inappropriate to them. How completely their efforts contradict Goethe's dictum:

The most reasonable thing is always that each pursue the metier into which he was born and which he has learned, and that he not hinder his neighbor from

whose principal demand from man is to consider the other more eternal than his ego, to dedicate himself to the other, but not to place himself above the other, and to perpetuate himself through it so as to conquer eternity. Thus it is precisely trade that threatens culture, and thereby the true immortality of mankind: it questions the survival of the genius, the real connection to posterity, and barricades the pathways to a deeper understanding.

---

Art may be recommended to mankind as the only help in time of need, the only means of reconstruction! Let mankind learn to tame through art the chaos that lurks in any matter—to tame it through selection and synthesis.

I remind the reader of what I have said about tonality already in the first volume [*Harmony*]: No key at all could have been established, had not the way of pure Nature been abandoned, and the natural sequence of perfect fifths been adulterated with the admixture of the artificial, false, diminished fifth interval between the VII and IV steps. [See *Harmony,* §17ff.] There they sit for centuries, those faithful to utopian ideals, bourgeois and worker, snob by snob, and enthusiastically applaud masterworks that could be born only because they used the false fifth! Do they think that the synthesis of the state can be achieved without a false fifth, and do they expect of their product that it will appear more just and perfect than the state-syntheses of the past? They deceive themselves. Posterity will certainly applaud more heartily all those state-syntheses of the past, with their false fifths, than those allegedly natural, and yet so falsified, state-monstrosities of today. Schopenhauer puts it as follows:

> In general, one could hypothesize that the law were of a quality analogous to certain chemical substances that cannot be presented in their pure and isolated form, but only with the aid of a small admixture that serves as a carrier or provides them with the necessary consistency—chemicals such as fluoride, even alcohol, hydrocyanic acid, and so forth. Accordingly, if the law wanted to gain a foothold and even prevail in the real world, it would necessarily require a small admixture of arbitrariness and force in order to be effective and lasting in this concrete and material world (in spite of its actual ideal and thus ethereal nature) without evaporating and flying off into the sky, as happens in Hesiod. All birthrights, all privileges by inheritance, all state religions and much besides may be regarded as the necessary chemical basis or amalgam described above; the law could be effectively and consistently practiced only on a firm foundation of this nature which thus would function, in a sense, as the δός μοι ποῦ στῶ[7] of law.

Let mankind observe in art the continuous natural growth of phenomena from the basis of a few principal laws, and learn to trust the power of growing outward from within more than the whims of that low plateau of humanity which believes it possible (or even necessary) to create new laws with each new motion of hand or mouth.

I have set forth in *Counterpoint I* the fundamental laws to the extent that they were revealed in two-voice counterpoint. Using the content of the present volume as a point of departure, I would like to give here an overview of the further growth [of these laws].

In three-voice counterpoint, the consonance is prolonged to $\frac{5}{3}$ and $\frac{6}{3}$. The intervals 5 and 6 signify the limits of the consonance-concept, which neither four- nor many-voice settings can transcend (p. 1f.). The fifth is the limit given by nature; the sixth is a derivative.

In $\frac{5}{3}$ is contained, at the same time, the roothood-tendency of the lowest tone; it reveals the desire of any lowest tone to be, above all, a root (p. 8).

In three-voice counterpoint, the setting of the outer voices becomes the vehicle of the basic two-voice counterpoint. The prolongation of two-voice counterpoint thus prevails over the three-voice format, and the voice-leading is the more beautiful the better it succeeds in resolving the conflict between the [demands of] three-voice format and setting of the outer voices in favor of the latter (p. 5f.).

Setting in three voices leads naturally to the necessity of distinguishing between open and close position (p. 25). Just an awareness of this distinction may lead to benefits for the voice leading.

The emergence of the $\frac{6}{4}$ sonority suggests particular new questions and possibilities (p. 37ff.).

The addition of a third voice often makes nonparallel similar motions [to perfect consonances] necessary if other important merits of voice leading are not to suffer. The basic prohibition of such successions in two-voice counterpoint, however, is not invalidated by this fact; compensation is provided, in a certain sense, only by means of other effects. The social relations between tones thus requires proof of necessity, and the poor effect of an unjustified license is evidence for the urgency of the prohibition (p. 27ff.).

Since only two leading tones are available for concluding a melodic line, and no others are conceivable, the third voice can do nothing but make use of a tone that is not a leading tone. This third tone has the function of contributing to completeness of harmony. Under certain circumstances it can be only that fundamental tone we know from free composition as that of scale degree V; but it has no further right to affect the laws of leading tones and thus the social relations between tones (pp. 45 and 65).

In the framework of three-voice settings, moreover, the essence of passing tones reveals new depths and prolongations. The dissonant passing tone in the lower voice points precisely toward the [concept of the] scale degree in that it causes the memory to retain the consonant point of departure for the whole duration of the passing motion (p. 56). The increment in harmony occasionally turns even consonant second-progressions into a type of consonant passing or neighboring tone (p. 60). Retention [in memory] of the more clearly defined harmony of the downbeat already provides a glimpse of the fourth-space (p. 73); at the same time, the possible rhythmic forms of the neighboring note become clearer (p. 75). Accordingly, the concept of composing-out makes a significant step forward (p. 58). The nodal points of the third are observed in passing motions (p. 58), while the neighboring note leads to the concept of substitution (p. 76). And the combined species reveal, for the first time, additional prolongations of the concept of the passing tone: an actual dissonant passing tone can even ensnare a leapwise interval, and this is the origin of the leaping passing tone (p. 182). The exchange of voices appears for the first time when two counterpoints are set in half- or quarter-notes (p. 179); and when two counterpoints are combined in different durations (half-notes together with quarters), a passing motion can produce for the first time a dissonant clash at the upbeat, which certainly extends the concept of the passing tone (p. 192). What brings us closest to the realm of free composition, however, is the experience that when several passing tones occur simultaneously, they join together in a kind of obbligato two-voice setting—that is, for the sake of their own clarification, they cultivate the consonance as the law of their relationship (p. 180). In a three- or four-voice setting with two or three counterpoints of the second species, this results most frequently in $\frac{6}{3}$-sonorities, which should be regarded as the soul of the passing-tone organism (p. 184). Just as downbeats, in the framework of cantus-firmus exercises, must take refuge in the consonance, so also must passing tones on the upbeat. And from the distance, the concept of passing harmonies of free composition already beckons; regardless of their passing-tone purpose, these harmonies want first to be understood in and for themselves, and, often enough, appear as consonant while fulfilling a dissonant function.

Three- and many-voice settings bring us closer to the distinction between the authentic suspensions $\frown 9 - 8, \frown 4 - 3$, and other indefinite syncopes which may (but need not) signify suspensions; this is a distinction that requires closest attention in free composition (p. 85). Even if the increment of harmony provides new interval-nourishment to the syncopes of two-voice counterpoint, the uniformity of the syncopation-concepts stands unaltered (p. 100). This uniformity leads us in the combined species to a freer use of syncopes as well as, in general, to new syncope-constructions that give rise to seventh-chords (p. 215). If it becomes especially obvious with the latter that the upbeat, although representing a resolution of a dissonant structure from the downbeat, nevertheless manifests more independence than an upbeat does in the case of authentic suspensions, we arrive at an interpretation of tying as ultimately a purely rhythmic phenomenon. And this conclusion in turn leads us to an application of the tie even to dissonant passing tones and neighboring notes, more in the service of the passing motion than with the intention of tying for its own sake. This occurs in its simplest form with sustained bass notes (in free composition they can be omitted); thus we have gained the first access to the organ point (p. 258).

The next and last volume of [*Neue musikalische*] *Theorien* [*und Phantasien*] will have the task of showing the further developments, up to that vast scope which they have been given by the German genius of music—and, in fact, *only* by him. As to the matter of synthesis, several works of mine are, as indicated before, already in print, and the "Entwurf einer neuen Formen-lehre"[8] previously announced will provide a concise overview. The sum total of my works present an image of art as self-contained, as growing of itself—but, despite all infinitude of appearance, as setting its own limits through selection and synthesis. It is my fervent wish that mankind may ultimately be permitted to be guided through the euphony of art to the noble spirit of selection and synthesis, and to shape all institutions of his earthly existence, such as state, marriage, love and friendship, into true works of art according to the laws of artistic synthesis!

# PART THREE

## Three-Voice Counterpoint

Semper idem, sed non eodem modo.

## *Chapter 1*

# The First Species: Note Against Note

### General Aspects

**§1.** *The two-voice foundation of voice leading remains present in three-voice counterpoint as well*

Three-voice counterpoint, too, is governed by the guiding principles of its two-voice counterpart, so much so that it is as if one were merely to add a third voice to a pair of voices constructed according to the precepts of two-voice counterpoint; this, however, can be done only by observing the same guiding principles (that is, those of two-voice counterpoint). In the light of this, then, it may be proclaimed as a basic principle that in three-voice settings, the [laws of] two-voice setting actually continue to apply; three-voice setting therefore represents merely a prolonged[1] phenomenon. And, as will be seen later on, the prolongation manifests itself, indeed, in all principles of three-voice counterpoint, both in the vertical direction, in relation to the fundamental law of consonance, and also in the horizontal, in relation to the other fundamental laws of voice leading.

**§2.** *Prolongation of the law of consonance*

To the extent that the three [simultaneous-sounding] tones of the counterpoint are to be of different pitch, the law of consonance itself (cf. Part 2, Chapter 1) restricts polyphony of three voices to $\frac{5}{3}$ or $\frac{6}{3}$. The concept of triad thus evolved in the vertical dimension of three-voice counterpoint, simply through the law of consonance first handed down by the voice leading of two-voice counterpoint. It had, to be sure, long since found fulfillment in appropriately constructed melodies of the horizontal dimension (see *Harmony*, p. 211ff., and *Cpt. I*, p. 17ff.). Now the triad reaches us by both routes, but with only this difference of effect: in the vertical dimension, it sounds in its complete, palpable, physical totality, so to speak, while the horizontal dimension unrolls it only step by step, through the detour of a melodic evolution—but, for precisely that reason, all the more cogently.[2]

### §3.  *Rejection of the ⁶₅-, ⁶₄-, and ⁶ᵇ₃sonorities*

Since the concept of triad was thus restricted, for the domain of three-voice counterpoint, to ⁵₃ and ⁶₃, the necessity of rejecting the sonority ⁶₅ followed as a natural consequence, although both of its intervals are consonant with the bass. For purely contrapuntal experience alone has taught that the triad as such can be bounded by either 5 or 6, but not with both of these intervals at the same time. (The theory of harmony confirms in its own way this result of voice-leading theory, in that it distinguishes the fundamental position of the triad from the so-called inversions as mere derivatives, and thus denies the possibility of a phenomenon that could appear as both original position and inversion at the same time.)

Concerning the sonority ⁶₄, one might have expected that the added third interval [in three-voice counterpoint] would at last have been able to make the equivocal, and therefore dubious, effect of the fourth (*Cpt. I*, p. 112ff.) clearer than it could have been made in two-voice counterpoint. Why this decisive clarification still is not achieved even by three-voice counterpoint, however, can best be learned from free composition. The latter shows that ⁶₄ can be understood as consonant only when the sonority reveals itself to be an inversion of a triad that manifests true scale-degree character, thereby expressing the scale degree itself (*Cpt. I*, Example 155). Whatever reasons may have motivated the voice leading in a given case to take the path of ⁶₄ instead of ⁶₃ or ⁵₃, the decisive question in this matter always remains whether the scale degree actually underlies the ⁶₄-sonority. If it does, then ⁶₄ by itself ceases to function as ⁶₄ in the company of the scale degree, since the latter immediately converts ⁶₄ into ⁸₅₃:

**Example 1**

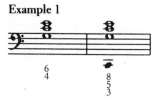

as though the triad stood simply in its fundamental position, which indeed knows nothing of a fourth above the root. (A merely passing ⁶₄-sound, however, must—precisely because it is merely passing—be interpreted only as a horizontal product; such a sound, therefore, simply never comes into consideration in evaluating a $\frac{6}{4}$-sonority that is to be understood vertically.) But since three-voice strict counterpoint lacks from the outset everything pertaining to scale degrees (see below, §15), the possibility of hearing $\frac{6}{4}$ from the vantage point of a scale degree accordingly vanishes. For that reason, the fourth, when it occupies the lowest position, continues to pose an obstacle for recognition of the quality of consonance, just as in two-voice counterpoint, so that the final consequence must be the fundamental inadmissibility of $\frac{6}{4}$ in three-voice counterpoint. It is important to formulate this result also in the following way: in contrast to free composition, strict counterpoint is not yet able to recognize a fourth in the vertical direction and a fifth in the same direction as fully equivalent.

It will be shown in subsequent chapters how the space of a fourth can be expressed already in strict counterpoint in the horizontal direction, by being filled in with passing tones. (The horizontal direction has, indeed, been available to the fourth from the outset, *Cpt. I,* p. 79ff.) This possibility at least paves the way for the ultimate prolongation reserved for free composition—a prolongation that culminates in recognition, under certain circumstances, of full equivalence of the fourth and fifth even in the vertical direction.

That finally the triad with diminished fifth—for example:

**Example 2**

—is also prohibited in three-voice counterpoint is likewise adequately grounded in the law of consonance found here in a prolonged form. It is no contradiction of this prohibition, however, if, in the case of $\frac{6}{4}$ the diminished fifth or augmented fourth is permitted in the inner voices:

**Example 3**

(Compare also *Cpt. I,* p. 114.) For through these positions, those intervals become thirds and sixths, which, as such, now adequately satisfy the law of consonance.[3] Granted, if scale degrees could manifest themselves in three-voice strict counterpoint, their force would undoubtedly be able even here, just as in free composition, to establish justification for the existence of the diminished triad, perhaps as scale degree VII in major or II in minor (see *FrC.,* "Musical Causality"[4]). Thus in the final analysis it is merely the absence of scale degrees that prevents the diminished triad in strict three-voice counterpoint from being included in the category of triads that are consonant or to be treated as consonant.[5] In a different formulation, included here expressly as a link to the theory of free composition, this result can be stated as follows: strict counterpoint knows nothing of that free treatment of the diminished fifth which inevitably becomes necessary in free composition, depending upon the circumstances, either by reason of scale degree or of a passing tone ([when the diminished triad occurs] as a passing-tone harmony).

### §4.  *Completeness of triads as the principal demand[6] of three-voice counterpoint*

The nature of three-voice polyphony itself (see above, §2) imposes first of all the demand that the three tones be of different pitch, or, which comes to the same thing, that each individual tone of the cantus firmus become wherever possible a constituent of a complete triad, $\frac{5}{3}$ or $\frac{6}{3}$.

By being able to stimulate the power of imagination from the outset in working out a three-voice exercise, the law of *completeness of triads* reveals itself as a heretofore unknown force of voice leading that is brought to life for the first time precisely in three-voice counterpoint, and, in conjunction with other forces, becomes a decisive ingredient of three-voice setting.

It remains to be shown, however, that, in spite of such considerations, three-voice counterpoint will appear the more convincing the more perfectly the two-voice counterpoint of the outer voices, above all, is manifested in it. And, likewise, it can be shown only later how the effect differs for the triadic postulate of strict counterpoint, on the one hand, and for the scale-degree postulate of free composition on the other—although even in free composition, in spite of all its display of scale degrees and prolonged laws, it is still, as always, only the two-voice counterpoint of the outer voices that remains in the foreground.

### §5.  *Prolongation of the voice-leading laws of two-voice counterpoint in counterpoint of three voices*

Often enough, on the other hand, it is the voice leading which—bound above all to the cantus firmus as something foreordained, and, through it, to the laws that took effect already in two-voice writing—nevertheless renders impossible the realization of that complete three-voice polyphony for all vertical sonorities. Thus there arises a constant interaction between the demand for triadic completeness and the laws of voice leading, so that in truth it is only the act of reconciling the two forces that represents the essence of three-voice counterpoint.

### §6.  *Incompleteness of triads as a product of reconciliation*

In the light of the necessity of reconciliation just mentioned, it is both permissible and obligatory in three-voice counterpoint that use be made not only of $\frac{5}{3}$ and $\frac{6}{3}$, but also of other sounds that get along without the property of completeness. Although these various harmonies, as will be shown below, certainly have different kinds of significance for contrapuntal usage, in strict counterpoint they are nevertheless conceived only in the sense of sonorities per se—that is, exclusively with reference to the intervals as they are presented by voice leading. No specific additional nomenclature is used for them, as it is in the theory of harmony, where terminology such as "sixth-chord" or "six-four chord" is common. For the theory of voice leading, it is perfectly adequate to derive the defining property from the demand for completeness of triads, and, accordingly, to classify sonorities first of all simply as *complete* and *incomplete.*

### §7. How the principles of two-voice counterpoint continue to apply, in a fundamental way, in the outer voices of three-voice counterpoint

The addition of the third voice by itself compels a discrimination of the high, the middle, and the low. If our ear then automatically focuses its attention on the upper and lower boundaries of the setting—that is, on the high and the low voice—, that simply lies in the nature of things that require no further explanation. The attraction of the outer voices, however, consequently leads to the quite natural demand that their setting above all be kept in view, and, optimally, that it be carried out in the manner of, precisely, a two-voice setting. This, then, is the meaning of the formulation enunciated already in §1, which now gains its ultimate precision through the following addendum: it is the outer voices that are to be regarded as the primary vehicles of the continued application, in three-voice counterpoint, of the principles of two-voice counterpoint.

Yet this demand is by no means to be interpreted as a recommendation that the three-voice setting always be prepared simply by first constructing an actual two-voice setting which is then to be filled out with a third, inner voice. Rather, it seeks only to make the student aware how thoroughly he must attend above all to the construction of the outer voices as a good two-voice setting—indeed, even in the event that the cantus firmus lies in the inner voices, and therefore in a position that seems to resist that demand and in which the executant is compelled to be guided at the same time by a mental image of three-voice polyphony (see above, §4). It is thus a matter of complete indifference in what manner the outer-voice counterpoint is achieved, so long as it exhibits that construction which is desired of a good two-voice setting.

It is clear, however, that when the cantus firmus lies in one of the outer voices, its very property of fluency cannot fail to benefit the totality of the two-voice counterpoint of the outer parts. But the student should not deceive himself on account of this advantage, which automatically attends such settings; he should not prematurely regard it as a possible merit of his activity. The latter smiles on him above all when the cantus firmus lies in the middle, and a good two-voice counterpoint is nevertheless formed between the outer voices.

It is most thoroughly in free composition that the secret of the outer voices gains new and elevated significance. There, finally, the transcendental world of scale degrees casts a light of its own on the physicality of the outer voices, in that it causes both, in a mysterious way, to be recognized ultimately as merely two upper voices of the posited lower third voice (that of the scale degree).

In the earlier literature the term "filler-interval" is encountered now and again; yet the authors, clearly, seem to have understood this term in a mere craftsmanly-external sense, and not at all as they should have in view of the profundity of the outer-voice problem.

### §8. *Ramifications of outer-voice intervals for triadic possibilities in general*

In consideration of the significance of the two-voice counterpoint of the outer parts as set down in the preceding paragraphs, it is perhaps advisable to take that counterpoint as the point of departure for any investigation that seeks to deal in a general way with triadic possibilities in three-voice counterpoint. In any case, such a procedure is more appropriate than an attempt to consider triadic possibilities merely in and for themselves, without any background. Therefore in the following paragraphs triadic possibilities will be presented and examined in terms of the intervals of the outer voices, to which end we will show the consequences of each interval, taken in turn, for three-voice polyphony.

This investigation, however, will at the same time be decisively influenced by the fact that wherever a multiplicity of possibilities is available (as is often the case here), it is precisely because of that multiplicity that the various possibilities with their different effects testify, so to speak, for or against each other, in that an available better possibility in a given case always prevails over one that is less good. I have already referred to this posture of judging a given situation with reference to other, merely possible, ones, incidentally, on several occasions in my treatment of two-voice counterpoint (*Cpt. I,* pp. 84, 92, and 207ff.). Now it is obvious, however, that the ear discovers hidden possibilities more easily the more it is cogently prepared by causal connections for what is to come. Thus in two-voice counterpoint it is still rather difficult to infer from a preceding harmony the one that is to follow, since against any given tone any of several consonances may be set, among which the selection is determined almost exclusively by the requirement of melodic fluency. There, in two-voice counterpoint, the clue to the coming consonance flows from a still very meager source, that is, the sense of overall line; and because the amount of causality is still so small, we perceive everything in a way only dimly. Causalities assert themselves with greater force in three-voice counterpoint, however; here, three voices are used as the basis of succession, and consequently, to the extent that the laws of consonance and of voice leading continue to be observed, a more accurately calculable range of possibilities is provided. This, then, is also the true content of that causal force of three-voice polyphony to which I referred above in §4 as newly originated by three-voice counterpoint. But the more calculable the range of possibilities, the more clearly one can survey hidden possibilities; and thus it happens that in every situation of three-voice counterpoint, it is not only the directly given voice leading—that is, the one actually executed—that speaks to our ear, but also the several others which, simply because they are possible at all, help to decide whether or not the solution used is the best of all possible solutions.

In four-voice counterpoint, naturally, still more causality will result from the further increased number of voices; it will make the ear still more conscious of hidden possibilities than in three-voice, and will serve as a standard for the judgment of a given voice leading. This capability of the ear to sense possible voice leadings reaches full precision, it is true, only in free composition, where the world of causalties is further augmented by scale degrees.

If bad composers had any notion of how a well-trained musical ear is able to hear, beyond the written version that they offer, several additional versions that are better, they would finally begin to believe in the actual validity of principles that manifest themselves not only when a great master brings his own drafts to fruition through emendations, but also when an astute artist passes judgment on poorly executed compositions. Indeed, it is high time to do away with the nonsense that everything in music is good just as it is written, and therefore that only taste determines the effect. It cannot be denied: there is badly written music, exactly as there are badly written essays, badly built houses, and so forth.[7]

### §9.  *Triadic possibilities: (a)* When the outer voices form a unison

It cannot easily happen that the outer voices coincide at the unison in the main body of a three-voice setting. In consideration of the fact that more advantageous intervals (8, 5, 3, 6) are available to the outer-voice structure, the same must be said of such a unison as was already established for the domain of two-voice counterpoint (Part 2, Chapter 1, §23)—namely, that the unison always has too empty an effect in the main body of the setting.

### §10.  *(b)* When the outer voices form an octave

When the outer voices form an octave, naturally, the triad of which they are a part can only be incomplete.

Addition of one of the perfect consonances would lead to [one of] the sonorities $\frac{8}{8}$ | $\frac{8}{5}$ | 88,[8] which suffer not only from the incompleteness caused by the 8, but also from the particularly inappropriate peculiar effect (especially in this situation) of the intervals combined with it: the unison or the fifth. For precisely in the company of 8, the unison, because of its empty effect, must be rejected, just as it was rejected as an outer-voice interval for the same reason (see the preceding paragraph). The same likewise applies to 88.

But even the interval 5 discloses too blatantly in the company of 8 its intrinsically too limited nature (see *Cpt. I*, p. 129ff.), so that $\frac{8}{5}$ must be abjured in the main body of a three-voice setting. Three-voice writing involving $\frac{8}{5}$ | $\frac{8}{5}$, however, undoubtedly offers more appropriate forms of supplementation of 8; but these, by virtue of the contrast they provide, expose the sounds $\frac{5}{1}$ and $\frac{8}{5}$ as the less appropriate ones. (Concerning $\frac{6}{3}$ | $\frac{8}{6}$, see below, §§12 and 13.)

### §11.  (c) *When the outer voices form a fifth*

Since in the case of a fifth between the outer voices, $\frac{5}{1}$ and $\frac{8}{5}$ are ruled out by §§9 and 10, and $\frac{6}{5}$ is eliminated by §2, only the third remains available as a supplement, thus [leading to] $\frac{5}{3}$. This very limitation confirms the "unyielding" quality (*das Nichtumgängliche*) of the fifth, as already revealed for the first time by two-voice counterpoint; this is compounded by the fact that access to 5, according to the principles of voice leading of two-voice counterpoint, has been made more arduous from the outset than access to the imperfect intervals.

If, however, the fifth on the other hand constitutes the ultimate triadic boundary of a given root, and if it is thus obvious that, simply according to the law of the overtone series, only the third can exist alongside the fifth, just the voice leading of three-voice counterpoint itself presents $\frac{5}{3}$ as the most perfect embodiment of a triad, in which the lowest tone is actually the root.

And thus, behind the demand for completeness of triads, a new demand suddenly appears on the scene: the postulate of the *roothood-tendency of the lowest tone*. In fact, it is as though the lowest tone in each case, striving to fulfill the law of nature, would seek above all to be the root of a $\frac{5}{3}$-sonority (concerning $\frac{6}{3}$, see below, §12). At one with nature, and as though her echo, our soul mirrors this law in itself in such a way that we are always first inclined to assume root-value for each lowest tone—a secret urge that bears its fullest fruit, to be sure, only in free composition. (See also *Harmony*, pp. 251ff.)

But however certain it may be that the $\frac{5}{3}$-sound per se, by virtue of its satisfaction of both demands—that of completeness of triads and that of roothood-tendency of the lowest tone—, represents the most perfect phenomenon, and is at the same time able, like no other sound in strict counterpoint, to evoke and underscore the quality of perfect independence, it is nevertheless advisable to avoid an exclusive use of $\frac{5}{3}$, just for reasons having to do with the 5 itself, which persist no less in three-voice counterpoint than in two-voice.

### §12.  (d) *When the outer voices form a third*

Among the possible supplementations of 3 in the outer voices—that is, the sonorities $\frac{3}{1}$ | $\frac{3}{8}$ | $\frac{3}{5}$ | $\frac{3}{6}$ | 33—the least advantageous is $\frac{3}{1}$, because of the unison; it is obvious that $\frac{3}{6}$ preserves the roothood-tendency of the lowest tone just as well as $\frac{5}{3}$ (see §11).

The sonority $\frac{3}{8}$ is to be favored, in spite of its incompleteness, caused by the 8. The decisive factor here is that the third, by virtue of its ancestry (*Cpt.*

I, p. 125), at least does not contradict our assumption of root-value for the lowest tone, and that the 8 likewise poses no hindrance to this assumption (see above, §10), so that the roothood-tendency of the lowest tone is supported by $\frac{3}{6}$.

The sixth and third together merge into a complete triad, in the form of $\frac{3}{6}$, which, however, is distinguished from $\frac{5}{3}$ by the hallmark of the sixth (§13).

As soon as the third is doubled, however, we arrive again at an incomplete sound, which, as noted in §10, I designate as 33. This sound has, indeed, the advantage of the third, but, on the other hand, also the disadvantage that in it—by contrast with the other possible supplementations $\frac{3}{3} \mid \frac{3}{6} \mid \frac{3}{8}$, which provide in 5, 6, and 8 a more desirable foil for the third—an interval already so vividly imprinted (as the third is) is subjected to doubling. Such a doubling certainly will always be perceived as gratuitous unless the strictest, virtually unavoidable necessity for it is impressed upon our senses by the surrounding voice leading—that is, by what precedes and follows.

## §13. (e) When the outer voices form a sixth

Since $\frac{6}{?}$ suffers equally from the unison and from the sixth,[9] the only remaining appropriate combinations are $\frac{5}{6} \mid \frac{8}{6}$ and 66.

As an inversion of the third (*Cpt. I*, p. 81f.), the sixth from the outset contradicts the roothood-tendency of the lowest tone (see above, §11). This contradiction logically occurs, then, with all combinations involving 6 as well, irrespective of whether the triad is complete or incomplete. Thus three-voice counterpoint itself already provides an occasion to discover the artificial and artistic appeal of the $\frac{8}{6}$-sound. And it is by no means unimportant to investigate how, in the case of $\frac{8}{6}$, our sense is forced to overcome the initially intrusive assumption of roothood-tendency of the lowest tone, in order to attend only afterward to the artistically taxing labor of inversion—that is, to add belatedly, in this way, that which was lost by the non-fulfillment of that assumption.

The sound $\frac{8}{6}$ can, at least, be credited with the advantage of the 8, which in fact illuminates the sixth better than does the doubling sixth in 66.

## §14. Conclusions drawn from the above considerations

When we survey the results of the above series of paragraphs in §§9–13, we arrive at the following conclusions:

The sonorities $\frac{6}{?} \mid \frac{3}{?}$ and also 88, $\frac{5}{8}$, and 55 are to be excluded completely from use in the main body of the exercise; $\frac{3}{3} \mid \frac{6}{?}$ are only just tolerable; thus the remaining usable sonorities are:

$\frac{5}{3}$ and $\frac{6}{3}$, which are complete;
$\frac{8}{3}$ and $\frac{8}{6}$, which, although incomplete, nevertheless exhibit the advantageous doubling interval of 8, which corresponds to nature; and finally

33 and 66, which, under certain circumstances—that is, to the extent that no compelling necessity for them is established—are sullied by the fault of having presented, instead of the octave, just the less appropriate doubling.

If we observe moreover the appearance of:

> the third in four sounds: $\frac{5}{3}$ | $\frac{6}{3}$ | $\frac{8}{3}$ and 33;
> the sixth in only three: $\frac{6}{3}$ | $\frac{8}{6}$ and 66;
> the octave in two: $\frac{8}{3}$ and $\frac{8}{6}$; and finally
> the fifth in but one sound: $\frac{5}{3}$;

then we derive from this overview the most impressive confirmation of the superiority of the third and sixth as over against the perfect consonances—a result that is proclaimed even earlier, by two-voice counterpoint.

This survey also reveals, with no less clarity, the greater range of application of the third in comparison to the sixth, and of the octave in comparison to the fifth, which only reconfirms for three-voice counterpoint the experience gained in two-voice.

And finally, the dubious quality of the fifth is perhaps most blatantly revealed by its limitation to only a single possibility of application.

It should now also be understood why I was able, and even obliged, to proclaim in §1 the continued applicability in three-voice counterpoint of the principles of two-voice.

In conclusion, notice should be taken of an aid for writing procedure in the first stage of study which, although derived from the theory of harmony and apparently only of mnemonic value, in fact encompasses in different words what has just come to light as a purely contrapuntal result: regardless of whether they are complete or incomplete, all sonorities to which three-voice strict counterpoint provides any access at all merge into the conception of only two triadic regions (*Dreiklangsbezirke*) (see below, Example 4, a and b), the second of which lies a third lower than the first; the triadic region a fifth lower (at c) remains completely out of consideration:

**Example 4**

The remarks by *Fux* concerning this question are as follows (p. 87):

*Aloys:* The first thing to be noted is that the harmonic triad is to be used in each bar, if other circumstances do not preclude it.

*Joseph:* What is the harmonic triad?

*Aloys:* It is a system that consists of third and fifth, as follows:

**Example 5**
Fux, Tab. VII, Fig. 1

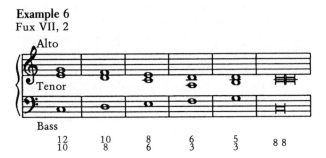

*Joseph:* But what manner of circumstances sometimes precludes the use of this triad?

*Aloys:* It is often the euphony of the melody that causes a different consonance—either the sixth or the octave—to be used occasionally instead of the triad. Sometimes the triad must be omitted in order to avoid the direct succession of two fifths or octaves, and instead of the fifth, the sixth or octave (or both together) must be used, as I shall show you in the following example:

**Example 6**
Fux VII, 2

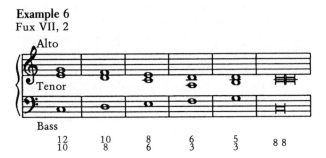

Fux discusses and defends the particular setting of the *first* bar[10] as follows (pp. 88–89):

Haven't you noticed that the bass of the same example consistently rises by step? For this reason, the other voices had to be separated from the bass, so that enough space would be available for the voices to move toward one another in contrary motion.

Fux thus emphasized the necessity of precluding, under certain circumstances, possible subsequent difficulties of voice leading by means of a suitable disposition in the first bar itself.

Fux does not stop at this explanation, however; rather, he expressly adds to the above example two other versions in order to defend his choice of initial sonority as accurately as possible:

**Example 7**
Fux VII, 10

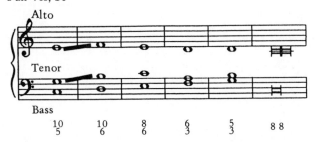

**Example 8**

Fux VII, 11

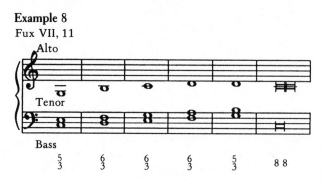

Regarding the first example, Fux comments (p. 89):

> I have little objection to these examples; but you see that in the first example, from the first bar to the second, all three voices proceed upward, partly by step, partly by a leap, which cannot easily occur without some measure of error, such as is present here in the relation of the tenor to the alto from the first bar to the second: [example follows, showing tenor and alto parts of bars 1–2].

Here it is the nonparallel similar motion to the fifth (see below, §22) that is to be avoided by the voice leading of Example 6 (Fux's Table VII, Figure 2). On the second example, Fux comments as follows (p. 92): "Nothing further [is wrong] except that the ascending sixths on the downbeat sound rather harsh. If they occur on the upbeat (which, however, has no place in this species) they are more tolerable since they seem to be less distinct. . . ."

Regarding the fact that in Example 6 a complete triad ⅜ could perfectly well have been used in the second bar as well:

**Example 9**

Fux VII, 3

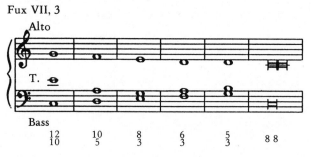

he finds the following explanation necessary:

> This idea pleases me, and your example, too, cannot be rejected. But who can fail to see that the first example—my own—corresponds more to Nature, order and variety? It is in accord with Nature and order because its tenor voice descends beautifully, stepwise and without leap, up to and including the third bar.

And further on:

> Now let us return . . . to a consideration of the reasons why my example has more variety. The note *a* occurs there only once in the tenor, while it occurs

twice in your example . . . I should like to tell you once and for all, that one should always take great care to achieve this sort of variety.

How beautiful the words with which the master is able to call attention to hidden, apparently insignificant tendencies of voice leading, such as the fact that even an inner voice (here the tenor) must be guaranteed a claim to melodic fluency, or that it must be preserved from monotony in the broader sense (Part 1, Chapter 2, §21). These deliberations of Fux's may also serve the student as the strongest proof of what was set forth above in §8—how a given solution in a particular situation has a good, and therefore beautiful, effect only when it can withstand comparison with other possible solutions, which, however, presupposes that the latter are also present in our imagination.

Fux speaks again in other contexts of different reasons for the possible absence of triadic completeness. A case in point here is the prohibition, already cited in Part 1, Chapter 2, §2, of going "beyond the limits of the five lines [of the staff] unless absolutely necessary"; moreover, his reference to the limitations imposed on exercises by the cantus firmus (p. 95): "I believe that the composition could have been more enriched by the harmonic triad in many places if my freedom had not been restricted by the necessity of the cantus firmus (*Choralgesang*)." The superiority of the imperfect consonances 3 and 6 (see above, §14) to the perfect ones is expressed by Fux, in his discussion of two-voice counterpoint, in words that are more suggestive than comprehensive (p. 66): "You should know that the imperfect consonances are more harmonious than perfect ones. . . ."

Fux understandably pays no heed to whether the fourth in the $\frac{6}{4}$-chord is perfect or augmented. Yet he supplies the reason for this practice only later, in four-voice counterpoint, where he writes (p. 109): "However, one must remember that the nature of the consonances and dissonances is to be measured in relation to the bass regardless of what may occur between the inner voices, so long as mistakes such as the succession of two fifths or two octaves are avoided."

Compare the remark on p. 116, concerning the syncopated species in four-voice counterpoint: ". . . the fourth between inner voices either is not taken into consideration at all, or else serves as an imperfect consonance."

It should further be mentioned that Fux makes no use of any differentiating terminology; his only technical term is "harmonic triad," or simply "triad," the content of which has already been explained above. Even characterizations such as "incomplete" or "imperfect triad," for example, are foreign to him (see the section below on Albrechtsberger); this shows how completely he is influenced by purely contrapuntal ways of thinking. Voice leading alone signifies everything for him, and in comparison to its necessities, any other discrimination obviously appears superfluous to him. It is no contradiction of this standpoint that he occasionally writes (as on p. 93) about a sonority such as $\frac{6}{3}$ in the following way: "Afterward, the bass and tenor form a unison, which contributes less to the harmony than an octave." Finally it should be noted that Fux's example, Table VII, Figure 2 (Example 6 here), has since made the rounds of almost all treatises on counterpoint. Regardless of whether the authors acknowledge its origin with Fux or not (as is the case with Cherubini, for example), they use it again and again for the same purpose of explaining the principles of three-voice counterpoint.

*Albrechtsberger* makes use of the following technical terms in three-voice counterpoint (p. 79ff.; see also p. 26):

When the perfect fifth and the major or minor third are added to a bass note, the resulting combination is called the perfect harmonic triad, *trias harmonica perfecta.* If a minor or major third and a minor or major sixth are added to a bass note, the result is an imperfect harmonic triad, *trias harmonica imperfecta.* . . .

From the examples that he provides, it can moreover be inferred that he conceives all chords in general as "perfect chords" if they contain 8, 5, 3 (but not 6!), irrespective of whether they are otherwise complete or incomplete. In the latter case, to be sure, he speaks of a "doubled dyad (*Zweyklang*) in *à tre*" (or of a "doubled triad in *à quattre*"), "all of which are good and, to avoid flaws, permissible."

Even these artistic formulations alone demonstrate Albrechtsberger's strong instinctive grasp of the different values of the fifth and sixth from the contrapuntal standpoint. And his account of the perfect chords by itself certainly expresses an awareness that in contrast to the sixth, the third at least supports the assumption of roothood for the lowest tone, in the sense of a complete triad (see above, §§11 and 12).

On p. 78ff., Albrechtsberger remarks:

> Chords of the second, the fourth, the seventh, and the ninth—even those marked above with NB—can never be used in the first species, because they are dissonant chords; for here, and in four-voice settings, only the two perfect chords and the three kinds of sixth-chords in any key (in which the sixth must never be augmented or diminished) are allowed. Also excluded are the three-four chord $\frac{4}{3}$, the four-six chord $\frac{6}{4}$, and the essential seventh chord $\frac{\flat 7}{\sharp 3}$.

Albrechtsberger further provides, on pp. 75–77, a comprehensive table of all possible three-voice sounds, such as can be used only in free composition; as is so often the case, however, he fails to make the slightest attempt to explain why only a certain type of triad is allowed in strict counterpoint, in contrast to which a far larger number are reserved only for free composition. If his presentation thus discloses that he wanted to keep the theory of strict counterpoint in direct proximity to free composition, it also supports the conclusion, on the other hand, that although he was indeed interested in the puzzle of how to reconcile strict counterpoint with free composition, he was nevertheless unable to find a solution to it—to the extent that one is disinclined to acknowledge as a solution (the solution to the puzzle, that is) the mere juxtaposition, such as he provides without further explanation, of phenomena of free and strict writing. Thus it happens that he finally states (p. 81): "For the rest, the remaining bars, as said earlier, have the following chords: chiefly, $\frac{5}{3}$, $\frac{6}{5}$; or $\frac{8}{5}$, $\frac{8}{8}$; or $\frac{10}{3}$, $\frac{6}{5}$, when these latter are not leading tones."

*Cherubini* reproduces, along with the example by Fux (see above), also the latter's teaching (p. 27, first Rule, Examples 81 and 82), except that he speaks of a "complete" rather than a "perfect" triad. Rule 6 on p. 29 is expressly concerned with the prohibition of $\frac{6}{4}$. (Concerning incomplete chords, see the citation below, in §18.)

*Bellermann* follows Fux most strictly, perhaps, in that like Fux, he prefers to restrict the concept of triad exclusively to $\frac{5}{3}$. He does, to be sure, subsequently present all possible doublings in turn, but in doing so he avoids—again, exactly like Fux—basing the matter on a definite solution; he then announces, finally, without providing any justification (p. 190ff.): "Those combinations in which the bass tone is doubled by the octave [meaning $\frac{8}{3}$, $\frac{8}{5}$ (!), and $\frac{8}{8}$] are preferable to these three last named [by which he means $\frac{10}{3}$ (=$\frac{3}{3}$ ), $\frac{6}{6}$, and $\frac{12}{5}$]." It is singular that Bellermann himself expresses no objection to doubling at the unison, and sets as a condition for it only the availability of a suitable mode of departure from the unison (*Cpt. I*, p. 146).

### §15. On the difference between the meaning of sonorities in strict counterpoint and in free composition

The more three-voice counterpoint has gained in fullness of sonority, the more it appears, at least at first glance, to come closer to free composition. Without doubt, when we listen to even a small three-voice exercise—see the exercises below, and compare what was said already in *Harmony*, p. 154ff., in the chapter "Scale-Step and Counterpoint"—we tend to read all kinds of scale degrees into its consonant sonorities. And our ear shows itself to be particularly sensitive in respect to apparent cadences and—especially in connection with the sixth as an interval by inversion—effects that evoke various associations with free composition (such as suspensions or passing tones, for example).

That tendency is explained, however, simply by the fact that in all compositions that we have occasion to hear, we never hear "strict" setting merely in the sense of the world of exercises, but rather an actual free setting based on scale degrees, and that we therefore—that is, through such familiarity with scale degrees—automatically cultivate in ourselves the capacity for connections and comparisons, which then accompany us constantly and reawaken in us whenever we encounter anything musical at all, even if it be only an exercise of strict counterpoint. It is more difficult to account for the reasons that subsequently cause us to recognize the earlier tendency as an error. First of all—and I cited this reason even in *Harmony*, p. 155—it is the undeniable lack of sense and goal-directedness in the progression of the harmonies, from the standpoint of scale degrees, that speaks against the assumption of their presence. For as we know, scale degrees are subject more to Nature than to Art; they have a course originally predetermined by the former alone, and therefore a deliberate wantonness in the succession of sonorities such as that found in a configuration of strict counterpoint can in no way be reconciled with the essence of a scale-degree progression that is truly in accord with Nature.

The ultimate reason, however, that the three-voice polyphony of strict counterpoint cannot advance to the full effect of scale degrees is this: the pre-existing cantus firmus, posited as the foundation for the voice-leading exercise, is itself already the composing out of a triad (or, under certain circumstances, of several triads); this means that in it, even though in the horizontal plane, an already definite harmonic sound is brought into existence (for example, the triad $f-a-c$ in the cantus firmus by Fux in exercise No. 1 of Example 81 below; cf. also *Cpt. I*, pp. 94–95 and 100–101).

Just as the pre-existence of the cantus firmus necessarily had its consequences even in two-voice counterpoint—for example, the fact that certain traces of subservience were imprinted on the added voice—it likewise manifests consequences in three-voice counterpoint as well, specifically in that the sonorities of the vertical dimension in their significance as individual entities must yield before the significance of the horizontally expressed sonority. The horizontal harmony proves to be stronger than the relationships of the vertical sounds to one another. This effect, to which our attention is first drawn by three-voice counterpoint—three-voice counterpoint has the first opportunity to do so because it is the first to introduce such three-voice polyphony as is the content and corporeality of the scale degrees (see *Harmony*, p. 152)—weaves, as will be shown in the further course of this presentation, like a "red thread" through all similar phenomena of strict counterpoint as well as free composition. As a main principle, it may rightly be expressed in general as follows:

Any closed melodic line weakens the vertical chords [that accompany it] with respect to their meanings as individuals in the same measure that the melodic line itself effects the composing out of a particular chord in the horizontal direction.

How this discovery helps to buttress and deepen the concept of scale degrees in particular, and also that of forms, will subsequently be shown more clearly.

For the reasons just presented, I consider the following statement by the early master *Fux* (p. 88) concerning bars 3 and 4 of Example 6 (his Table VII, Figure 2) to be confusing, and indeed in total contradiction to his own teaching, which is otherwise so scrupulously pure:[11]

> . . . in which the sixth occurs, which is more suitable than other consonances for the note *mi* that stands below the bass. I have already said this elsewhere, but I want to emphasize it again still more clearly. Consider first this example of the sixth:

**Example 10**

Fux VII, 4

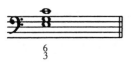

Here the note that forms the sixth stands out of its normal position, in an unusual place, so to speak; for in its proper place it would appear thus:

**Example 11**

Fux VII, 5

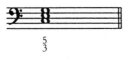

Therefore the C in its usual position completes the harmonic triad; since it stands an octave higher, while the remaining components keep their place, it necessarily becomes a sixth. This holds true, however, only when *mi* is followed by *fa,* as in this example:

**Example 12**
Fux VII, 6

But when *mi* moves elsewhere, the fifth rather is to be preferred to the sixth, as in the following examples:

**Example 13**
Fux VII, 7

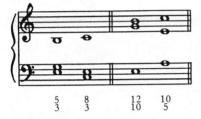

$$\begin{matrix} 5 & 8 & 12 & 10 \\ 3 & 3 & 10 & 5 \end{matrix}$$

Only by assuming that Fux here suddenly yields to the instinct for scale degrees—specifically, in bars 3-4 of Example 6, the feeling of a progression by second (I — II), and in Example 13 that of progressions by third (III — I) and by fifth (III — VI)—can we understand why he recommends for the bass note *E* in the first case the sixth, *c*, but in the last two cases the fifth, *b*. That it is none other than Fux, however, who invokes the spirit of scale degrees—and thereby appeals to harmonic theory—in the midst of contrapuntal teaching is as unexpected as it is regrettable, however much this development is, on the other hand, to be appraised as the first trace of an awareness, dawning in him as well, of the world of scale degrees. (See the Preface to *Counterpoint I*.)

Such errors on the part of *Albrechtsberger* are less surprising—as for example on pp. 105-106, where, to the following configuration of syncopes, constructed with deliberate flaws for the sake of illustration:

**Example 14**

he compares the following one:

**Example 15**
No. 2

$$\begin{matrix} & 7 & 6 & \begin{matrix}6\\4\end{matrix} & 3 & \begin{matrix}8\\4\end{matrix} & 3 \end{matrix}$$

and comments as follows:

> The ninth mistake is again an inharmonic cross relation in the eleventh and
> twelfth bars[12] ♮ in soprano and alto with the tenor; this augmented-fourth
> suspension B can be used in three-voice counterpoint only with the natural
> major sixth D, when this B derives from the key of A minor, and not from C
> major, as can be seen above in No. 2.

### §16.   *The concept of tone-repetition, too, is determined by the purely voice-leading significance of the sonorities in strict counterpoint*

As is well known, conventional harmonic doctrine sets down the rule that in
connecting two triads, any previously present common tone, or two common
tones, should be retained in the same position—that is, in the same voice. At
first glance, this rule seems to express the same thing that contrapuntal theory
seeks to express by the license, appropriate to it (*Cpt. I*, p. 164), of repeating
a tone so that it occurs twice, or even three or four times—that is, allowing
the tone simply to remain in the same place. The similarity of result of that
rule of harmonic doctrine and the license of contrapuntal theory, however, is
only apparent: there is a fundamental difference between the two, for, while
the former *directs* the student to retain the common tone, the latter leaves it
only to the judgment of the writer of the exercise whether he chooses to repeat
the tone or whether, for the sake of a subsequent advantage for the voice
leading, he would not perhaps prefer to substitute for the repetition a different,
better course of motion. Thus the rule of harmonic doctrine causes voice
leading to originate as though out of the rule itself, while contrapuntal theory,
on the contrary, leaves it up to us to decide on the basis of the situation at
hand whether to use tone-repetition or not.

Free composition, which, despite its scale degrees, also completely
preserves voice leading's independent nature (*FrC.*, [§§22, 66]), now retains
the concept of tone-repetition in exactly the same sense as strict counterpoint.
By making use, specifically, of passing tones and suspensions in all possible
prolonged forms and, further, of all kinds of liberties in abbreviations and in
substitutions of intervals, octave registers, and the like—all for the sake of
melodic content and of diminutions—free composition presents tone-repeti-
tions (however much it might disguise them) as completely contingent on the
needs of the given situation—that is, exactly as is the case in strict counterpoint.

The agreement of strict counterpoint and free composition with respect to
the use of tone-repetition—an agreement born in both cases of the same
preservation of the independent nature of voice leading—then lays bare all the
more glaringly the falsity of the rule of conventional harmonic doctrine
mentioned above. Why this rule, if it has no validity for strict settings, and
still less for free? When and where does it claim true validity, if neither strict
counterpoint nor free composition is bound by it? It is altogether false and
has no justification. This is explained quite simply, however, by the fact that
the whole plan of the conventional harmonic doctrine, as I have demonstrated

in *Harmony,* p. 175ff., is false from the outset, since it pretends to teach voice leading in terms of scale degrees, without first having indicated the nature of both by means of fundamental concepts. And only the fact that young students are still subjected to this type of harmonic doctrine, in spite of its obvious contradictory quality and in spite of the crassest failures in the real world, compelled me to speak here about one of its non-rules (*Irr-Regeln*).

To return to strict counterpoint, it should be stated explicitly at this opportunity that whenever an advantage for the melodic line can thereby be gained, even two voices may simultaneously retain their tones.

In exercises by Fux, [for example] Table VII, Figure 22, and Table VIII, Figure 4, we sometimes find a three- or even a four-fold tone-repetition.

### §17.   *How the essential independence of voice leading yields the concept of interval-doubling only in a similarly unconditional sense*

By prohibiting parallel ("open") octaves and permitting introduction of the octave only in contrary [or oblique] motion (*Cpt. I,* p. 127ff.), two-voice counterpoint establishes for the first time the concept of *doubling,* which, there, in two-voice counterpoint, is possible with no other interval except 8.[13] Two-voice principles base this concept on the necessity of avoiding parallel 8-successions, which is the precondition of obbligato voice leading, and thereby sets a boundary between doubling and the concept of reinforcement, which, on the contrary, goes beyond doubling precisely by making use of 8-successions.

Three-voice counterpoint now makes possible a prolongation, in that it admits not only doubling of the octave, but also doubling of other intervals, the third and sixth. Again, however, as in two-voice counterpoint, obbligato voice leading is the precondition of such a doubling. Therefore, so long as parallel octaves are avoided between all [pairs of] the three voices, any doubling of an 8, 3, or 6 here falls under the concept of an admissible doubling, and not under that of an inadmissible reinforcement.

To abide by this in strict counterpoint is all the more practicable because the voice leading, since it is free of scale degrees, exhibits an unrestricted character in any case. Each interval here remains just what it is—thus the third is nothing but a third, the sixth nothing but a sixth, and so forth—, so that a doubling of third or sixth is truly nothing other than a doubling of third or sixth.

But even in free composition, which, in spite of scale degrees, preserves independence for voice leading, that quality extends most strictly to the independent nature of doubling. It is therefore permitted in free composition, as an extension of the principles of strict counterpoint, to double octaves, thirds, and sixths within a texture of obbligato voice leading, however they may be expressed by it; thus there can be no talk of prohibition of doubling, for example, a third (excepting only the ascending leading tone), as is rumored in the conventional harmony treatises. In free composition, therefore—to sketch only briefly what will be presented in greater detail by the examples in *Free Composition*[14]—, a doubling such as the following:

**Example 16**

3 3

may, if the logic of harmonies points to a C scale degree, appear from that standpoint also as a fifth-doubling:

**Example 17**

And similarly, the following:

**Example 18**

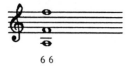

6 6

could also appear as an octave- or even a third-doubling, depending on whether *F* or *D* were the scale degree in question:

**Example 19**

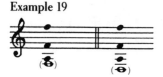

Regardless of which is the case, the voice leading first of all follows its independent nature, and freely presents such doublings of thirds and sixths precisely according to its own need, while the scale degrees restrict themselves to activating the composing-out process in general, and to imprinting it with scale-degree logic.

### §18. *Prohibition of doubling the ascending leading tone*

The only tone that must not be doubled is the ascending leading tone, which belongs conceptually to the pure theory of voice leading (*Cpt. I*, p. 102ff.); the doubling of this tone, in consideration of its foreordained path to the tonic, would result in parallel octaves.

The question of why the descending leading tone is not also affected by the doubling-prohibition, however, is answered as follows. If the leading tone in the contrapuntal sense is based on relationship only to the tonic tone—that is, if both leading tones appear as such only when they pull toward the tonic tone (as is shown best by the cadence formula[15] in strict counterpoint)—then, by virtue of this similar determination, no initial distinction should be made between the two leading tones with respect to a doubling-prohibition. But three-voice counterpoint reveals an important difference between the two leading tones which subsequently had to effect a limitation of the prohibition to only the ascending leading tone. (It should be remembered that in two-voice counterpoint a doubling of leading tones could not be considered at all, and, consequently, no opportunity arose there to become aware of any possible distinction between the two leading tones!) In particular, three-voice counterpoint shows that the ascending leading tone, if led downward (see a of the following example), would arrive at a tone that is no longer even a harmonic tone of the tonic harmony, while the descending tone, even if led upward (see b), still leads to the third of the tonic harmony:

**Example 20**

Two paths, then, are open to the descending leading tone; and if, as stated above, it counts as leading tone in the strictest sense only when it actually leads to the tonic, it nevertheless retains leading-tone value even when, for one or another pertinent reason, it after all ascends to the third of the tonic harmony. For the ascending leading tone, on the contrary, there is but one path: that to the tonic tone itself, if it is not to fall away completely from the tonic harmony and thus from its conceptual essence. In this light it can be understood that a doubling of the ascending leading tone would have to result in a prohibited succession of octaves or unisons, while a possible doubling of the descending leading tone, on the other hand, is by no means necessarily associated with such a succession.

The doubling-prohibition of the ascending leading tone—and only of that tone—is then incorporated by free composition as well, except that the latter, in the context of various chromatic processes, manifests the leading tone in various prolonged forms and metamorphoses.

On the question of doublings, *Fux,* as I have already shown in §14, adheres so strictly to the standpoint of independent voice leading that he even finds it unnecessary to mention explicitly a doubling-prohibition for the ascending leading tone. He obviously considers it sufficient that, through the pure nature of voice leading itself, such a doubling must be excluded.

*Albrechtsberger* addresses this question all the more zealously, although it can readily be seen that he is moved to do so only because he has his eye constantly turned toward free composition. Thus we read, already in the first species of two-voice counterpoint (p. 27), a remark that properly belongs to four-voice counterpoint, in which he explains:

> Another rule [of good melody] requires that the seventh large tone,[16] which is also called the sensitive note or *nota sensibilis,* be led upward by a half-step to the eighth, and the regular fourth tone, especially in major scales, be led downward to the third, though it is not necessary that the expected chord follow in every case.

(The quotation cited in Part 2, Chapter 1, §23 follows upon this one.) Here the discussion is, to be sure, of an ascending leading tone (to use a different technical term), but at the same time also of a "fourth tone," to which Albrechtsberger is no less inclined to attribute leading-tone quality in the falling direction than to the former one in the rising direction. Such a confusion of ideas, occasioned by insufficient mastery of the subject! Instead of first conceiving the leading tone in strict counterpoint in terms of purely melodic considerations (Part 1, Chapter 2, §23) and subsequently applying its conceptual basis also to the cadence of two-voice counterpoint (Part 2, Chapter 1, §29), which would automatically have had to lead to the first encounter between the two possible and conceivable leading tones in strict counterpoint, he speaks in the context of strict writing of "full and partial cadences" completely in the sense of harmonic theory (V — I), and, in the above quotation, again in the same sense, of another alleged leading tone in the scale-degree progression IV — I. (The solution of the whole question will follow in *Free Composition.*)

Albrechtsberger speaks explicitly, however, of a doubling-prohibition for the ascending leading tone on p. 81 (see the quotation in §14), and takes the further opportunity on p. 84 to return to it indirectly in that he remarks, concerning two doublings that he uses in bars 5 and 11 of the exercise given below (see Example 81) as no. 5: "The NB at the tone *B* in the alto, and also at *F♯* in the tenor,[17] means that it would not be an error to double these tones, since neither of them is the *semitonium modi, D♯.*"

Similarly, in a syncopation-exercise of three-voice counterpoint on p. 104 he deliberately commits the following offense:

**Example 21**

in order to be able to comment (p. 105): "The third error is the following *B* in the alto, because through it the sensitive note of the following *C* chord has been doubled, which is allowed only at the upbeat."

Compare also the remark on p. 362, in the context of five-voice counterpoint: "NB. If the latter [the seventh large tone] were also a third or sixth (as a doubled bass-note—that is, as an octave—it is tolerated in an inner voice), then it would always be prohibited on the strong beat in counterpoint of five and also of more than five voices."

And finally, observe Albrechtsberger's correction of voice leading in a Beethoven exercise violating the prohibition (Nottebohm, p. 54):

**Example 22**

Concerning the permissible doubling of third and sixth (except when the tones involved have leading-tone character), see the citation in §14. It should be noted finally that in his discussion of doubling-prohibition Albrechtsberger never again mentions that other alleged leading tone (IV—I) that he cites so surprisingly on p. 27.

*Cherubini* writes as follows (p. 28f., fifth rule):

> In incomplete chords, one must avoid allowing the third or sixth to be heard in two voices at the same time [i.e., doubling the third or sixth]. This is prohibited because of the imperfection of those intervals, and because the harmony would appear too impoverished. For converse reasons, doubling of the octave and fifth is recommended, since they are the most perfect consonances. But even this rule is not without exception; the imperfect consonances, too, can be doubled for the sake of good harmony, better voice leading, and, finally, to avoid still worse faults, when no other means is available.

Examples of application of the strict rule:

**Example 23**

Ex. 83

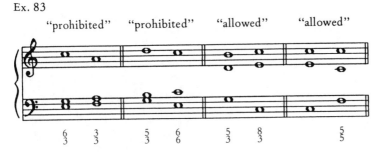

*Bellermann* likewise makes no explicit mention of a prohibition of leading-tone doubling; and in fact, we find in his exercises just such a usage—under especially difficult circumstances, to be sure:

**Example 24**

Although Bellermann undoubtedly had in mind here the Dorian mode, in which *B* is not a leading tone, the above progression of chords can be understood as a modulation, within that mode, to *C* major, so that a doubling of *B* would automatically be ruled out.

## Beginning

### §19.  *Construction of the beginning*

The following sounds are suitable for constructing the beginning:
    (a) among *complete* triads, only:

$$\begin{smallmatrix}5\\3\end{smallmatrix}$$

since $\begin{smallmatrix}5\\3\end{smallmatrix}$, for lack of perfect consonances, must be excluded at the beginning, in spite of its completeness as a three-voice chord; next,
    (b) among *incomplete* triads, first of all:

$$\begin{smallmatrix}8\\5\end{smallmatrix}\;\Big|\;\begin{smallmatrix}8\\1\end{smallmatrix}\text{ and }\begin{smallmatrix}5\\1\end{smallmatrix}$$

as chords that do exhibit two perfect consonances;[18] as a second choice, however, also chords with imperfect consonances:

$$\begin{smallmatrix}8\\3\end{smallmatrix}\;\Big|\;\begin{smallmatrix}10\\3\end{smallmatrix}\;\Big|\;\begin{smallmatrix}3\\1\end{smallmatrix}$$

but only in the event that a significant advantage for the voice leading in subsequent bars can be attained only through their use.

*Fux* makes frequent use even at the beginning of chords with imperfect consonances: $\begin{smallmatrix}10\\8\end{smallmatrix}\;\big|\;\begin{smallmatrix}8\\3\end{smallmatrix}\;\big|\;\begin{smallmatrix}3\\1\end{smallmatrix}\;\big|\;\begin{smallmatrix}10\\1\end{smallmatrix}$. Significantly, however, for the Dorian, Phrygian, and Aeolian modes he uses the minor third, while on the other hand he avoids it in the closing chord, as we shall see later in §27.

*Albrechtsberger* (p. 81): "The beginning and ending must be perfect." According to his terminology, this does not mean, however, that the opening chord must, for this reason, also be complete. Thus he is able to write on p. 79 that "the empty chords $\begin{smallmatrix}8\\5\end{smallmatrix}\;\big|\;\begin{smallmatrix}8\\1\end{smallmatrix}$ may be used only in the first bar."

*Cherubini's* remarks (p. 28, rule 2) are similar to those of Albrechtsberger.

## Main Body

### §20. *Recollection of several earlier principles*

The more strictly the exercises of three-voice counterpoint are to be executed in terms of a vocal orientation alone (*Cpt. I*, p. 11), the more carefully one must attend to a consistently suitable spacing of the voices (cf. Part 2, Chapter 1, §24).

Crossing of voices is permitted, when necessary, not only for two adjacent voices, but even for the two outer voices.

The prescription of variety of intervals, which was set forth in two-voice counterpoint (cf. Part 2, Chapter 1, §22f.), now finds its prolongation in three-voice as well. In this respect the voice leading will be better the more it exudes such variety above all in the setting of the outer voices; most of the time, this will be attended by a variety of triadic phenomena in general.

*Fux* writes, on p. 71 (as early as his treatment of two-voice counterpoint), "But it is to be noted that preference is given to combinations using adjacent clefs, so that the simple consonances can be distinguished more readily from the compound ones."

In contrast to his misleading practice in two-voice counterpoint, *Albrechtsberger* employs incomparably better spacings of voices in three-voice (necessity is the mother of invention), which provides another counter-argument against his earlier procedure.

*Cherubini* writes (p. 28, third rule), ". . . the more they [the voices] stay close to one another, the better the effect will be."

### §21. *On open and close position*

Of greatest significance with respect to effect, however, is to pay careful attention in constructing triads to the difference between close and open position (*enge und weite Lage*). First, let it be recalled that only the open position corresponds to the triad of nature, since only in it does the model of the overtone series—in which, as we know, the fifth occurs before the third (see *Harmony*, §39ff.)—find exact fulfillment:

**Example 25**

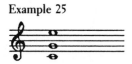

If we may interpret Nature's purpose, it is as though she wishes at least to grant the third, as the weaker overtone, the advantage and protection of the higher position in comparison to the stronger fifth. Its position above the fifth—its height—, then, is what secures for the third the ear's attention.

If to the open position we now compare the close position (which originates in the artificial domain of music) and place the fifth above the third:

**Example 26**

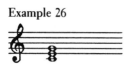

the high position, which inevitably attracts the attention of the ear, now accrues to the fifth, which is by nature stronger than. the third. If it runs counter to Nature to strengthen gratuitously that which is already strong, and likewise to weaken that which is already weak—and this, to be exact, is a form of self-repetition, which is always alien to Nature—, it is, then, on the contrary, entirely appropriate for a synthetic culture such as music to seek out such effects as needed. Therefore let the student learn to perceive, even in the domain of exercises of strict counterpoint, how the open position always confers special emphasis on the highest tone in any given case—an emphasis that could not be attained by the same tone as an inner voice in close position.

It is clear, however, that what has been said here initially about only $\frac{5}{3}$ and $\frac{3}{5}$ with direct reference to the model of Nature holds good no less, by free and extended application, of $\frac{6}{3}$ and $\frac{3}{6}$, and ultimately of the incomplete triads $\frac{8}{3}$ and $\frac{3}{8}$ as well. For these sonorities, too, it is possible to distinguish between a close and an open position; and transposition to the highest location at the same time means accentuation of the interval in question. *The third therefore shall count as the hallmark of the open position,* and indeed, for all sonorities without exception, *only* the third, while the intervals 5, 6, and 8 shall remain from the outset signs of only the close position (see Examples 25 and 26):

**Example 27**

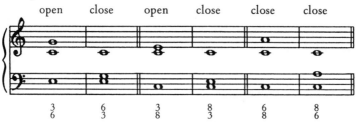

From this we see the significance enjoyed by the setting of the outer voices, which, apart from its various other powers of determination, is also the sole determinant of open and close position.

It is a different matter to contemplate the relationship of the inner voice to the outer voices: it is true that the inner voice has no power to alter the fact of an open or close position; nevertheless, it is a good practice also to speak of an internally open position whenever, within a close position, the inner voice bears a relationship to either the upper or the lower voice that exceeds a third, as the following examples show:

**Example 28**

That the octave registers in Example 25 appear better connected, in a purely sonic sense, than those of Example 28 requires no explanation; but a higher requirement of voice leading may nevertheless impel the setting to a form exactly like those of Example 28, in which case even such a position, demanded of necessity, sounds good and beautiful.

The discrimination of close position in the strictest sense (Example 26) from that with a merely internally open position (Example 28) teaches at the same time, however, that the spacing of voices must be completely literal; for how could an internally open position be identified if the spacings counted as merely figurative? Admittedly, the importance of this question at first remains small in three-voice counterpoint (it is perhaps most noticeable in the case of ⁶₄, which will be considered in more detail in §23); the differentiations appear more distinctly in four-voice counterpoint, and most distinctly of all in free composition, where the basic principles of open and close positions are applied to seventh chords (*Vierklänge*) as well, and where, moreover, the whole network of reinforcements finds its ultimate foundation in the various positions, together with, specifically, the corporeality of the voices.

It should be mentioned finally that an element of good voice leading is alternation of positions, since variety in the spacing of voices, or—which comes to the same thing—variation in the density of sonority engages the ear in the most effective way.

### §22.  *The permissible nonparallel similar motions*

It has been explained already in *Counterpoint I*, p. 130, and subsequently often repeated, that parallel octaves (8 — 8) must continue to be prohibited in three-voice counterpoint for the same reason [as in two-voice], and that only by this means can we establish the obbligato nature of the voices, which would otherwise function [merely] as "reinforcements."

The three-voice counterpoint also offers no means to counteract parallel fifths (5 — 5). While free composition has access to means that can cause the two fifths to be recognized under certain circumstances only as an innocent collision of tones [*FrC.*, Fig. 54, 12] which—because they are assigned the mission of a passing tone, a neighboring tone, or the like—have not the slightest wish to place their vertical relation to one another in the foreground (so that in reality there can be no talk of parallel fifths), strict counterpoint still lacks the means to generate this type of camouflage. Therefore parallel fifths, which here would always have to be interpreted in their absolute significance as such, remain unusable for the same reasons as in two-voice counterpoint.

Nonparallel similar motions, on the other hand, are a different matter in three-voice counterpoint; under certain circumstances, as will be shown presently, they must be admitted. But the admission of nonparallel similar motion in three-voice counterpoint—to repeat this important idea expressed earlier in *Counterpoint I,* p. 142ff.—absolutely does not constitute any kind of "exception" to the governing prohibition. Rather, three-voice counterpoint is already able to *improve* the otherwise poor effect of nonparallel similar motion, and therefore, by virtue of so favorably altered circumstances, to make permissible a voice leading which, if the setting were of only two voices, would have to be prohibited now as before because of its poor effect. The very presence of a third voice in three-voice counterpoint in general, as well as the possibility of having complete triads [in particular], provides for the first time the opportunity for a simultaneous contrary motion, or for the generation of new sonic impressions made of strong enough material to lead the ear away from the poor effect of the otherwise prohibited succession—in short, to absorb that effect (*Cpt. I,* p. 141ff.).

In spite of the basic admissibility of nonparallel similar motion, it is once again the obligation (discussed above in §8) to invoke, for purpose of comparison, all hidden possibilities of voice leading that compels us to test the various licenses concerning their respective values and to establish a gradation of those values. It can be established with complete accuracy whether, and for what reason, the one license is more appropriate than the other.

Since the inner necessity inherent in voice leading is always conceived as the first and absolute precondition, the value of a license depends solely on the extent to which the primary requirements of three-voice counterpoint have been fulfilled in spite of it; this means: the license will have all the better an effect and will appear all the more justified the more closely the guiding rules have been observed—or, to say the same thing differently, the shorter the step away from them that has, of necessity, been taken.

If we regard the prescription of melodic fluency (casuality in the horizontal dimension) together with that of completeness of triads (causality in the vertical dimension) as the two main postulates of three-voice counterpoint, and add to those the element of contrary motion as a procedure which, in itself, serves as a countermeasure against forbidden progressions in general, then it follows from the foregoing that a case of nonparallel similar motion will be justifiable in proportion to the extent to which the following conditions have been met:

1. to satisfy the prescription of melodic fluency, at least one of the three voices moves by the *step of a second;*
2. to satisfy the prescription of completeness of triads, the second chord of the pair appears as a *complete triad;* and finally,

3. at least the third voice, the one not involved in the forbidden motion, proceeds in *contrary motion.*

The following comments are in order regarding these conditions:

*Ad* 1.    Basically, it perhaps makes no difference which of the three voices executes the progression by second, whether it be one of those involved in the forbidden motion or the third, uninvolved, voice. It should however be remembered that, as remarked in Part 2, Chapter 2, §12 concerning the "ottava battuta," a larger leap is more suitable for the lower voice than for the higher, from which it follows that in the case of a forbidden motion as well, the particular motion by second is better reserved for the higher of the two voices than for the lower.

*Ad* 2.    In the case of nonparallel similar motion to 8, completeness of the triad is inherently impossible to attain because of the 8 itself; but if one adheres to the principle stated above in point 1 that the motion by second is preferably given to the upper voice, such an octave will not easily arise unless the second involved voice leaps by a fourth or a fifth:

**Example 29**

less good

Triadic completeness in nonparallel similar motions to 5, however, is in itself possible, and therefore should also be sought.

*Ad* 3.    It is *only* contrary motion that can counteract the forbidden progression, not oblique motion as well. The latter, just because of its own motionlessness, necessarily lacks all power to distract the ear in some way from the forbidden progression.

What has been said so far will now be amplified with a few examples.

In a voice leading such as the following:

**Example 30**

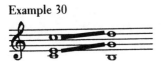

we find completeness of the second triad, contrary motion of the third voice, and, in the nonparallel similar motion itself, the favorable attribute that the higher voice moves by second, while the lower (here the inner voice) makes a leap of a third. For all of these reasons, such a leading of voices represents a more fully justified license than, for example, the following one:

**Example 31**

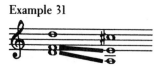

in which there is no contrary motion at all.

In a voice leading like the following, however:

**Example 32**

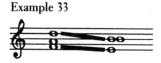

it is true that the step of a second is not lacking, nor is contrary motion and triadic completeness; yet its value is diminished in comparison to the preceding example to the extent that in the nonparallel similar motion it is precisely the higher voice—the one that most attracts the ear's attention—that makes the larger leap, while the lower voice, on the contrary, brings the step of a second.

Still more faulty, therefore, is a voice leading such as:

**Example 33**

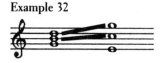

One would almost be tempted to establish a hierarchy of licenses, ranging from those most easily justified (and therefore best) to those least permissible (and therefore most remote), if it were not for the fact that still greater benefit can be derived if each license in exercises is judged not in and for itself, but purely contextually, with respect to its individual situation (see above, §8). In other words: if the voice leading occasionally exacts the price of a license that is more remote from the demands of the exercise, one should confidently pay that price, so long as one knows what price is being paid.

Concerning the leaps that occur in permissible nonparallel similar motions, the reader is referred once again to the fundamental observations in *Counterpoint I,* pp. 84, 92, and 129ff. While it was possible in principle even in two-voice counterpoint to measure, in terms of the still meager—but nevertheless already present—causalities, whether instead of:

**Example 34**

the following would not be better:

**Example 35**

(we know, of course, that two-voice counterpoint admits no nonparallel similar motions [to perfect consonances] at all), in the case of such a leap in three-voice counterpoint, we can sense all the more clearly which different, smaller leap is possible at the point in question;[19] for example:

**Example 37**

To avoid prohibited motions, contrary or oblique motion should be used if possible, or the voices should be crossed. It is true that contrary motion requires a larger space, but on the other hand it has the advantage of causing the triads to occur sometimes in open and sometimes in close position (see above, §21).

Crossing of voices, for its part, can also occasionally avoid a forbidden motion; one should be aware, however, that under certain circumstances it can, on the contrary, actually cause such a motion; for example:

**Example 38**

*Antiparallels* exhibit the same poor effect in three-voice counterpoint as in two-voice (*Cpt. I*, p. 128). An additional fault is revealed by three-voice writing, for as the following examples show:

**Example 39**

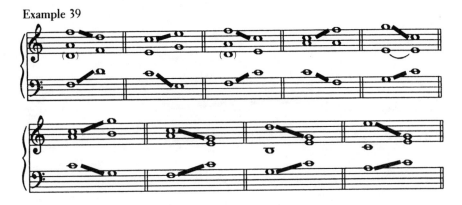

just the situation of the voices in these cases betrays the fact that countless other voice-leading possibilities are available which—because they spare the outer voices the succession of empty octaves, protect the setting from the triadic incompleteness caused by 8, and also require less space—have a more natural and better effect than the antiparallels. In the light of such latent, more appropriate voice leadings, our ear therefore rejects antiparallels in three-voice counterpoint as well.

*Fux* addresses this question on p. 90 in the following basic formulation:

> The rules should be observed not only with respect to the bass, but also, where possible, with respect to the relationship of the other parts one to another, although such rules cannot be observed very strictly in combinations of several voices; even in three voices it is permitted sometimes to depart, for good reasons, from strict observance of the rules.

For the rest, however, his treatment of this question is not systematically unified, and emerges only case by case. Thus in Fux's view, to cite selections from his discussion, a nonparallel similar motion to an octave,[20] for example, is inevitably associated with the cadence (pp. 91–92):

**Example 40**
Fux VII, 13

To the student's question of whether a better solution could not perhaps have been found here in the tenth (that is, the third) instead of the octave, Fux replies:

> [The similar motion] could indeed have been avoided [in that way], but the imperfect consonance [of the tenth] appears unsuitable to represent the perfection and repose required by the ending. It is a different matter in four-voice settings, since the addition of the fifth provides adequately for those qualities, and inclusion of the third poses no obstacle.[21]

To take another example, Fux criticizes (p. 93) a voice leading such as this:

**Example 41**
Fux VII, 15

because of the two nonparallel similar motions in direct succession in bars 3 – 4 and 4 – 5, and also because of the thin sonority ⁀ in bar 3; he also criticizes the following voice leading:

**Example 42**
Fux VII, 16

because of the prohibited seventh-leap of the bass in bars 2 – 3, and writes instead, against the same cantus-firmus tones, the following:

**Example 43**
Fux VII, 14

in order to confirm finally, with reference to the nonparallel similar motion to a fifth used here, the teaching that "in three voices, to avoid still worse errors it is permitted occasionally to depart from strict observance of the rule if there is no other possibility." In each situation, then, what is important to him is only to seek out all conceivable voice-leading possibilities; in doing so, he discovers the most appropriate among them (see above, §8), so that under certain circumstances, when nothing different and better is available, he nevertheless ventures even two successive nonparallel similar motions to fifths, as in Table VIII, Figure 12; Table XIII, Figure 3; etc.[22]

Concerning the voice leading in Example 7, bars 1 – 2, Fux remarks on p. 89:

> From this it is clear that if the bass is omitted the progression is faulty, not only because it moves from an imperfect [consonance] to a "perfect" one, but—still worse—because this fifth is not even a consonance, but only the diminished fifth.[23]

It follows from this that for him, a nonparallel similar motion to a diminished fifth is a doubly serious error. (How in free composition, on the other hand, the defining property of a diminished fifth as originating in a passing tone secures complete freedom for that interval even in parallel successions of fifths will be treated in *Free Composition*.)

Finally even voice leadings such as the following are found in Fux:

**Example 44**
Fux VIII, 6        Fux IX, 7

That at a shows a third-leap in the upper voice—undoubtedly one of the more remote licenses in comparison to those that exhibit only the step of a second; the second one, at b, however, also openly presents so-called antiparallel fifths. (Concerning such fifths, see Albrechtsberger's opinion below, and Example 49.)

*Albrechtsberger* makes a strong approach to a systematic treatment of this issue by writing, on p. 80:

> Moreover, hidden fifths, octaves, and unisons are permitted here, especially when the third voice is led in contrary motion; or also, when the lowest voice makes a leap of a fourth. In such liberties (licenses), however, the higher of the two faulty voices must proceed by step; for example:

**Example 45**

Observe in particular that he requires, under all circumstances, stepwise motion in the upper of the "two faulty" voices.

In the continuation, however, he loses all security of direction, and writes first of all on pp. 84ff.: "Finally, it should be remembered that Handel, J.S. Bach, and also several other good masters of correct writing have very often used the following three settings, which contain hidden fifths":

**Example 46**

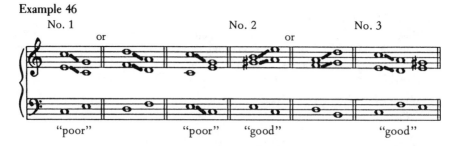

No. 1            No. 2            No. 3
     or                 or

"poor"           "poor"   "good"           "good"

If these words permit no secure inference concerning whether he would actually have approved such progressions even in strict counterpoint, it must be remarked that in all cases they show serious infractions of the rule that he himself established at the outset.

have been attained in previous ages in regions below that of genius. In short, we live in an epoch which future historians will consider an era of asininity, and which—I repeat—is most inimical to art.

---

If one sees how mankind is generally not lacking in dedication, but always strives with much greater perseverance and thoroughness for deception rather than truth, then one is tempted, in a jovial mood, to call in a Jacques Offenbach, who would drive away today's delusions by putting all the false gods of the West and their German imitators, including Marx and comrades, onto the operetta stage for the purpose of general ridicule. The Germans in particular would, of course, have at their disposal a more noble tool for liberating themselves, once and for all, from serfdom to the incompetent West. Having assured their panderers—as superfluous as they are detrimental—of unemployment compensation and having given them their walking papers, the German bourgeois and worker should band together, become musicians, and, under the baton of a chosen one, thunder the last movement of Beethoven's Fifth Symphony to the West with the force thirty million strong until the people there, deeply moved by the German genius, would gladly kiss any German hand in gratitude that a German man had opened his chamber to them. But since we live in a completely depraved world in which, because of German treachery, the *capitis diminutio maxima*[5] of the super-merchant has unfortunately failed to take place, we must content ourselves with such noble flights of fancy.

The mercenary spirit and politics of violence of the West have assumed the task of rebuilding and cleansing the world that they crushed and polluted. In keeping with his limited vision, the supermerchant thinks he can cure the thousandfold discontents of mankind[6] by just one means, namely trade. He does not grasp that although trade may lead to wealth, the latter provides only the means to the goods, never the goods themselves; he does not grasp that the rich can find satisfaction only through the means, but never through the goods, and therefore can never arrive at that wealth of mind guaranteed only by the possession of the spiritual goods bestowed by the genius. Just as the rich have at all times stolen religions from the poor (who were wealthier in spirit and humanity) only to be able all the more safely—as "brothers" among brothers—to keep their possessions for themselves alone, so today the rich man, bourgeois as well as worker, may want to ally himself nominally, for reasons of self-protection, to the temple of culture. But since this practice has always been vain self-deception, it will reveal itself no less as such today. Trade is incapable of reconstruction. As it has caused most wars [in the past], it will continue—after a brief breathing space of peace—again to crave and steal land and people, for it is not the way of trade to be content with exchanging commodities alone. Imperialism sneers at the sovereignty of nations and freedom of trade.

Trade implies advantage, egoism, and thus is the deadly enemy of culture, pursuing his own activity. Let the shoemaker remain with his last, the peasant walk behind his plow, and the prince know how to govern. For even this is a metier that needs to be studied, and which nobody should be so presumptuous as to venture into without understanding it.

Disrespect for any kind of labor other than that pursued by a disciple of Marx has led to granting even a right of idleness to such a disciple, who is remunerated at the expense of the work of women and intellectual laborers. Isn't this the reason we have arrived at a time when the worker so frequently misuses his free time for profiteering, racketeering, and other such vices? It is significant that in Goethe's *Torquato Tasso* the prince approves of both Antonio and Tasso; the democrat easily simplifies the matter by readily eliminating from his state the intellectual as a bothersome parasite.

One thing is irrevocably ingrained in the mad democrat's mind: human progress can and must be achieved solely by means of Western democracy. And, as a symbol of his cultural qualifications, the democrat attaches himself to the genius. But how? He readily embraces, for example, Goethe, as has happened recently, even though Goethe stated clearly: "My works cannot become popular; whoever strives for that goal is in error. They are not written for the masses, but only for individuals who want and seek something similar, and who pursue similar directions." The democrat has no inkling that just as sound ricochets off a wall, the genius ricochets off the wall of the masses (but does the wall know it?); rather, he considers connection with the genius as simple as connecting a plug to an electrical outlet on the spur of the moment. That, on the contrary, only true receptivity, hence organic depth, can be the precondition of understanding the genius is entirely beyond his grasp. As little as a dull schoolboy tends to blame himself rather than Homer (or the teachers) for not having learned to read Homer at school, so little does it occur to the democrat to blame mankind—an eternally dull schoolboy—for not having learned anything in the school of the genius. To the average person, the one who discovers and solves problems is never the genius, but always only the average person's equal—that is, the other average person. Therefore, he believes himself to "progress" if only he runs past as many novel products of the democratic intellect as possible, as if they were display windows, and sees as many lands and peoples as possible—in short: simply takes in with his eyes the greatest possible turnover. Thus he sees "progress" rushing and careening forward person by person, second by second, issue by issue, faster than it could in fact move even among geniuses for millennia. Presumably he even considers city horses today, just because they are not afraid of a streetcar, more advanced than the horses of Antiquity or the Middle Ages.

Especially for music, the people-panderer has certain knowledge that its salvation can come only from the "people" rather than the individual genius. It escapes him that charlatans have already destroyed the pure tonal material—the art of voice leading and harmony—to such an extent that it is no longer possible to achieve even mediocre results, such as could at least

In the same context, Albrechtsberger adds the following remark: "The remaining [settings], however, in which all three voices proceed in direct motion, and those in which both upper voices have leaps (even though the bass may proceed in contrary motion), are almost all prohibited":

**Example 47**

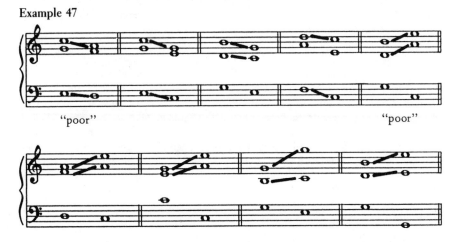

"poor"                                      "poor"

But wouldn't the prohibition of the fourth example on the contrary have to be considered remarkable, since its voice leading, strictly speaking, satisfies Albrechtsberger's fundamental rule? (Obviously, he was moved to reject it because of the lack of contrary motion and the larger leap in the inner voices.) And if one notes that he also approves motions such as the following:

**Example 48**

p. 84            p. 85

"good"                            "acceptable"

then Albrechtsberger's illogical position is, without doubt, adequately documented. The reason for this is that Albrechtsberger, failing to recognize the true purpose of contrapuntal theory and misunderstanding the relationship of strict counterpoint to free composition, was unable to formulate the license in such a way that it could first of all have satisfied the needs of strict counterpoint, and only later, in extended forms, have adapted itself to the vastly increased demands of free counterpoint as well. As a result, he was forced—ultimately without judgment or plan—to intermingle cases of strict counterpoint with those of free composition. Just observe, on the other hand, how easily cases such as those of Example 46 can be taken care of according to the formulation I have given in the text: under certain circumstances, all of these progressions must be approved, even for the domain of exercises—but, to be sure, in full consciousness of their advantage or disadvantage in comparison with other possible and more natural licenses. Thus in No. 1, although the requirements of contrary motion and complete-ness of the second triad are met, melodic fluency suffers from the leaps in all three voices, so that the value of such a voice leading, considered in and for itself, is inferior. In Nos. 2 and 3 the value of the voice leading is reduced by the fact that it is precisely the upper of the "two faulty" voices that makes the larger leap.

Only in treating the second species of three-voice counterpoint, on p. 88, does Albrechtsberger remark: "Two perfect consonances of like name are, of necessity, allowed here in contrary motion between the outer voices from upbeat to downbeat." It follows from this that antiparallels, except those that occur "of necessity," are obviously better avoided, and should under all circumstances be avoided here in the first species. To elucidate, he presents the example by Fux quoted here in Example 44, and comments: "We find this exception or license in the two fifths that Herr Fux has written in bars 8 – 9 in his last example, in F, of this same species." For use in free composition, "where any voice may move when and where it pleases," he takes it upon himself to "improve" Fux's voice leading as follows:

**Example 49**

Albrechtsberger's suggestion for improvement can scarcely be described as other than childish, for the freedom of antiparallels in free composition rests less on the fact that in it "any voice may move when and where it pleases" than on their justification by the stronger necessities of scale-degree progression, composing out, and the like, so that in free composition, antiparallels have no need of "improvement," since they far more often appear to be urgently demanded.

As far as voice-crossing is concerned, Albrechtsberger often enough makes excessive use of it (see p. 98, bars 5 – 7, for example).

*Cherubini* exaggerates beyond all measure in permitting no licenses in the outer voices under any circumstances (p. 28, fourth rule): "No license at all is permissible where the two outer voices are concerned." This prohibition is prefaced, however, with the following words: "One can disregard this rule (but only very seldom), at least with respect to the inner voice, in cases where its strict observance would encumber the progression of the other voices or would have still worse consequences for subsequent bars"; this clearly retains the flavor of Fux's teaching, which certainly cannot be reconciled with the above absolute prohibition that is Cherubini's own brain-child. If this constitutes a notable failure of logical continuity in the text itself, it is all the more astonishing suddenly to come across the following voice leading in Cherubini's exercises:

**Example 50**

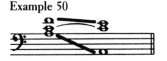

(Concerning [Cherubini on] antiparallels, see the citation below with respect to four-voice counterpoint, in Part 4, Chapter 1, §7.)

Stricter than Albrechtsberger (but not so contradictory as Cherubini), *Bellermann* requires (p. 192ff.) that

1. of the two faulty voices, the upper always move by step;
2. the lower voice at the same time make a leap of a fourth or fifth;
3. a complete triad be produced by the leap, except in the closing cadence (see above, Fux's illustration in Example 40).

Thus he differs from Albrechtsberger not only in the third point, but also in the second (which implies that many licenses involving contrary motion of the third voice that are permitted by Albrechtsberger remain excluded according to Bellermann). The only point of complete agreement between the two is their prohibition of nonparallel similar motion combined with oblique motion with respect to the third voice. (As a counterexample, see the above quotation from Cherubini, [Example 50].)

### §23. A few special remarks concerning the ⁶₄-chord

To lead all three voices in similar motion with constant preservation of triadic completeness is possible only through use of the ⁶₄ chord. However, even here (compare the first species of two-voice counterpoint, *Cpt. I*, pp. 160–161), it is not advisable to use too many of such ⁶₄-chords in succession. In part it is the monotony that threatens the so sensitive outer-voice setting by a protracted use of the sixth (close position!) in such cases and in part also the continuing deception concerning the roothood-tendency of the lowest tone (see above, §11) that has an unfavorable effect.

The notion of a succession of ⁶₄-chords also raises the question—to my knowledge it has never before been considered—of why, since the fourth in the ⁶₄-chord has newly been declared a consonance, the prohibition of parallel successions would not extend to the succession of fourths that arises here as actual parallels. Should the succession of fourths in an example such as the following:

**Example 51**

perhaps be regarded as faulty parallels of perfect consonances, then, or—all logical consistency to the contrary—is the situation again different in this case, in spite of our recognition of the consonant character of the fourth?

This question shall now be answered as follows:

In fact, we differentiate very precisely in strict counterpoint between fourth-successions like those of Example 51 and fifth-successions like these:

**Example 52**

If strict counterpoint accepts the former without hesitation but discards the latter as poor-sounding, it is obviously only because of the unqualified perfection and distinctness of the fifths (*Cpt. I*, pp. 79–80 and p. 112ff.), whose direct succession manifests their inherently poor effect in strict counterpoint even where, as here, the fifths do not even come into consideration as boundary intervals, and three-voice polyphony moreover contributes its effect of absorbency. The fourth, on the other hand, because of its far lower degree of perfection, is much less sensitive, and therefore readily admits similar motion.

A longer succession of $\frac{6}{3}$-chords in stepwise motion has a better effect descending than ascending. The reasons for this are obviously the following:

Since in strict counterpoint we are still completely unable to attribute mere passing value to such $\frac{6}{3}$-chains, as we can do frequently (indeed, most of the time) in free composition, in such a case the question of roothood-tendency of the lowest tone ($\frac{5}{3}$) necessarily becomes more pressing in strict counterpoint than in free composition. But in descending stepwise progressions of $\frac{6}{3}$- chords, such as these:

**Example 53**

a much shorter path (motion of only one voice) leads to fulfillment of the roothood-tendency than in ascending stepwise progressions (which require motion of two voices):

**Example 54**

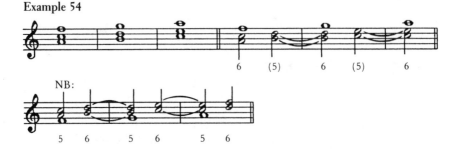

In Example 53, the lowest tone actually becomes the root once the subsequent tone [of the upper voice] is brought into relationship with it through anticipation, while in Example 54, the low tones *a, b, c,* etc., can in no way achieve the status of actual roots.

But even disregarding the sixths,[24] here it is also the fourths which—as though they were actually dissonant suspensions—prefer, in keeping with the resolution-rule familiar from *Counterpoint I,* p. 261, to resolve downward rather than to rise.

In so far as possible, the voices of the ⁶₄-chord should be kept close together, just because of the sonic density that attends close position; yet the distance of a tenth from the lowest voice is also permitted, to the extent that it is demanded and justified by the voice leading.

*Fux* speaks expressly about progression to the fourth (p. 116): "Therefore, this progression is to be viewed as motion from a perfect consonance to an imperfect consonance by similar motion—an interpretation that should be noted well."[25] (See the quotation above, in §14.) Concerning the ascending progression of several successive sixth-chords, see above, in §14, the quotation regarding Example 8.

*Albrechtsberger* deals with the problem of the ⁶₄-chord on p. 83 with the following comment: "The two NB's . . . signify that in simple counterpoint it is no error to place two or three sixth-chords in direct succession, because they are not [to be] inverted; in double counterpoint at the octave, however, they would be faulty, because [when inverted] . . ." and so forth. And also:

> At one time there was a rule that sixth-chords in succession should be kept in close spacing, so that the fourth-succession in the upper voices would not be perceived as so detrimental [examples follow]. But it is not always possible, in the first place, to move soprano and alto into the low register or the bass into the high register so quickly without harming the melodic flow; in the second place, often it is the cantus firmus or the fugal subject or countersubject that causes the [voices of the] sixth-chords to be set so far apart. As a consequence, this rule was a severe constraint.

Apart from an inherently indefensible—and thus under all circumstances reproachable—appeal to the compositional technique of the sixteenth century, *Bellermann's* explanation on p. 193 must otherwise be acknowledged to be perfectly correct:

> Just as one attempted in two-voice counterpoint to avoid prolonged successions of parallel thirds and sixths, in three-voice counterpoint as well an extended series of sixth-chords cannot be considered good. On the contrary, attention must be given to variation in tonal combinations, so that the triad occurs sometimes in close and sometimes in open position, sometimes with the third as the upper voice and sometimes with the fifth, and so forth. This, however, can be achieved only through an adept employment of contrary and oblique motion.

## §24. *The succession of two major thirds*

To the ideas presented already in *Counterpoint I,* p. 146ff., it must be added here that with three-voice polyphony, under appropriate circumstances a new remedy against the hazard of the tritone is given: specifically, it is the

again, only free composition (see *Free Composition,* [pp. 92–93]) can use it
with the full force of necessity as a transformation of a chromatic progression.

*Albrechtsberger* writes on p. 80: "We fall into the error of an inharmonic cross-
relation if we write [tones that form] an augmented or diminished octave in two
successive beats (even when one third is minor and the other is major, or both are
minor); for example:"

**Example 60**

(Compare several similar faulty progressions deliberately constructed by Albrechtsberger himself in the syncope-species on pp. 104–105.) In spite of the fact that for the
first time in his entire treatise he speaks here of a cross-relation produced by an
augmented or diminished octave (cf. *Cpt. I,* p. 152), he still neglects to elucidate the
inner nature of such a thing. That the reason for this neglect is to be sought only in
an insufficient penetration of the problem follows clearly from a transgression that he
commits on p. 147—only in four-voice counterpoint, to be sure:

**Example 61**

He comments upon it as follows, on p. 148:

> The license at the **F♯** here does not offend the ear at all, since in the present
> day the chromatic genre is very frequently mixed with the diatonic in order to
> invigorate the harmony. Yet in counterpoint it must not be done often. The
> chromatic fugal movements that are constructed deliberately for the purpose of
> expressing darker sentiments are exempt from this rule. The chromatic passage-
> work, however, that we see and hear ad nauseam in recent concertos and pieces
> in the galant style, make a poor effect on our ear in a gay allegro or rondo. But
> another reason this license is good is that the inharmonic cross-relation F/F♯
> forms not a diminished, but an augmented octave, which is more tolerable.
> Finally, this accidentally raised note is only a leading tone, which makes the
> following G of the harmony easier for the singer and more agreeable to the
> listener.

(Compare also Albrechtsberger, p. 144, bar 7 of the exercise.)

Diffusion, confusion! Just to confirm the teaching of strict counterpoint, as he
understood it, Albrechtsberger moves himself to such prejudice against "chromatic

passage-work . . . in recent concertos and pieces in the galant style," a prejudice which, however, because of its complete baselessness, is also completely out of place in strict counterpoint, and which, moreover, he contradictorily rescinds for "chromatic fugal movements," although such movements have as little to do with strict counterpoint as "galant" pieces. Add to this that he criticizes, on the one hand, the use of chromaticism even in free composition (!), but on the other hand takes refuge exactly therein to justify the license of the chromatic progression $F — F\sharp$ that he has used in the above passage. Such vacillation! We see clearly again on this occasion where the teacher's lack of secure footing leads when he is unable to distinguish clearly between the theory of pure voice leading and that of free composition (which is based at once on voice leading and scale degrees): first he tethers free composition—as happens so often with Albrechtsberger—in the name of counterpoint, then, vice versa, he oversteps the limits of counterpoint in the name of free composition. How much simpler and more natural, by comparison, my own teaching on this point: chromatic progression is completely prohibited without exception in the exercises of strict counterpoint, and this automatically excludes any cross-relation of chromatic tones, regardless of any further differentiation among the types of octaves that might be produced by it.

I therefore also reject what Albrechtsberger has to say about the same question later on concerning the second species of two-voice counterpoint, on p. 87: "In this species and in the following ones, all inharmonic cross-relations are already permitted, if they do not offend the ear too severely." Such a standpoint must be described as too premature under all circumstances for exercises that should confer only the understanding of pure voice leading, regardless of whether they are in three or four voices or in one or another species. Finally, it should be mentioned that in Albrechtsberger's exercises, examples can certainly be found of modulations that are completely permissible in strict counterpoint, such as p. 84, bar 5ff; p. 89 (as though C major to F major); p. 92 (as though E minor to G major); p. 96, bar 8ff.; etc.

When *Cherubini* writes on p. 48, in third exercise [of four-voice third-species counterpoint]:

**Example 62**

it can only deserve reproof as a contradiction of his invariably strict position. For the two major thirds in the lower voices of bars 1 – 2 produce as a sum an augmented fifth $(F — C\sharp,$ cf. *Cpt. I,* p. 147f.), which in this context unfortunately is not at all disguised by the voice leading. Very unpleasant, too, is the gratuitous doubling of the leading tone, $c\sharp$.

*Bellermann* writes on p. 103:

On the other hand, it can happen in polyphonic settings that a major triad is followed by a minor triad on the same scale degree, or, conversely, a minor triad is followed by a major. In such cases the earlier composers avoided raising or lowering the tone of the voice that had the third; they preferred instead to transfer the interval in question to a different voice; for example:

**Example 63**

The reason is that it is very difficult to demarcate the small minor second with perfect purity [in singing], while the minor and major third are far easier to sing. But if the small half step is used actually as an ascending progression in one voice, as Goudimel has done, then this movement must continue in the same direction to the nearest diatonic step. A progression like that sung by the alto voice in the following example is very unattractive and extremely difficult to execute well, for which reason it should be completely avoided in a capella settings:

**Example 64**

So far Bellermann. He is right to prohibit such cross-relations and chromatic progressions in strict counterpoint, but when he moreover prohibits them for use in free composition, it is error and presumption, which surely rest on a flagrant misunderstanding of the true purpose of contrapuntal doctrine. For, to repeat once again: the cross-relations shown above in Example 63 are prohibited here in strict counterpoint only because they are components of purely harmonic phenomena, such as mixture, tonicization, and actual modulation, which, however, can by no means be adequately certified as such here in strict counterpoint. The comparison with free composition is, to be sure, suggestive of an interpretation of the first progression of Example 63 as a mixture of C major and C minor, and the second progression of the same example (as well as the progression in Example 64) as a chromatic modulation and a tonicization process; but, as I have said, that is only a comparison, and, as such, lacks the demonstrative power inherent in a true mixture or tonicization in free composition.

### §26. *Partial cadences* (Halbkadenzen) *in the main body*

Since three-voice counterpoint, as we shall see in §27, already has access to the form of the "full cadence," it naturally shows less sensitivity to "partial cadences," which two-voice counterpoint by its nature still had to prohibit.

Therefore partial cadences, such as the following, for example:

**Example 65**

are to be admitted even in the main body without restriction.

*Albrechtsberger* writes (p. 81): "The partial cadences $\begin{smallmatrix}6\\3\\e\end{smallmatrix}\ |\ \begin{smallmatrix}8\\3\\d\end{smallmatrix}\ ||\ \begin{smallmatrix}6\\3\\b\end{smallmatrix}\ |\ \begin{smallmatrix}3\\1\\c\end{smallmatrix}$ are allowed throughout."

## Cadence

### §27.  *Construction of the cadence*

In three-voice counterpoint as well, construction of the cadence is initially influenced only by the aspect of the two leading tones: it is precisely the principles of voice leading of a melodic line that make an actual closure without a leading tone—whether the ascending or the descending—unthinkable (*Cpt. I*, p. 172). In seeking a concluding formula for the additional, third voice, we find that it too could cadence by means of a leading tone, provided that the latter were the descending one, which is the only one that admits doubling (see above, §18); this, however, would necessarily lead only to an incomplete triad in the penultimate bar and only to $\frac{6}{3}$ [or $\frac{6}{3}$] in the final bar:

**Example 66**

If, on the other hand, the primary requirement of completeness of triads is to be met in the penultimate bar as well, then, depending on the situation, only the following possibilities are available:

1.  If the two leading tones are in the inner and highest voices, then, since $\frac{6}{4}$ (see Example 67) is inadmissible, the third, lowest, voice is assigned exclu-

**Example 67**

sively to the tone of the *dominant* lying a third below the ascending leading tone; from here, it can leap down by fifth to the tonic tone, or up by fourth:

**Example 68**

The last bar in such cases presents 88, a sound which, because of its complete perfection, is better suited to the close than $\frac{8}{3}$:

**Example 69**

2.   When on the contrary the lowest voice has one of the two leading tones, the following additional distinctions are necessary:

(a) If it has the ascending leading tone, since Example 70 is prohibited

**Example 70**

because of the diminished fifth, the third voice is once again assigned only to the tone of the dominant:

**Example 71**

which, however, may fall to the third in the last bar:

**Example 72**

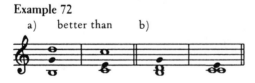

Here the effect is better in the first example than in the second.

(b) If the lowest voice has the descending leading tone, since Example 73

**Example 73**

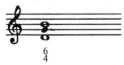

is inadmissible, the third voice, in whatever position it may be, can present only the third of that leading tone:

**Example 74**

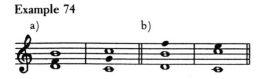

In this case, however, the following progression is allowed:

**Example 75**

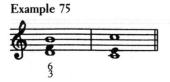

while this is prohibited under all circumstances:

**Example 76**

The result to which the theory of closure of a melodic line (cf. *Cpt. I,* §23) leads us in relation to cadential formulas in three-voice counterpoint corresponds in a surprising way to the result with which we are familiar from the theory of harmony, which speaks of scale degree V or VII at the penultimate position in a cadence. Consider, in particular, how strict counterpoint itself exposes the conceptual closeness and the inner kinship—obviously a product of exactly the same voice-leading necessity—of these two sonorities (cf. *Harmony,* pp. 190ff., and *Free Composition*). There is no doubt that it has been the purely contrapuntal collaboration of leading-tone principles together with the demand for completeness of triads that has introduced us for the first time to the dominant-concept in any form (*Harmony,* p. 139ff.); in strict counterpoint, however, the two complete triads [available] in the penultimate bar signify the last rally, as it were, of triadic completeness shortly before its dissolution into the perfect oneness of the last bar.

In particular, however, the following additional results, of the most far-reaching significance, must be underscored:

Not just any major third of a randomly chosen complete (major) triad is to be viewed as an ascending leading tone, but only the major third of that fundamental which is actually the dominant tone of the key (=V − I). This affirmation absolutely does not constitute an arbitrary stipulation, but only formulates in different words the recognition that in three-voice writing, if the penultimate chord is to be complete, there is no tone other than the dominant

No. 6. Bar 7 shows a modulation; the inner voice crosses with the cantus firmus, but the use of this technique deteriorates in bars 9 – 12. Moreover, the line of the soprano, with its lame circling about $c^1$, is, like the whole character of the exercise, too monotonous.

No. 7. Concerning the octave-leap in bars 8 – 9, see §22. From bar 8 on, the line of the bass is shaped in a purely instrumental fashion: just observe the leaps of third, octave and third in direct succession and in the same direction. In bar 11 we see ⁶₄ in the internally open position, which, however, is too poorly justified by the voice leading.

# Chapter 2

# The Second Species: Two Notes Against One

### §1.   *The guiding principles in general*

In the second species of three-voice counterpoint, the principles of two-voice second-species writing are augmented by those of three-voice writing. In the paragraphs that follow, it will be shown what kind of influence three-voice polyphony exerts on those principles, and in what way they are prolonged and deepened.

### §2.   *The relationship of the vertical harmony of the downbeat to the half-notes of the horizontal direction, specifically to the consonant or dissonant upbeat*

Along with the completely independent character of voice leading, in the second species of two-voice counterpoint a more or less definite relationship is expressed between the vertical harmony of the downbeat and the half-notes moving in the horizontal direction (see *Cpt. I*, p. 213ff.). The content of this relationship varies, depending upon whether the half-note is in the upper or lower voice, and whether it is consonant or dissonant; but every effect that is produced is limited by the general character of strict counterpoint, which, as we know, can under no circumstances lend the sonorities such definiteness as that with which they are infused by free composition.

   If we take as a beginning the *consonant* upbeat, we see how, under certain circumstances, as for example here:

**Example 84**

the harmony of the downbeat is continued by the upbeat, so that one and the same complete or incomplete triad is produced by the sum of upbeat and downbeat. In the next example, on the other hand:

**Example 85**

the upbeat either is not contained at all in the harmony of the downbeat, as at a, making it necessary to speak of a change of harmony (5 — 6), or, as at b, a doubt at least may be raised about whether the unchallenged roothood-tendency at the downbeat implies a change of harmony, or whether the sixth can be assumed to have a retrospective effect.

We reach similarly uncertain conclusions when the counterpoints are in the lower voice: sometimes, to be sure, an indisputable triadic sum is produced, as at a in the following example; but sometimes, as at b and c, it is doubtful whether a change of harmony is present or not:

**Example 86**

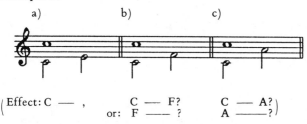

As mentioned before, the harmony of the downbeat, therefore, can control our hearing in such a way that, wherever the upbeat permits, we imagine the first half-note as sustaining—that is, as continuing to sound; but strict counterpoint does not yet have the power to eliminate the doubt that may arise concerning a change of harmony (except in the indisputable case of 5 — 6, Example 85a), to say nothing of yielding a complete precision of meaning.

The situation is more distinct for the effect of a dissonant passing tone in two-voice counterpoint:

**Example 87**

If the motion into the second half-note introduces a dissonance, there is present on the upbeat, strictly speaking, only an interval dissonant against the lower voice; nevertheless, the second interval still remains under the influence of the harmony of the preceding downbeat. It is as if the harmony of the downbeat were still present at the upbeat—as if it were still sounding:

**Example 88**

This effect is present in both cases [a and b], but, in the case of a passing tone in the lower voice [see b], it is, moreover, extended and deepened in a special way: because at a the lower tone is sustained, that act of sustaining alone prolongs in one's memory the sound of the consonant first interval, and all the more clearly so because all intervallic definitions are based on the lowest voice. In the second case, at b, on the other hand, the lower voice gives up the means to do what it was above all obliged to do, namely to provide an audible continuation of the harmony established on the downbeat; therefore it is particularly necessary in this case to retain the harmony of the downbeat at least in memory. If, for the sake of greater clarity, we write at b the tone to be prolonged in a lower register—since it is purely imaginary (*geistig*) in nature—:

**Example 89**

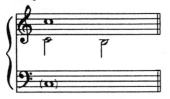

then we gain an insight into the true nature of the lower voice (to be presented more fully in *Free Composition* [§56]), and how, in relation to the scale degree conceived as lying still lower, it actually takes on the meaning of another upper voice. In other words, it is precisely the dissonant passing tone that confirms the harmony of the downbeat more reliably and emphatically than the consonant upbeat, which, as we saw earlier, does not imply a unity of harmonic effect [within the bar] and often leads even to a more or less explicit change of harmony.

Alongside all of the corporeality (which is always to be understood as independent) of the intervals available in strict counterpoint, the first appearance of the dissonant passing tone produces a curious intrusion of the imaginary: it consists in the covert retention, by the ear, of the consonant point of departure that accompanies the dissonant passing tone on its journey through the third-space. It is as though the dissonance would always carry along with it the impression of its consonant origin, and thus we comprehend in the deepest sense the stipulation of strict counterpoint, which demands of the dissonant passing tone that it always proceed only by the step of a second and always only in the same direction [as that by which it was introduced].

The implications of this effect are of great importance: we recognize in the dissonant passing tone the most dependable—indeed the only—vehicle of melodic content. While in the first species the melodic line still unfolds laboriously, sound by sound, in the second species we see it move ahead within the framework of a sustaining vertical sonority. Therefore even two-voice counterpoint shows the beginnings of melodic *composing-out*—that is, the *simultaneous unfolding of the same harmony in both vertical and horizontal directions*—to the extent that it is capable of setting up a relationship of downbeat and upbeat such that both express the same harmony. When the upbeat is consonant, this relationship of downbeat and upbeat may or may not be present, depending on the particular interval; but it is always present when the upbeat is dissonant.

The concept of *nodal point (Knotenpunkt),* which plays such an important role in the voice leading of free composition (see *Free Composition*) should perhaps be taken up first of all in connection with dissonant passing tones. Since the dissonant passing tone fills out the space of a third, it gives both of the consonant points the significance of beginning and end of a third-space that is to be understood as a unit; at the same time, it releases the concluding tone for service as the beginning of a newly adjoined tonal event:

**Example 90**

For the dissonant passing tone itself, the interval it forms in relation to the other voice (9, 7, 4, etc.) is a matter of complete indifference—this is how completely it is generated by the horizontal direction. This characteristic, too, carries over into free composition, so·that there, whether the passing event is a single tone or a harmony, it is inappropriate to discriminate among the dissonant intervals, to say nothing of attempting to measure the degree of dissonance and to evaluate one interval as more dissonant than another.

In three-voice setting, the consonance of the downbeat acquires clearer content. In like measure, clarification and intensification of all adumbrations of composing out are advanced. Regardless of whether the upbeat is consonant or dissonant, the increased accumulation of consonance on the downbeat can already make available a considerable spiritual abutment, which is particularly beneficial to the dissonant passing tone in the lower voice.

We shall see later, in the combined species as well (see Part 6), how the necessity of holding fast to the harmony of the downbeat becomes all the more urgent the more the other voices simultaneously moving in half-notes threaten to imperil the unity of the harmony of the downbeat. Then, particularly for the dissonant passing tone in the bass, our power of imagination must on its own carry forward the harmony of the downbeat; and by doing so, it prepares itself most appropriately to grasp that greatest marvel of imagination which governs free composition: the scale degree, which represents the highest ramification of that lingering of a harmony through the duration of passing events. Even there, in free composition, in spite of maximized possibilities of composing out, the consonant harmony of sustaining tones (either actual or assumed) remains the sole measure of all that pertains to passing dissonances; and in whatever guise (resulting from substitution or other abbreviation-processes) the dissonant passing tone may be used there, the consonance lying a second higher or lower always stands at its cradle—just as is demanded by the original phenomenon.

To return to three-voice strict counterpoint, all that remains is to show, with a few examples, how here (just as in two-voice counterpoint), in case of triadic completeness at the downbeat, a consonant upbeat can either continue or change the harmony, while a dissonant upbeat invariably only confirms it:

**Example 91**

and, further, how an incomplete initial harmony can be (but need not be) completed by a consonant upbeat, while a dissonant upbeat always leaves it unchanged:

**Example 92**

*Fux* addresses this question, only in the third species, to be sure, on p. 98: ". . . as in all species of counterpoint, so also in this one, attention is given to the notes that fall on the downbeat." And further: "But take care whenever you cannot use the harmonic triad on the first quarter occurring on the downbeat to bring it about on the second or third quarters." (Our inference from the third species back to the second is no doubt justified by his own words.) But for Fux, the first and last criterion for deciding among all these possibilities is the coherence of voice leading, and therefore three-voice chords which do not achieve completion even by the upbeat occur often enough in his exercise.

*Albrechtsberger* (p. 88): "Every downbeat must have a complete or an incomplete chord, namely ⁵₃ ⁸₅ | or ⁶₃ ⁸₅ | or ³₃ ⁶₆." And further, on p. 87: "Here too it is allowed—specifically, in passing—frequently to apply $\frac{6}{4}$ $\frac{5}{3}$ $\frac{5}{4}$ $\frac{6}{4}$ $\frac{6}{3}$ at the upbeat above the bass note."

When *Cherubini* teaches, on p. 30 in the third rule, "the third may never be doubled on the strong beat, but this is allowed on the weak beat," and then immediately states, "there are cases in which doubling of the third on the strong beat cannot be avoided, but such cases are rare," it is a formulation, quite inept and not without danger, of the awareness that among all doublings, those of the imperfect consonances rank lowest in the scale of value (cf. Part 3, Chapter 1, §17). Cherubini (like Fux) speaks of completion of the downbeat harmony through the upbeat only in the third species (p. 33, first rule).

### §3.   5—6 (6—5): *Change of harmony or consonant passing tone?*

According to what has been said already in §2, in the following case, for example:

**Example 93**

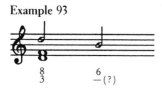

because of incompleteness of the first harmony and because of the sixth at the upbeat (cf. Example 85b), our impression must vacillate between a triadic sum $\frac{6}{3}$ on the one hand and a change of harmony on the other—specifically, as though at the downbeat, by virtue of the roothood-tendency of the lowest tone, we were to assume the sonority $\frac{8}{3}$, which would imply a succession $\frac{8}{3}$—6. Thus the first prerequisite of a genuine change of harmony would appear to be that the harmony of the downbeat also be actually complete with 5 (see above, §2, Example 85a).

It is no less true, however, that in a succession of 5 — 6 (6 — 5), in spite of triadic completeness at the downbeat, we often find an uncertainty, or at least a variation of effect, which casts doubt in a different way on the concept of change of harmony:

**Example 94**

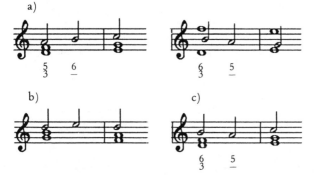

Since we tend, in the midst of the mechanism of a composing-out process (even though very simple), to interpret the harmony of the downbeat as continuing through the complete bar, wouldn't the perception of a passing tone take precedence at a over that of a true change of harmony—especially when the continuation of the half-notes so completely fulfills the rule of the passing tone?

Or can it be precluded that we hear at b a neighboring note, and accept by preference at c the effect of 5 (which brings fulfillment of the roothood-tendency of the lowest tone), and accordingly, despite all emphasis of the downbeat-harmony, hear 6 before 5 as an accented passing tone?

Strict counterpoint, to be sure, cannot supply a final disposition of these questions. But neither is that its business: all we can say is that strict counterpoint, with its exclusive concern for voice leading, cannot prevent secondary effects such as passing tones, neighboring notes and accented passing tones, as in the above example, wherever we may encounter more or less definite preconditions for their occurrence.

In this sense, then, even in strict counterpoint, to be sure, we find the first traces of a *consonant passing tone,* a *consonant neighboring note* and an *accented passing tone,* which play such an important role in free composition (see *FrC.*).

## Beginning

### §4. *Construction of the beginning*

To the possibilities for beginning as presented in the first species of three-voice counterpoint is now added the license, familiar from the second species of two-voice counterpoint (*Cpt. I,* p. 195), of the *half-rest.* This very possibility, however, raises the question in the domain of three-voice polyphony of whether instead of $\overline{8}\ \underline{3}$ sometimes even $\underline{3}\ \overline{8}$ might not be written—that is, whether the perfect consonance could be introduced only belatedly, on the upbeat. Basically there is, surely, no objection to the latter order; it may be used any time special advantages can thereby be gained for the voice leading, but one should be aware that the value of the former, as an inherently more natural one, nevertheless persists. Thus at the beginning not only the following are permitted:

Example 95

etc.

but also these:

**Example 96**

10          —          10
—          5          —          8

A formation such as this, on the other hand:

**Example 97**

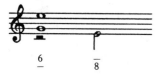

6          —
—          8

—because of the sixth, which first excludes roothood-tendency—is better regarded as ranking lower in the hierarchy.

In *Fux's* exercises we come across a license such as, for example, $\frac{10}{-}$ $\frac{-}{5}$ only in the fourth species of three-voice counterpoint (e.g., Table XI, Figure 9).

*Albrechtsberger:* "$\frac{8}{3}$ and $\frac{5}{3}$ may be used even in the first chords, if the upper voice has the counterpoint and there is no place for the third." Should and may we infer from this that he preferred $\frac{8}{3}$? Concerning the license of a rest and the attendant question of ranking of intervals, we read for the first time in Albrechtsberger concerning the third species, on p. 93:

> Now it should be noted that counterpoints may be initiated with a rest *(Suspir)*, which has the value of only a half-stroke; but these counterpoints following a rest, both here and in four-voice writing, or even counterpoints without a rest, no longer need begin with a fifth or octave as their first note (as they had to do formerly, in two-voice writing), but may also take the third, if the filling voice has the fifth or octave. In short, the perfect[1] chord, which every species must have in the first bar, can be used at liberty in counterpoint of three and more voices.

Obviously he refers, with these last words, to opening configurations in which the imperfect consonance precedes the perfect. In fact, Albrechtsberger uses such beginnings in exercises quite copiously: $\frac{10}{-}$ $\frac{-}{8}$ (p. 90); $\frac{10}{-}$ $\frac{-}{5}$ (pp. 92, 96); even $\frac{6}{-}$ $\frac{-}{8}$ (p. 92).[2]

*Cherubini* has this to say about the rest (p. 31, fifth rule): ". . . that is more elegant than beginning with a complete bar." "More elegant"? What is that supposed to mean, here in strict counterpoint?

# Main Body

### §5.  *Recollection of several earlier principles*

There is no objection to the *unison* at the upbeat (cf. Chapter 1, §12).

Since it is always possible here, through use of a consonance or a dissonant passing tone, to enlist the upbeat as well in support of the general equilibrium required in strict counterpoint, the *neighboring note,* which all too easily imperils that equilibrium, is superfluous, and is therefore better avoided (*Cpt. I,* p. 178ff. and p. 230ff.).

Variety is particularly well served here if complete and incomplete chords are used in alternation on both down- and upbeats.

> Concerning *Fux's* position on the neighboring note, see *Counterpoint I,* p. 180f.
>
> Oddly, in *Albrechtsberger's* exercises of [three-voice] second-species counterpoint there is no neighboring note, although he is otherwise fully in favor of it (see *Cpt. I,* p. 181); can this be accidental?
>
> *Cherubini* (p. 31, fourth rule): "The unison is not allowed on the downbeat, unless there is really no other possibility. It is allowed in the first and last bars as well as tolerated [elsewhere] on the upbeat."[3]

### §6. *How otherwise prohibited parallel fifths or octaves between downbeats can be improved by a third-leap*

In the relationship of downbeat to downbeat in this species—that is, the relationship shown by bracket 2 (*Cpt. I,* p. 197ff.):

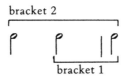

a third-leap in the inner voice can render parallel successions (involving the inner voice) harmless, since the outer-voice setting causes the poor effect to recede into the background. (For a counterexample, see *Cpt. I,* Example 279.)

It is obvious that, by the same token, in the case of a fourth-leap (of an inner or an outer voice), just as with respect to afterbeat-successions, three-voice counterpoint is shown to be less sensitive than two-voice to parallel motion between consecutive downbeats.

But a third-leap such as the following, for example:

**Example 98**

is all the more strictly prohibited here, finally, because voice leadings such as the following are available as a substitute:[4]

**Example 99**

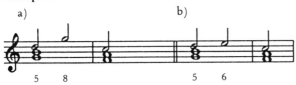

is, to be sure, prohibited here, just for the reason that the second half-note—despite appearances to the contrary—absolutely cannot function as ascending leading tone: since the second half-note here appears only as a dissonant passing tone, it renounces that chief precondition which, according to Chapter 1, §27, is indispensable for the essence of the ascending leading tone—namely, a consonant third-relation to the tone of the dominant.

To counter at the downbeat the errors of a unison or a fifth-doubling—for example:

**Example 105**

—or any other improprieties of voice leading, one may take refuge at the penultimate bar in the syncopated form:

**Example 106**

—just as it was often necessary in the same species of two-voice counterpoint to return to the whole-note of the first species (*Cpt. I*, p. 217ff.). This not only makes it possible to retain the half-note motion to the end, but, further, three different tones are after all made to sound at the downbeat, wherein the dissonant syncope moreover functions as a place-holder for the ascending leading tone.

Such a syncopated form is suitable only for the ascending leading tone, however. If the latter is in the lowest voice, in the *close position*, instead of the following:

**Example 107**

there is more justification for use of the diminished fifth:

**Example 108**

The pressure, specifically, that the postulate of melodic fluency exerts on the outer voice is so strong that, yielding to it, we opt for a second-step instead of a third-leap even at the cost of a diminished fifth. And if as a by-product it also appears as though, because of the need to avoid parallel fifths, the syncopated form was perhaps on the contrary caused only by the diminished fifth, this deception merely promotes all the more effectively the impression of that particular necessity which, in this situation, cannot be better satisfied than with the voice leading of example 108.

This pressure [exerted by the requirement] of melodic fluency vanishes, however, in the *open position,* where the voice in question is in the middle, and the second-step in the outer voice in any case does full justice to melodic fluency. With the reduction in the inner voice of such pressure, however, the compulsion to use a second-step (and also a diminished fifth) disappears, so that in the end, the deception that the syncope would be necessary here to avoid parallel fifths simply cannot arise at all. If, for all of these reasons, there is no longer any necessity at all to write, for example:

**Example 109**

then it follows just from this that the open position is better avoided, simply to eliminate use of the syncope, whose necessity here is far less compelling than in the close position.

Syncopation of the descending leading tone, however, is better avoided, especially when the cantus firmus is in minor (see below, Chapter 4, §10).

It should also not be overlooked that the leading tone need by no means always be reserved for and forced upon the voice that moves in half notes; rather, the process used in exercises in the Phrygian mode (see below, Example 113, first illustration) of assigning the leading tones to the two whole-note voices and relieving the counterpoint in half-notes of its leading-tone obligation may also be adopted for exercises in major and minor (cf. Example 113, last illustration):

**Example 110**

—unless one prefers to renounce in principle such a cadential formation whenever the half-notes are in the lowest voice. The final arbiter concerning the assignment of leading tones, certainly, is the commandment of voice leading, which, under certain circumstances, can thus be served very well by writing:

Example 111

Strict observance of diatony in minor, on the other hand, causes a voice leading such as this:

Example 112

to sound undesirable, since the raised leading tone collides with the minor third [scale-degree tone].[7]

> *Fux* devotes the following explanation (p. 96ff.) to the syncopated version:

> But since almost no rule is without exception, such a rule must be understood as applying specifically where the circumstances for its applicability are present; this is always the case in two-voice writing, but is not so in three-voice, as can be noted from the preceding examples. For where tying has been used, if one wanted to set two untied half-notes [instead], either a faulty unison or an empty sounding octave would result.

For the rest, we also find closing formulas such as the following in Fux:

Example 113
Fux IX, 2                    Fux IX, 3                    Fux IX, 7

Without providing a word of explanation, *Albrechtsberger* makes the attempt to illustrate all kinds of cadential formulas in a table (p. 88). He presents there along with various forms in half-notes—curiously, in one of them the ascending leading tone is approached by the leap of a diminished fifth (but see his Example 103):

Example 114

—also the syncopated forms, including the syncopation with diminished fifth. If we compare with the latter the cadential formulas of the exercises on pp. 90, 91, etc., we see that in the syncopation with diminished fifth he made no additional distinction between close and open position, just as he has nothing at all to say about the irregularity of the diminished fifth that it contains.

   *Cherubini* initially follows Fux's teaching and even shows expressly, with an example, the faulty doublings (11, 55) that would have to be produced if the penultimate bar were in principle restricted to two half-notes. But when he recommends a usage such as the following to solve these difficulties:

**Example 115**

he himself commits an inexcusable error, since he neglects here to place the leading tone directly after the tonic tone (Part 2, Chapter 2, §17). It is obvious that he recommends the syncope as a counter-measure; but his foundation for this sounds all too naive:

> By using the aforementioned exception in this way, one avoids the error of the unison on the strong beat; and since there is no rule that prohibits syncopation in this species, it may be used without causing error, at least so long as it occurs only in the penultimate bar. Nevertheless, we advise using it only seldom. The following examples will show that in many cases it is very easy to avoid the syncope in the penultimate bar.

(Examples follow—his Example 92—among which a quotation of Fux may also be found.)

*Bellermann* characterizes the syncopated version of the cadence as "the most satisfactory" (p. 200), and adds:

> If the ascending leading tone is in the lower voice and the cantus firmus in the middle, then here in three-voice [counterpoint]—contrary to all usual rules—we may also form the close in the following way, with the aid of tying and of the diminished triad on the weak beat. [Example follows.] This is permitted, however, only when the voices are close together, and would be objectionable if, for example, the cantus firmus, which now lies in the middle, were placed an octave higher, or the lower voice an octave lower. [Examples follow.]

We see the difference between his viewpoint and that of Albrechtsberger; but I must confess that in this question I am more inclined to support Bellermann, precisely in consideration of the fact that the interweaving and interaction of voices that attends close position is of better and more natural benefit to the cadence (Part 2, Chapter 1, §29) than the dispersion of tenths which is associated with the open position.

## Exercises

**Example 116**
Fux VIII, 12

is related to the rejection of $^6_3$ in strict counterpoint (cf. Chapter 1, §3), and subsequently also to the prohibition of a leap to a dissonant interval.

It is obvious that a consonant neighboring note in the third species of three-voice counterpoint can occur with greater clarity than in the second species (cf. Chapter 2, §3):

**Example 119**

6    5    6

The neighboring note, which is used with more justification in the third species than in the second (*Cpt. I*, p. 230), however, suggests a question that, to my knowledge, is raised here for the first time: are both neighboring notes in each individual case—that is, the upper and the lower—of similar effect and similar value? It is noteworthy, in particular, that our instinct in each individual case—contrary to theory, which counts the two neighboring notes as equal—often admits only the one, while rejecting the other. To be convinced of this, compare the effects at a and b, for example, in the following passages:

**Example 120**

The reason the effect of the lower neighboring note in the second bar at a is better than that of the upper neighboring note at b clearly must be sought in the fact that only the former, and not the latter, reflects the underlying passing tone:

**Example 121**

Thus is confirmed the priority of the passing-tone concept, as a fundamental concept, to the neighboring-note concept, as a concept merely derived from it (*Cpt. I,* p. 178ff.); similarly, the neighboring note is shown already in strict counterpoint to be the harbinger of an underlying note, hidden within the given line, which it serves as an embellishment (diminution).

With the upper neighboring note in the third bar at a, on the other hand, a fourfold repetition of the tone $f^1$ is avoided (see b); the upper neighbor moreover introduces an element of particularly delicate appeal in that the tone *a,* used first in the form of a neighboring note and on the weak beat, potently suggests and at the same time prepares the coming *a,* which arrives decisively at the third quarter of the next bar. As we see, it is the altered rhythmic placement of the same tone—how often our great masters have sought such things in their works!—that plays the chief role in establishing this attractive effect.

As simple as these examples are, it may be just as difficult in many other cases to decide between the two neighboring notes. The sensitive nature of tonal life reveals itself in the fact that such decisions cannot be made without awareness of so many diverse and concealed imponderables as are present—for example, the overall shape of the melody, the fundamental line, strictest satisfaction of basic concepts, number of repetitions of a tone, and so forth.

Strict counterpoint at the same time, however, provides also the first opportunity to observe how much the effect varies depending upon the placement of the neighboring note in the bar:

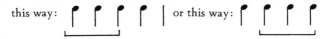

That the first form is the more natural (see above, Example 120, bar 3) requires no further proof; but the second form (bar 2 of Example 120) occasionally is not undesirable, provided only that it is justified by the situation. This difference plays an important role even in free composition (see *FrC.*).

A precisely similar variety of effects, incidentally, emerges also when 5 followed by 6 (or 6 by 5) enters the picture less in the sense of a consonant neighboring note (or accented passing tone) than in that of a change of harmony, as can be seen by comparing the regular ordering in a of the following example with the irregular cases at b and c:

**Example 122**

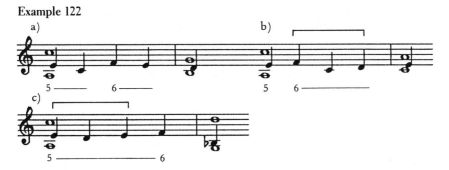

If we reflect that, considered purely horizontally, the endpoint of an actual passing motion is consonant with its point of departure—that is, remains in the same harmony with it (see above, Example 90)—then we may espy in the neighboring-note figure (derived from the passing tone) at the same time the first germ of the technique, used so often in free composition, of *substitution,* by favor of which one component of a harmony may appear in place of another:

**Example 123**

Substitution becomes much more distinct, to be sure, in the third species, when the neighboring-note figure extends from the first to the third quarter; there, retention of the same harmony is clearly evident:

**Example 124**

c.f.

If, however, the neighboring-note figure goes from the third quarter to the first of the following bar, the returning principal tone is already subsumed within a new harmony (in the contrapuntal sense, the harmony of each successive downbeat always counts as new, even if in the sense of harmonic theory it is an extension of the preceding one!), from which a new harmonic light now falls on the endpoint of the figure:

**Example 125**

In this sense, though, such a neighboring-note formation can be designated as irregular. If we reflect that the second species would have access to only this less regular variant (see Example 123), then we understand still better why the neighboring note is preferably eschewed there (*Cpt. I,* pp. 178–180).

The accented passing-tone effect of a dissonance used on the third quarter was already discussed in two-voice counterpoint (*Cpt. I,* p. 227ff.). The following observations can be added:

The justification for using a dissonance on the third quarter derives not only as an inevitable result from the law of the passing tone, which finds fulfillment any time the succession consonance-dissonance-consonance is achieved, but also from the principle that applies to the fundamental rhythmic subdivision into half-notes (two-voice counterpoint, second species), according to which the upbeat half-note may also be dissonant.

The dissonant passing tone is not allowed on the downbeat, because the accented passing-tone effect inevitably associated with it—for example:

**Example 126**

—would necessarily obscure for now the [more] fundamental concept of the suspension (⌐9 — 8). In the first stage of study, the student would have to deal immediately with two different effects which he would not so easily be able to keep separate. Since the task of strict counterpoint is to demarcate the fundamental concepts in the most precise way in order to secure understanding and usage of the prolongations, it must consequently decline to permit the actual accented passing tone alongside the fundamental concept of suspension.

I have said already in *Counterpoint I*, p. 239, that the nota cambiata is a phenomenon of free composition, which was adopted by the older teachers in their counterpoint textbooks only because of its abundant usage. Here it must be said further that this figure, which consists of two passing motions interwoven in a particular way, causes, in the final analysis, only a second-step by the melodic line—a descending step in the descending nota cambiata, and an ascending step in the ascending one:

**Example 127**

This reveals the ultimate meaning of the figure, to the extent that, as will be shown later in *Free Composition*, the line has the last word concerning the phenomena of the setting.[2]

### §3. *Parallel motion*

It should be remembered only that in the third species (*Cpt. I*, p. 232), parallel successions even in the relationship of downbeat to downbeat are to be avoided, except in a case involving parallel octaves or fifths that arise with the nota cambiata and, for its sake, must in the end be tolerated and permitted:

**Example 128**

from Fux's exercises:

Fux X, 1    Fux X, 3

from Albrechtsberger, p. 95    p. 97

p. 98

Concerning the seventh approached by leap in Albrechtsberger's second example, see *Counterpoint I*, p. 243ff.

## Cadence

### §4.  *Construction of the cadence*

In cadence formulas it should not be forgotten that in accord with the teaching of Chapter 2, §7, the second leading tone also can very well be left to the other whole-note voice. For the rest, one should take the opportunity of the cadence especially to put the nota cambiata and the neighboring note to good use. If we compare the normal and permissible cadence formula at a in the following example with the insupportable one at b:

**Example 129**

a)    b)

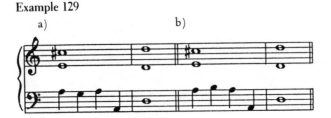

it appears as though the unquestionably better effect of the lower neighboring note at a derives from the reference contained in it to a hidden scale degree IV of the key, but at the same time, however, also from the fact that the lower neighboring note (as a derivative form of passing tone—compare the comments on Examples 120 and 121) paves the way to the third of the tonic, while the upper neighbor bogs down as the first passing tone in a fourth-space *a — b — c♯ — d (Cpt. I,* p. 239).

But in no case may one commit the infraction of a chromatic progression, for example:

**Example 130**

A leap to the ascending leading tone must also be avoided:

**Example 131**

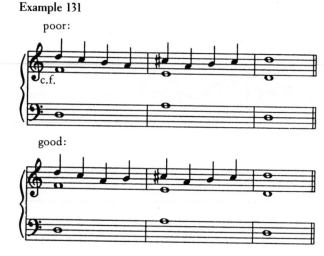

Concerning the inadmissibility of a cadential formula such as this, for example:

**Example 132**

see Chapter 2, §7.

attention of the student cannot be directed emphatically enough to the outer-voice setting as the alpha and omega of voice leading, even that of free composition.

## §2. *Review and clarification of the result derived in two-voice counterpoint concerning the nature of the syncope*

Concerning *consonant* syncopes, it was established in two-voice counterpoint that their content seems, like that of the dissonant syncopes, to comprise three beats: ♩♩♩, but that in truth only two beats come into consideration: ♩♩ . The reason for this was that because of the consonance on the downbeat, a true necessity, in the strictest sense, for one or another kind of continuation at the upbeat vanishes. It is only the general rhythm of the exercises (intended from the outset to be in the syncopated species) which, by demanding a tied upbeat after every downbeat, in itself produces the effect of an apparently indivisible unit of three beats. Recall too in this connection that in the matter of parallels (8 or 5) in two-voice counterpoint, for consonant syncopes the downbeat itself was found to be sufficiently weighty to eliminate the poor progression, which may count as a further proof of the co-determinative effect of the downbeat, and thus also of the inseparability of only two beats. All of this, however, leads to the following suggestive result.

Whereas in strict counterpoint the syncope need not always be dissonant, and whereas, moreover, in the consonant syncope only two beats (♩♩) come into consideration, the fundamental content of the syncope, through a scarcely noticeable hint, is revealed already in the domain of strict counterpoint to be a tying-over from upbeat to downbeat that is to be interpreted as purely rhythmic, encompassing only two beats. We shall see later what significance this recognition assumes especially in the prolonged application of free composition.

As far as the *dissonant* syncope is concerned, two-voice counterpoint's legacy to three-voice is as follows:

1. The voice leading of strict counterpoint can never be constituted in such a way as to carry with it a compulsion to particular foreordained paths for the voices as is so often the case in free composition, where the compulsion derives, for example, from motive, passing motion, or—to cite the most obvious instance—in suspensions of the leading tone, what is known in thoroughbass theory as the chord of the major seventh:

**Example 135**

where the leading tone as such, despite the tie, must ascend (*Cpt. I*, p. 263ff. and examples 395–397). The impossibility of giving the harmonies in strict counterpoint such definiteness that the paths of the individual voices can be predetermined at the outset with similar forcefulness—this impossibility is what must necessarily make all voice leading here independent, that is, uninfluenced. This in turn is also expressed in an extremely significant manner by the irrevocable demand of preparation of the dissonant syncope by means of a consonance, which, as such, has no wish to stipulate anything in advance, and also is completely unable to do so.

Also connected with the true and ultimate sense of this basic rule of the syncopated species as it is formulated here is the fact that we grasp the nature of the dissonant syncope directly from the sonority of the downbeat, and thus imagine the dissonant passing tone concealed within the dissonant syncope (*Cpt. I*, p. 266ff., and here §3) as entering on the downbeat, and not still earlier (as is often possible in free composition).

2.  The compulsion of the dissonance, on the other hand, necessarily points to a third time-unit—specifically, the upbeat that follows the tied downbeat: ♩♩♩ ♩—by virtue of which the dissonant syncope distinguishes itself at the outset from the consonant (see above).

3.  Nevertheless, the dissonant syncopes divide into two groups: ⁀9—8 and ⁀4—3 of the upper counterpoint on the one hand, and ⁀7—6 of the upper counterpoint together with ⁀2—3 and ⁀4—5 of the lower on the other hand.

Because of their origin, specifically the first group alone represents that category of tied phenomena which, encompassing three time-units, also flow at the third unit (the upbeat) into the harmony of the downbeat. These, then, are the *authentic suspensions.*

The syncope ⁀7—6, as well as ⁀2—3 and ⁀4—5, on the other hand, must at first raise doubt about whether the harmony of the downbeat still continues at the third (final) time-unit or whether, because of the interval 6 in the upper (or 3 or 5 in the lower) counterpoint, a second harmony should not perhaps be assumed. In particular, since 6 relates as an inversion to a different fundamental, and since 3 and 5 in the lower voice, when they occur at the upbeat, are no less able to effect a change of fundamental, in the case of these syncopes the harmony of the upbeat (the third time–unit) clearly must be described as somewhat uncertain for the domain of strict counterpoint.[1] That the effect here nevertheless appears to shift in favor of suspensions in the sense of three time-units, as in ⁀9—8 and ⁀4—3, must on closer inspection be recognized only as a reflection of these genuine suspensions, and also of the total situation of a syncopation-exercise in general.

4.  The falling 6—5↑6—5 syncope (in the upper counterpoint) occupies a middle position (*Cpt. I*, p. 294ff.), since the sixth—although consonant from the outset and therefore eligible for any kind of continuation, not just the progression to 5—borrows from the dissonant syncope the apparent compulsion

of a falling second-step (moving exactly to 5), and thus demands treatment in the same manner.

All of these relationships of consonant and dissonant syncopes return in three-voice writing; specifically, here, in spite of the three-voice texture, the situation is the same with respect to the uncertainty of harmony described above in the suspensions $\frown 7-6$, $\frown 2-3$, and $\frown 4-5$.

Concerning the latter, it should be mentioned here, for better understanding, that their equivocal condition persists even in the combined species (see below, Part 6), but there it tends to be decided in the opposite direction: since in the four-voice combined species those syncopes can receive supplementation on the downbeat such as $\frown{7 \atop 3}$, $-{6 \atop 4}$, and $-{8 \atop 2}$, they reveal, differently than in two- and three-voice settings, the incipient independence of the harmonies of the downbeat in relation to those that follow on the upbeat, to the extent that in contrast to the compulsion toward a third time-unit which derives from the tied dissonance of the downbeat, in another sense once again only two time-units ($\flat\uparrow\flat$) appear to come into consideration, and the syncopes appear to enter a state of more definite contrast to the authentic suspensions (see above, under 1). These syncopes are divested of all uncertainty, to be sure, only in free composition (see *FrC.*).

### §3. How three-voice counterpoint definitively clarifies and confirms the necessity of a downward resolution of the dissonant syncope[2]

The postulate of descending resolution of all syncopes in strict counterpoint is now definitively confirmed in three-voice counterpoint by the standards of the increased resources. This will now be shown for the individual syncopes taken in order.

(a) $\frown 7-6$. According to the explanation given in *Counterpoint I*, p. 265ff., $\frown 7-6$ is to be traced back to a descending passing tone, not an ascending one; thus, in two-voice counterpoint, as follows:

**Example 136**

The difference in effect of these two passing motions is clear enough already in two-voice counterpoint, since in the ascending passing tone—regardless of whether one assumes only one chord (A) or a succession of two (A and C)—abbreviation of the passing motion through omission of the point of departure, as is demanded by my interpretation of the syncope, turns out to be impossible, specifically for the reason that we do not have the right to violate at the outset the roothood-tendency of the given bass note and to assume the presence of its sixth.

Three-voice counterpoint now adds to this argument further reasons in support of the descending resolution.

If we imagine as the third voice the *octave* of the bass:

**Example 137**

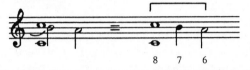

then this only confirms expressly the point of departure, which in any case represents the beginning of the passing motion when the tie is removed.

For an ascending passing tone, on the other hand:

**Example 138**

the effect of a neighboring note would have to be perceived:

**Example 139**

because the added octave here strengthens the roothood-tendency of the lowest tone to such an extent that it is even less possible to imagine the sixth *a* as the point of departure of a passing tone than in two-voice counterpoint (see above, Example 136).

If we take a *third* as the third voice, it is again the impossibility of assuming a sixth as the beginning of a passing motion that prevents the question of what effect a third would make from arising at all; thus:

**Example 140**

In the ascending passing motion, the bass note, precisely because of the presence of the third, would have to awaken in us the impression of an octave

more easily than that of a sixth, in which case ⌐7 — 8 would, however, again
have to have the effect of a neighboring note (see Example 139):

**Example 141**

That the third voice may not have the *fifth,* however, is obvious: apart
from the empty effect of the fifth, at the downward resolution, a dissonant
sonority $\frac{6}{3}$ would have to be present on the upbeat:

**Example 142**

and, in the case of the ascending passing motion, even on the downbeat:

**Example 143**

For who would want to assume a sixth along with the fifth just to save the
impetus of the passing motion, when it is possible to hear the dissonance
either in the sense of a neighboring note:

**Example 144**

or finally even in the sense of a passing motion unfolding in the space of a
fourth (*Cpt. I,* p. 240):

**Example 145**

(b) ⌐4 — 3. The resolution of the dissonant syncope 4 (*Cpt. I,* p. 267) rests on the descending ( ⌐4 — 3) passing tone, and not on the ascending one ( ⌐4 — 5):

**Example 146**

If we consider that in the first case the passing tone leads to the third, which, in the horizontal direction, points backward to the fifth no less than the bass tone points upward to it in the vertical direction, this alone provides truly a surfeit of advantages for the descending passing tone in comparison to the ascending one, which at its conclusion leads to an empty fifth that is undesirable in two-voice counterpoint; this remains correct even if it must otherwise be acknowledged that one would have to be allowed to assume the third just as well as the fifth as a point of departure for the passing tone.

In three-voice settings it is most natural to assign the *fifth* to the added voice, a tone which, in the descending passing motion, explicitly acknowledges the point of departure of the passing motion along with the passing tone itself:

**Example 147**

One sees clearly in this instance the advantage of the suspension, which—by filling the space of a fifth with a dissonant passing tone and, by that means, setting up our expectation of the third—is the only thing that makes possible use of the fifth in the first place, since it would otherwise be indefensible because of its emptiness.

In the case of an upward resolution, the fifth would not only lead to the completely insupportable result of a doubled fifth at the upbeat:

**Example 148**

but would also bring into the foreground the impression of a neighboring note:

**Example 149**

In this way, then, in three-voice counterpoint as well, an interval so decisive as the fifth speaks in favor of only the descending resolution of the syncope of the fourth.

Further still: instead of the fifth, the sixth can also be assigned without hesitation to the third voice; in this case, for a descending passing tone:

**Example 150**

the sixth represents the explicitly incorporated point of departure of a passing tone in the space of a fourth (between the sixth and the third of the chord), in which the choice between the two possible passing tones in a fourth-space is decided in favor of the more natural one that lies only one tone removed from the endpoint. But with the sixth too, ⌒4—3 remains within the same sonority, which follows unequivocally from the fact that it would be inadmissible (because of $^6_5$) to imagine, along with the sixth, also a fifth as point of departure for the passing tone.

For the assumption of an ascending passing tone, on the other hand, the dissonant sound $^6_5$ would have to appear at the upbeat:

**Example 151**

not:

unless one prefers to use this passing tone:

**Example 152**

which, however, is too unnatural to be assumed by random choice.

Finally, in regard to the assignment of a *third* to the third voice in ⌒4—3, in the case of the descending passing tone we would have the disadvantage of a neighboring-note effect:

**Example 153**

not:

which is all the more unnecessary in that by assignment of a fifth, sixth, or octave [to the third voice] such a thing can be precluded under all circumstances. For the ascending passing tone, on the contrary, the third would certainly be appropriate as point of departure:

**Example 154**

if it were not for the fact that the roothood-tendency of the lowest tone, supported by both of the thirds, would cause a fifth to arise in our imagination, which would produce a neighboring-note effect.

**Example 155**

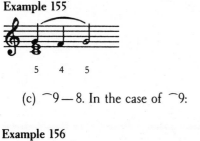

(c) ⌢9—8. In the case of ⌢9:

**Example 156**

it is true that we remain in the same harmony with both forms of passing motion (the descending as well as the ascending); but the third-space in question here, between octave and tenth, reveals itself as such to our understanding only under the assumption of the tenth as initial interval, as is the case in the descending passing tone. This matter is decided by what is actually presented to the ear: if, as in the case of the ascending passing motion, one must first posit the octave, one inevitably runs the risk of equating this at first with the fundamental, and of imagining a unison; from there, however, the upward motion would lead only to a third rather than to an actual tenth. In the descending passing motion, on the other hand, where the octave occurs after a literal 9, that sound cannot be disregarded as an octave, so that the inference concerning the true distance above the bass note—that is, the inference of the third-space between tenth and octave—emerges in the most convincing way possible. Just this was the reason I gave priority in *Counterpoint I* to the descending passing motion over the ascending in the case of ⌢9—8, and distinguished between ⌢9—8 and ⌢2—1.

Three-voice counterpoint opts even more decisively than two-voice for the descending resolution. Here the most obvious possibility is to assign a *third* to the third voice, in which case, along with the descending passing tone, its point of departure is inserted at the same time, irrespective of whether the spacing amounts to a tenth (for the upper voice) or only to a third (for an inner voice):

**Example 157**

With the third, then, the sonority is adequately saturated especially as the dissonant passing tone aims for the interval of the octave, which yields either $\frac{8}{3}$ or $\frac{10}{8}$ (see above, Chapter 1, §14).

An ascending passing motion in the case of the third, however, would sooner tilt toward the effect of a neighboring-note motion:

**Example 158**

not:

and this could not be avoided by imagining the octave as point of departure. For, as has seen said, in the context of completely independent voice leading such as that which characterizes strict counterpoint, what actually sounds always has a stronger effect than what is only imagined. An additional result of the above voice leading would be a doubled third at the upbeat, which—since other, better results are possible—must be designated as less desirable according to what was set forth in Chapter 1, §14.

The adjoining of a fifth to ⌐9—8 in the case of the descending passing motion would still mark the sound as empty:

**Example 159**

not:

since the mental image of the third—precisely only as a mental image—could not be nearly sufficient to eliminate the actually presented emptiness while the octave, and with it the completely empty harmony $\frac{8}{3}$, awaits us at the upbeat. The objections to a mentally posited octave as point of departure for an ascending passing tone have been stated already in reference to Example 156, and apply to $\overset{\frown}{\underset{3}{9}}{-}^8$ as well:

**Example 160**

not:

The addition of an *octave* to a descending passing motion would have the effect of a neighboring note:

**Example 161**

not:

In the ascending passing motion, on the other hand, the octave would acknowledge the point of departure:

**Example 162**

not:

It would, however, presuppose nothing less than 88.

It is also possible to add a *sixth,* in which case, for the descending passing motion, we land on $\frac{8}{6}$:

**Example 163**

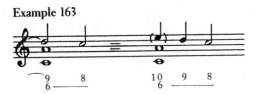

—a sonority that is not among the most desirable (see Chapter 1, §14), but which in the ascending passing motion:

**Example 164**

not:

would even have to be posited as a prerequisite.

Decisive for the assumption of a descending passing motion for ⌐9—8 from the standpoint of strict counterpoint, then, is the suitability of the 10 to demarcate more precisely the space above the octave, and also the availability of better combinations with 10 (or 3) and 6. It should not be overlooked, however, that, beyond such an independent standpoint of voice leading, the upward resolution in ⌐9—10 encounters less opposition even in strict counterpoint than the upward resolution in ⌐7—8 or ⌐4—5 (see above, under a and b) in the upper counterpoint; and this is in fact the reason ⌐9 more easily moves up as well as down than ⌐7 or ⌐4 in free composition, where the logic of harmonies can even stipulate the paths of voice leading in advance. There, in free composition, to state it even here, ⌐9—10 will be more readily perceived only as a second before the third—that is, as ⌐2—3—than as an actual ⌐9—10 syncope, whereby free composition acknowledges and confirms the danger that an octave that is only to be mentally posited as the departure-point of a passing motion can be confused with a unison far more easily than an actually sounding octave.

(d) ⌐2—1. The voice leading of two-voice counterpoint often finds it necessary to admit ⌐2—1 as well (*Cpt. I*, p. 274), especially since the unison (assuming the necessity of voice leading) has a less deleterious effect on the upbeat than on the downbeat; moreover, the downbeat is adequately filled with sonority by the dissonant second. That here (as in ⌐9—8) only the descending passing motion can be assumed—that is, only the third as a point of departure:

**Example 165**

—follows from the fact that in the contrary case, that of the ascending passing motion:

**Example 166**
not:

1  2  3

it is necessary to posit the undesirable situation of a unison on the downbeat. In this sense, in the case of ⌒2 — 1 the necessity of positing the third as departure-point is still stronger than in ⌒9 — 8; on the other hand, to guard against the neighboring-note effect:

**Example 167**

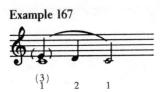

($^3_1$)  2  1

one prefers the higher octave, where the descending passing motion corresponds at least in the imagination to 10 — 9 — 8, which again precludes the neighboring note. Conventional theory nonetheless goes too far, however, when, by exaggerating the countereffect of imagination, it sees a necessity to equate ⌒2 — 1 and ⌒9 — 8 in all cases (*Cpt. I*, p. 275ff.); this would be correct only if the decision had been made to deny the unison altogether as an interval.

Three-voice counterpoint now also decides in favor of the descending passing tone (despite the danger of a neighboring-note effect, against which a defense similar to that in two-voice counterpoint is sought: reinterpretation as 10 — 9 — 8), here again, as in the case of ⌒9 — 8, because of the greater suitability of a third in comparison to a unison:

**Example 168**

thus:                              not:

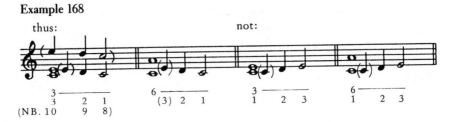

$^3_3$ ———   2   1      6 ——— (3) 2 1      $^3_1$ ——— 2 3      6 ——— 1 2 3
(NB. 10      9   8)

(e) ⌒2 — 3. The negative effect of the ascending passing tone is revealed far more decisively in syncopes in the lower voice than in the upper. For the initial tone of an ascending passing motion, when it is in the lower voice, automatically has associated with it the effect of a root, so it is doubtless clear that such a tone would be the last thing to be voluntarily posited in the world

of independent voice leading. This can be seen immediately for the syncope
⌒2 — 3 in two-voice counterpoint. If the descending passing tone is assumed
as its basis:

**Example 169**

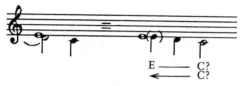

then the harmony of the cantus-firmus tone is initially preserved by the unison
on the downbeat, or at least is not impaired, while the endpoint of the passing
motion produces a tone of which one does not, to be sure, know whether it
is the root of the single harmony [of the bar] which first appears in its entirety
only at the upbeat or—and this is precisely the uncertain effect mentioned in
§2 under 3—the root of a new, second harmony. But what would give us the
right to imagine such a harmony—one based on a root a third lower—at the
outset, as would be the indispensable precondition in the case of an ascending
passing tone?:

**Example 170**

After all, there is a complete lack here of harmonic logic, which in free
composition could compel us to do this under certain circumstances. And
with an ascending passing motion, incidentally, wouldn't we moreover have
to arrive at a neighboring-note effect (see NB in the above example)?

And now three-voice counterpoint, too, confirms the preference for the
descending passing tone: if the third voice is given an interval that forms a
third with the passing tone's point of departure, as the following example
shows:

**Example 171**

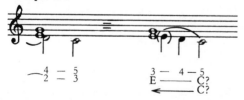

—with syncopation, to be sure, the figure for the downbeat reads $-\frac{4}{2}$—then a $\frac{5}{3}$-sound is obtained at the upbeat.

But $\frac{6}{3}$ can also be achieved at the upbeat, if an interval is taken at the downbeat which stands in the relationship of a fourth to the initial tone of the passing motion:

**Example 172**

With the syncopation, then, it is expressed as a fifth: $-\frac{5}{2}$. To the possible objection that the fourth is dissonant in the vertical direction, it should be replied that in the actual situation of the setting as in Example 172, because of the adjoined dissonant syncope the fourth is no longer in the lowest position, and is therefore consonant. As the consonant inversion of the fifth, it also creates the effect that only one harmony is admissible, precisely that of the upbeat: $\frac{6}{3}$.

Addition of the sixth to the point of departure of the passing motion:

**Example 173**

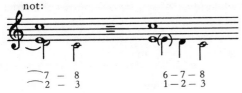

—that is, $\frac{7}{2}$ in syncopated form—produces $\widehat{\phantom{x}}7$—8 in the lower counterpoint, which will be discussed under g.

If we try on other hand to test the ascending passing tone as a basis for $-\frac{4}{2}$ or $-\frac{5}{2}$:

**Example 174**

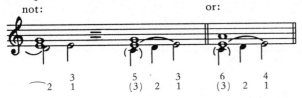

we see that in no case could adjunction by the imagination of the root in the lower position be supported and justified in any way. Further still, in the second case a fourth would have to result on the upbeat, which, as actually given and not merely posited, is excluded at the outset in the syncopated species.

(f) ⌐4 — 5. The preference for the descending passing tone over the ascending in the case of ⌐4 — 5:

**Example 175**

clearly rests, in strict counterpoint, on the fact that in the former, the point of departure of the passing motion demands [support of] its own roothood-tendency, but also leaves open the possibility of a subsequent new, lower root, while in the second case, the lower root, which signifies the ultimate boundary of the given sonority, would have to be assumed at the very outset. If we consider that for both passing motions the points of departure must, in a similar way, be posited below the cantus-firmus tone, and that both, therefore, influence the harmony, then we understand why the question first posed about preference for the descending or ascending passing tone would in the strict sense actually have to be reduced to the question of which of the two passing tones to be imagined is the more natural one. And so formulated, the question certainly can be decided only as has been done at the outset.

Again it is three-voice counterpoint which decides authoritatively in favor of the descending resolution. While in the ascending passing motion (apart from the fact that to posit a new root below cannot be permitted) a neighboring-note effect would be produced:

**Example 176**

the descending passing tone by contrast offers far more favorable combinations. If the third voice acknowledges the point of departure of the passing motion with the unison or octave:

**Example 177**

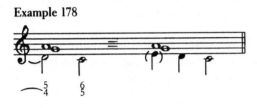

with the syncopation we gain, along with ⌐4 — 5, also ⌐2 — 3, so that precisely because of these intervals, the question must remain undecided whether we should assume here only one harmony, to which the upbeat points, or two harmonies (on the downbeat and upbeat, respectively). This produces an effect of uncertainty, as in the case of ⌐7 — 6 in the upper counterpoint.

To place a fifth along with the fourth, however:

**Example 178**

is not permissible, because of the ⁶₃ [which would result at the upbeat].

Concerning the impossibility of assigning the third voice the *sixth* above the point of departure (that is, the seventh above the passing tone itself), see under g.

(g) ⌐7 — 8. For reasons already mentioned several times, in the case of ⌐7 in the lower counterpoint even in two-voice setting, the descending passing tone would under all circumstances deserve preference over the ascending:

**Example 179**

if it were not for the fact that a certain effect here speaks against the former as well, an effect that unexpectedly turns the lower counterpoint actually into an upper counterpoint. For if one were to imagine the lower sixth as departure-point of the passing motion, one would at the same time, without expressly intending to do so, have carried out at once the inversion of the sixth into a third, and would have imagined, by virtue of the latter, the root once again in the low position:

sometimes a product only of the horizontal line, a true passing tone (as, for example, in the seventh-chord), which, whether tied as a result of abbreviation or freely attacked, by its nature presupposes that at the conclusion of the passing motion the harmony will have changed; at other times, however, the seventh as a vertical product emphasizes the effect of a suspension, which, as such, by encompassing three time-units (♩│♩ ♩)—irrespective of whether 7 is literally tied: ⌐7 — 6, or is (apparently) freely attacked: 7 — 6—finds its resolution in the same harmony (that is, with a tone that continues to sustain) (*FrC.,* [§176]).

There are probably few discoveries in tonal art that are so instructive and so salubrious as the discovery of the differences between the seventh in strict counterpoint and free composition in general, and, in the latter, between the seventh as passing tone as suspension.

That ⌐7 — 6 points more compellingly to the sixth than does 5 — 6 results from the nature of dissonance; a leap away from the consonant fifth is still imaginable, and therefore the path of the sixth is proportionately less definitely fixed.

(b) About ⌐9 — 8. It is thanks to the increase in harmony that in three-voice counterpoint the syncopes ⌐9 — 8 and ⌐2 — 1 in the upper counterpoint and ⌐4 — 5 in the lower—syncopes that were more tolerable than welcome in two-voice counterpoint (*Cpt. I,* p. 278)—begin to express a more convincing effect (as ⌐$\frac{9-8}{3--}$ │ ⌐$\frac{9-8}{6--}$ and ⌐$\frac{4-5}{2-3}$). Any reservations concerning these syncopes are directed only toward the intervals of resolution 8 (1) and 5 themselves—intervals which, especially when they belong to the outer-voice setting, can easily cause voice-leading difficulties.

(c) About ⌐2 — 3. ⌐2 — 3 and ⌐2 — 1 are completely different concepts: the first syncope belongs to the lower voice, the latter to the upper.

The lower syncope ⌐2 — 3 can be incorporated into two complete triads; specifically, with ⌐$\frac{4}{2}$—₃ it leads to $\frac{5}{3}$, and with ⌐$\frac{5}{2}$—₃ to $\frac{6}{3}$.

Whether with ⌐$\frac{4}{2}$—$\frac{5}{3}$ the diminished fifth can also be used at the upbeat:

**Example 183**

depends on the strictness of the point of view, which must be established by mutual agreement of teacher and student. All that is necessary is that one be able to hear and evaluate the differences of effect that result from the differences in location of the diminished fifth or from differences in the circumstances of accompaniment. [These will now be taken up in some detail.]

If introduced on the downbeat, the diminished fifth would have to bring about that effect characteristic of a passing tone which, as I shall show later,[7] is always inseparably associated with it. It was explained already in the first species of two-voice counterpoint (*Cpt. I*, p. 176) as well as of three-voice, however, that in strict counterpoint, where the principle of consonance must continuously attend to the equilibrium of harmonies, where fundamental concepts demand strictest purity and consistency, and where the dissonance may appear only on the upbeat, just for these reasons a passing tone on the downbeat remains prohibited. (Many theorists—for example, Albrechtsberger, as in the quotation in *Counterpoint I*, p. 270—permit the occasional diminished fifth even on the downbeat, although its passing-tone effect necessitates a joining of two bars.)

A similar effect results when, in the case of consonant downbeats, the diminished fifth is placed on the upbeat (see the succession $3 - 5b$ in Example 408 of *Cpt. I*); in such a case as that, too—Albrechtsberger allows it as a "license"—, the passing-tone effect, which again forces a joining of two bars, stands in the foreground.

It is different, however, for the diminished fifth formed on the upbeat along with the dissonant syncope $\frown 2 - 3$ or $\frown 4 - 5$; for here the syncopes $\frown 2 - 3$ and $\frown 4 - 5$ themselves are so clearly located in the foreground that the passing-tone effect of the diminished fifth, by contrast, remains in the background. And just because of this gradation of effects—specifically the foreground-effect of the syncope and the background-effect of the merely passing diminished fifth—the latter may after all be permitted, even though it contradicts full strictness and even though one can arrive at a complete triad in $\frown 2 - 3$, if one wishes, also with $5$ ($\frown\frac{5}{3}\overline{=}\frac{6}{3}$). Once permitted on the basis of such an understanding, however, it would then certainly have to be counted for the continuation, necessarily and by extension, as [equivalent to] a perfect fifth—specifically, in the sense that it would be considered just as suitable a preparation for some subsequent dissonance as would a perfect fifth (see below, Example 186).

It should be left up to the voice leading alone to decide whether necessity actually decrees a departure from the strictness of the viewpoint. The diminished fifth may be most acceptable in the cadence (see below, §10), since there all that remains is resolution into the tonic harmony; thus the hidden passing-tone effect may be allowed to emerge without hindrance, and the necessity vanishes of providing the diminished fifth with false credentials as a consonance for the purpose of continuing the syncopes.

(d) About $\frown 4 - 5$. The syncope $\frown 4 - 5$ of the lower voice, on the other hand, has only one possible resolution, namely $\frown\frac{4}{2}\overline{=}\frac{5}{3}$. This has to do with the appearance at the upbeat of the fifth, whose nature is appropriately illuminated in this way as well (cf. Chapter 1, §11).

(e) Finally, it is to be inferred from the above discussion that three-voice counterpoint still provides no opportunity at all for sounds such as $\frown\frac{6}{5}\,|\,\frown\frac{6}{2}$ or $\frown\frac{7}{}$. This is presented here only as a preliminary remark; its meaning, however, will become clear only in the further course of our account (see Part 6).

As purpose of the exercises in syncopation, *Fux* proposes the following (p. 104): ". . . Here too, the ties are the main purpose, a complete understanding of which can be achieved through practice of this kind. Therefore I recommend this exercise very specially to you as the most beautiful in composition." (Compare the quotations in *Cpt. I*, p. 291!)

Fux betrays the unseasoned quality of his viewpoint, however, by the following ideas (p. 103):

> You must remember that we are here concerned with studies and with a type of exercise in which there is a ligature in every bar, and therefore it is not so necessary to attend to consonances with the remaining voices, as we have discussed elsewhere and shall presently discuss again. It is a different matter in a free composition, where no law prevents the assignment to each dissonance of its own consonances.

With these recondite words Fux hints at the seventh-chords of free composition; but how little true understanding of the concept of seventh-chords (see below, Chapter 4, §2, the Fux quotation) is won by this hint.

Fux says the following about the question of which intervals should be added to the individual dissonant syncopes (p. 99):

> Therefore it appears remarkable that the third voice has to supply the same consonance that would have been used had the ligature been omitted. This is made clear by the following examples:

**Example 184**

Fux XI, 1

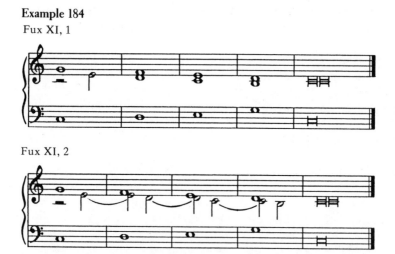

Fux XI, 2

Here it can be seen that the same consonances are given to the third voice in both examples, and the tying presents no obstacle to this. The same holds true of the ties in the lowest voice, or bass (see Table XI, Figure 3) [cited in *Cpt. I*, p. 298].

It should not be overlooked, however, that Fux is thinking here explicitly only of dissonant syncopes; that may have happened unconsciously, but in any case the reader has already been informed [in the present treatise] that the result for the consonant syncopes is not at all the same as that for the dissonant.

Let it be noted finally also that in the few exercises Fux presents, he used the following syncope-settings as the occasion demands:

$$\overset{\frown}{^7_3}{=}\!{^6_-} \mid \overset{\frown}{^7_8}{=}\!{^6_-} \mid \overset{\frown}{^4_5}{=}\!{^3_-} \mid \overset{\frown}{^9_3}{=}\!{^8_-} \mid \overset{\frown}{^2_3}{=}\!{^1_-}$$

(see Table X, Figure 3), and:

$$\overset{\frown}{^2_4}{=}\!{^3_3} \mid \overset{\frown}{^2_5}{=}\!{^3_6} \mid \overset{\frown}{^4_2}{=}\!{^3_3}$$

(in which the diminished fifth also finds use—cf. Example 116, no. 2), from which one may conclude, however, that on other occasions he would also have used $\overset{\frown}{^9_6}{-}^8 \mid \overset{\frown}{^4_6}{-}^3$ — or might he actually have allowed only $\overset{\frown}{^9_3}{-}^8$ and $\overset{\frown}{^5_4}{=}^-_3$?

He never explicitly states the prohibition of doubling the tone of resolution; for a remark that aims indirectly at the matter, however, see below, Part 4, Chapter 4, §2.

In conclusion it should also be mentioned here that Fux even teaches in this species of three-voice counterpoint the use of a figure encompassing two bars: $\overset{6}{^{-}_5}{^{-}_4}\overset{\frown}{}$ $+\,{^5_4}{^{-}_3}$, and the associated phenomenon of a still further extended setting of tied dissonances (Table XI, Figure 7 and 8). But more about this below, in a section expressly concerned with such things (see Part 6).

It would carry us too far afield to rebut *Albrechtsberger*'s table, as unnecessary as it is misleading, of the countless possible ligatures in free composition (see p. 100ff.; cf. also *Cpt. I*, pp. 269–270), especially since through misunderstanding of the true nature of prolongation itself he also binds free composition to nonsensically strict rules. Nevertheless, several items from among his scattered remarks may be highlighted. For example, on p. 105ff. he criticizes the setting:

**Example 185**

with the words, "the first [error] is the fifth A in the second bar instead of the third *f* along with the lowered ninth." From this it follows that he had no objection to $_{-}{^3_2}{=}\!{^-_1}$ or $_{-}{^{10}_2}{=}\!{^-_1}$ . That he permits in principle the diminished fifth on the upbeat was mentioned already in Chapter 2, §7 (see also below, §10). It is worth mention here, however, that in an exercise on p. 108 he uses the diminished fifth as preparation of a dissonant syncope:

**Example 186**

c.f.

"license"

In Nottebohm (pp. 53 and 56) we find Albrechtsberger's corrections pertaining to Beethoven's infractions against the prohibition of doubling the tone of resolution, and on the last correction, moreover, an explicit remark (relating, to be sure, to a four-voice setting): "To the fourth-ligature no third can be added, and to the seventh-ligature no sixth. If necessary, with 9 8, $\frac{6}{3}$ may be used below;[8] $\frac{6}{3}$ or $\frac{6}{4}$ is better, however." Here he enunciates most clearly the prohibition of doubling the tone of resolution.

Apparently it is to be traced back to the model of Fux when Albrechtsberger (on pp. 99–100) introduces $\frac{6}{5}\underline{-}4+\frac{5}{4}\underline{-}3$ already in the fourth species of three-voice counterpoint. (See below, Part 6.)

Without explicitly mentioning Fux, *Cherubini* employs his train of thought along with examples (p. 36, Examples 98, 99), but adds the following in his second rule: "All dissonances, the second, fourth, seventh, and ninth, can be used here. The second must be accompanied by the perfect fourth, and can occur only in the lower voice":

**Example 187**

We see that Cherubini freely permits the diminished fifth on the upbeat—or should the above example be understood as relating only to the cadential formula, even though the author did not himself expressly impose this qualification? [Cherubini continues:]

> There are cases in which the second can be accompanied by the fifth. This idiom is really even more in accord with the true principles of strict counterpoint than the former [with the fourth], because those principles in a certain way prohibit the diminished fifth, which prohibition however would not be possible if the procedure just described is accepted. [Cherubini's Example 104 follows.] The fourth as a dissonance should be accompanied by the fifth, and can occur in the upper voice or in one of the inner voices. [Cherubini's Example 105 follows.] The seventh should be accompanied by the third and should resolve to the sixth. It can occur only in the two upper voices. [Cherubini's Example 106 follows.] The ninth should be accompanied by the third and should resolve to the octave. It can be placed in the upper voice and also in the inner voice. [Cherubini's Example 107 follows.][9]

From this it can easily be judged how much of completeness and correctness remains absent from these rules.

Cherubini goes still further than Fux and Albrechtsberger, however, by presenting at the conclusion of the syncopated species not only the setting $\frac{6}{5}\underline{-}4+\frac{5}{4}\underline{-}3$ but also examples of the combined species, including combinations of the fourth and second as well as of the fourth and third species. (Concerning these matters, see below, Part 6.)

*Bellermann,* in a splendidly organized discussion (p. 212ff.), arrives at particular evaluations concerning the setting of dissonant syncopes; for the sake of brevity, I here present his main points opposite each individual figure:

$\overset{\frown}{7}-6$
$\phantom{}_{3}$    " . . . most suitable."

$\overset{\frown}{7}-6$
$\phantom{}_{8}$    " . . . a tone-combination in which the octave appears either as the upper or as the inner voice. The first sounds fuller and better, since the voices here lie closer to each other than when the seventh lies above the octave. Yet in many cases this second tone-combination is also justified by the voice leading."

⌐$\frac{4-3}{5}$   "... the best setting."

⌐$\frac{4-3}{8}$ } "Instead of the fifth, occasionally the octave or sixth of the bass tone may be
⌐$\frac{4-3}{6}$ } used, out of consideration for fluent voice leading."

⌐$\frac{9-8}{3}$   "... almost without exception in works of the better composers of the fifteenth and sixteenth centuries."

⌐$\frac{9-8}{6}$   "... in rare cases the sixth may also be used, although this is by far less good
sounding than the preceding [setting]."

⌐$\frac{9-8}{5}$   "... sounds empty, and is therefore to be completely avoided in the following
contrapuntal exercises."

⌐$\frac{4-5}{2-3}$ } "... best of all."
⌐$\frac{5-6}{2-3}$ }

⌐$\frac{2-3}{2-3}$   "... The progress of the voices can also occasionally demand that the two upper voices form an octave."

It should further be added that Bellermann does not concern himself expressly with
the filler-voice in the case of ⌐2 — 1, because he regards ⌐2 — 1 as equivalent to ⌐9 — 8
(*Cpt. I*, p. 277). Rather, on p. 215 he explains: "It can therefore very easily happen
that the dissonance designated as a ninth actually lies only a second away from the
voice that is dissonant with it, and that conversely, the dissonance designated as a
second may actually lie a ninth away." Bellermann's judgment about the diminished
fifth in ⌐$\frac{4-5}{2-3}$ has already been presented, in our discussion of the cadence in the second
species of three-voice counterpoint (see above, Chapter 2, §7).

Finally, Bellermann's digression (p. 214) concerning the ⌐9 — 8 syncope may be
noted:

The ninth is used in strict vocal setting with few exceptions only as a dissonance
occurring against the *bass*[10] (the lowest tone of the chord), thus not between the
upper and an inner voice or between two inner voices, as is quite possible in
settings of four or more voices, and as happens not infrequently among classical
composers of the preceding century—for example:

**Example 188**

etc.

When the older masters nevertheless use it between two upper voices out of
consideration for melodic fluency of the individual voices, we find its duration
limited almost always to only a quarter-note, as in the preceding example at B.

It is clear that with this remark, Bellermann probably meant to take a position
concerning the prohibition of doubling the tone of resolution; all the more regrettable,

then, that he failed to treat this difficult question in a manner fundamentally independent of the free ways of writing of "classical composers" and "older masters," whose invocation as authority for strict counterpoint is itself the gravest error imaginable.

I make only preliminary mention here finally of the fact that Bellermann, on the one hand following Fux's organization, speaks of $\frac{6}{-4} + \frac{5}{4-3}$ already in the fourth species of three-voice counterpoint under the title "consonant fourth," but, on the other hand, going beyond Fux, also speaks there—without waiting until the fourth species of four-voice counterpoint—of "resolution of the dissonance with moving voices," all of which leads him to combinations of the fourth and second, or of the fourth and third species. More detailed treatment of all these voice leadings is reserved, for reasons having to do with my own organization, for Part 6.

## Beginning

### §7. Construction of the beginning

Two examples by Fux may show how, by extension of the basic rules, under certain circumstances still other opening-possibilities are indeed available in the syncopated species of three-voice counterpoint. Thus Fux writes:

**Example 189**

Fux XI, 10                    Fux XII, 1

and explains as follows on p. 109:

> *Aloys:* Why have you used a rest in the first bar of the bass in the last example?
>
> *Joseph:* Since I saw that no tie was possible there, and believed that the space should not be filled with different species of counterpoint, I sought a solution in the form of a rest.
>
> *Aloys:* I am not displeased by your thoughts. However, it could have been done in the following way: [see the quotation from Table III, Figure 1 in example 189]. Here the tenor takes the place of the bass in the first bar—a thing that not only the tenor may do, but also the alto and, if such were possible, even the soprano, so long as the lowest voice, whichever it may be, is taken as the basis and the remaining tones are measured in relation to it.

Elsewhere, he prefers the first of the following two settings:

**Example 190**

Fux XIII, 2                    Fux XIII, 1

c.f.                           for

—a license which he again accompanies with the following words in the text (p. 104):

> For the rest, the first bar of the last example [see the quotation from Table XIII, Figure 1 in Example 190] could have been better executed. For an indirect hidden succession of two fifths occurs between the alto and the soprano, which is easily perceptible to the ear and should be avoided in three-voice writing. Here this may be accomplished by using a rest in the alto (Table XIII, Figure 2).

Compare to this the use by *Albrechtsberger* at the beginning of an exercise in the fourth species of four-voice counterpoint (p. 145)—printed there as No. 7 of the exercises—of the "license" according to which the syncope is absent from the first bar.

## Main Body

### §8. *How the postulates of three-voice setting are realized in the syncopated species*

Once voice leadings that could offend against the prohibition of doubling the tone of resolution have been excluded, in all other respects the applicability of the chief postulates of three-voice setting does remain in force in the syncopated species as well, except that here the postulate of completeness of triads naturally is subject to modifications.

In the case of dissonant syncopes, it is specifically the upbeat alone which can take over the complete triad and which, therefore, is obliged to do so; thus the former postulate is now applied to the upbeat. We arrive at $\frac{5}{3}$ with the following syncopes:

$$\overset{\frown}{\underline{4}}\!=\!\tfrac{3}{3} \mid \overset{\frown}{\underset{2}{\overline{\phantom{7}}}}\!=\!\tfrac{5}{3} \mid \overset{\frown}{\underset{4}{\overline{\phantom{7}}}}\!=\!\tfrac{3}{3}$$

and at $\frac{6}{3}$ with these:

$$\overset{\frown}{\underset{3}{\overline{7}}}\!\underline{=\!6} \mid \overset{\frown}{\underset{6}{\overline{4}}}\!\underline{=\!3} \mid \overset{\frown}{\underset{2}{\overline{\phantom{7}}}}\!=\!\tfrac{6}{3}.$$

The voice leading does not always permit the complete triad to be sought out in such a way; it often leads to incomplete triads. $\frac{6}{3}$ is yielded by the following syncopes:

$$ \overparen{^4_8}{-}^3_- \mid \overparen{^9_3}{-}^8_- \, , $$

and $\frac{6}{4}$ by these:

$$ \overparen{^7_8}{-}^6_- \mid \overparen{^9_6}{-}^8_- \, . $$

The consonant syncopes, on the other hand, automatically make it possible to adhere to the guideline given above in Chapter 2, §2—that is, to give the complete triad to the downbeat where possible, or to use the upbeat to complete the triad, although these possibilities do not abridge the right to eschew triadic completeness altogether.

*Albrechtsberger* remarks on p. 103 that "the upbeat, however, must always have a perfect or imperfect triad $\frac{5}{3}$ or $\frac{6}{3}$, or a consonant doubled dyad such as $\frac{8}{3}$, $\frac{8}{6}$, or $\frac{8}{5}$, $\frac{6}{6}$, or at least one of the empty chords $\frac{5}{1}$, $\frac{8}{5}$, $\frac{8}{3}$, $\frac{6}{1}$."

On p. 105 we read the following further particular remark: ". . . because the fifth on the downbeat . . . accompanied by the octave sounds too empty, and as previously noted, the empty chords are to be used only on upbeats."

In *Cherubini's* exercises, p. 40, Example 113—the first of which, incidentally, is identical to Fux's Table XII, Figure 5—we find the empty chord $\frac{8}{5}$ on the downbeat all too often; its effect is not improved by the fact that the upbeat brings its completion.

### §9. *Successions of fifths*

Successions of fifths can occur in the syncopated species of three-voice counterpoint not only in $5 \uparrow 6 - 5 \uparrow 6 - 5$ in the upper counterpoint and $5 \uparrow 4 - 5 \uparrow 4 - 5$ in the lower, as in two-voice counterpoint (*Cpt. I*, p. 292ff.), but also along with $\overparen{7} - 6$ when the syncopated voice lies in the middle. That the successive fifths on downbeats possible with $6 \uparrow 5 - 6 \uparrow 5 - 6$ in the lower counterpoint in two-voice counterpoint cannot be included in three-voice writing rests on the insupportability of the voice leading that would have to be used to produce them:

**Example 191**

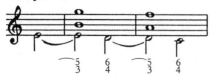

In particular, the following points should be noted:

1. Just the fulfillment of the complete triad at the upbeat, as occurs in $5 \uparrow \frac{6}{3} - 5 \uparrow \frac{6}{3} -$ :

**Example 192**

would have to emphasize the suspension-character of the sixth much more strongly than in two-voice counterpoint. Precisely for that reason, the use of such a voice leading in three-voice counterpoint would have to be more severely restricted than in two-voice if a satisfactory and complete counter-agent were not provided by the triadic completeness of $\frac{6}{3}$ along with the continuing compulsion of the syncopes. Add to this that when the inner voice is syncopated (see b), the outer-voice setting moving in thirds is able likewise to improve the effect considerably—an advantage which, naturally, had to be lacking in two-voice counterpoint.

 2.  With ⌒4—5↑4—5 in the lower counterpoint (*Cpt. I,* p. 294):

**Example 193**

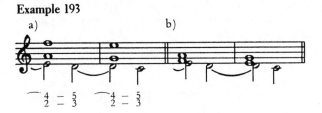

the mitigating circumstances of compulsion, as may reveal itself most often in the case of second-steps in the cantus firmus, for example, is joined here in three-voice counterpoint by fulfillment of triadic completeness as a further mitigating circumstance. Both the afterbeat placement of the fifths and also triadic completeness undoubtedly improve the effect, even when, as at b, the successions in question belong to the outer-voice setting.

 It will be shown in *Free Composition* [§164, and Figure 54,5] how free composition makes abundant use of exactly this voice leading in order to transform open parallel fifths at least into afterbeat successions.

 3.  When the thirds lie in the upper voice with ⌒7—6↑7—6:

**Example 194**

successions of fifths result between upper and inner voice; these are to be allowed not only because similar successions were admitted already in two-voice counterpoint, such as ⌒4—5↑4—5, [*Cpt. I,* p. 294], and in three-voice counterpoint even in the outer-voice setting (see above, under 2), but, above all, because the thirds of the counterpoint of the two outer voices, with the triadic completeness, likewise contribute to improvement of the effect.

**4.** In the case of ascending syncopes $^6\uparrow^5_3\underline{\text{—}}^6\uparrow^5_3\underline{\text{—}}^6$:

**Example 195**

the succession of fifths ($^5_3$) from downbeat to downbeat is improved by the intervening sixths ($^6_3$). To be sure, the suspension-effect appears weakened here from the outset because of the ascending direction, and for this reason the characteristic effect of such successions manifests itself already in the domain of strict counterpoint, in that the fifths on the downbeats and the sixths on the upbeats are of approximately equal weight. Specifically, since the consonant fifths do not completely take on the role of suspensions, by their fulfillment of the roothood-tendency of the lowest tone they emphasize themselves above all; on the other hand, it is precisely the tying-across that casts a stronger emphasis on the sixths. Also related to the tying is the fact that in the case of $5\uparrow6\text{—}5\uparrow6\text{—}5$ (see under 1) or $6\uparrow5\text{—}6\uparrow5\text{—}6$ (see under 4) the effect of a change of harmony, which in strict counterpoint is associated with the succession $5\text{—}6$ or $6\text{—}5$, recedes into the background—without, admittedly, being completely obliterated.

It will be shown in *Free Composition* how free composition now assimilates the ambivalence of the successions under 1 and 4—which, in view of their contrasting directions, might be considered opposites—so as to place in the foreground sometimes the sixths and sometimes the fifths according to need (specifically, the needs of the fundamental line[12]).

Both *Fux* and *Albrechtsberger* show little scruple in the use of $6\text{—}5\uparrow6\text{—}5$ and $4\text{—}5\uparrow4\text{—}5$, or that succession of fifths produced by $\text{—}^3_7\overline{\text{—}_6}$, as can be seen in the exercises that follow.

## Cadence

### §10. *Cadential formulas*

Regarding cadential formulas, the basic rule established in *Counterpoint I,* p. 302, continues to apply. If the cantus firmus permits no exact application of that rule (*Cpt. I,* examples 452–454), it is advisable to transfer the leading tone to the other voice—for example:

**Example 196**

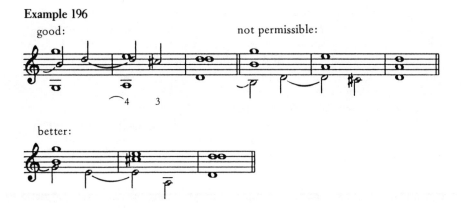

The effect of a syncopation of the descending leading tone may be illustrated as follows:

**Example 197**

Such a syncopation is often not sufficiently convincing, and thus often even impermissible. The form at a2 shows the consonant fifth, which need not point to a cadence, since it may also be left by leap; a3 and a4 show non-diatonic intervals (a diminished fourth and an augmented fifth), which we must reject. (The augmented fourth is a diatonic interval; nevertheless, its use in strict counterpoint is restricted.)

Among the forms at b, only that under 3 is convincing—indeed, by virtue of ⌐2 — 3. The forms in minor (4, 5, 6) all suffer from their inclusion of non-diatonic intervals. It is therefore advisable to avoid syncopation of the descending leading tone.

In no event, however, may the tying involve the root of the dominant:

**Example 198**

not:

major                              minor

Concerning the diminished fifth that may be used in the penultimate bar, see above, Chapter 2, §7.

A cadential formula such as this:

**Example 199**

is prohibited for reasons cited above in connection with Example 66.

*Albrechtsberger* (p. 103):

The end, or last bar, may have three tonic tones, or may have the diatonic third and the octave. The penultimate bar must have $-\frac{5}{4}-_3$ if the bass or lowest voice has the dominant; ⌐$\frac{7}{3}-^6$ if the lowest voice has the cantus firmus; and ⌐$\frac{4}{2}-\frac{5b}{3}$ or $-\frac{5}{2}-\frac{6}{3}$ if it has the tied notes.

On p. 105 (the relevant text is on p. 106) Albrechtsberger explicitly criticizes the following cadential formula:

**Example 200**

c.f.

"because there the fourth-ligature ⌐4 — 3 must occur." (Compare *Cpt. I,* p. 303).

In *Cherubini,* in spite of his fifth rule on p. 39, which agrees with Albrechtsberger's rule above, we nevertheless find in the second exercise on p. 40 the following cadential formula:

**Example 201**

## Exercises

**Example 202**
Fux XI, 3

**Example 202** *continued*

Fux XIII, 4

Albrechtsberger, p. 107

Cherubini, Ex. 113

**Example 202** *continued*

H. Schenker

Soprano

6.

Alto (c.f.)

Bass

## Comments on the Preceding Exercises

No. 1. Uninterrupted parallel tenths between bass (cantus firmus) and soprano; moreover (with a few exceptions), a succession of fifths between upper and inner voice, avoided by chains of ⌒7 — 6.

No. 2. In bars 5 – 6, a rising succession ⌒$\frac{5}{3}$—$\frac{6}{3}$ ↑$\frac{5}{3}$—$\frac{6}{3}$, with emphasis on the sixths. The almost uninterrupted thirds between bass and inner voice are not of good effect, and are also unnecessary.

No. 3. In bars 1 – 2, an afterbeat octave-succession (8 ↑6 — 8) between alto and bass; concerning this succession, see *Counterpoint I,* p. 294.

# Chapter 5

# The Fifth Species: Mixture of the Preceding Species

### §1. *Recollection and prolongation of several earlier principles*

**1.** The beginning may be introduced only with the second or the fourth species (*Cpt. I*, p. 311), not with the third; the following, for example, is therefore incorrect:

**Example 203**

This has to do with the fundamental significance of the half-notes as the true subdivision of the whole-notes of the cantus firmus; a beginning like that of Example 203 would accordingly be misleading and a stylistic contradiction.

With a cantus firmus in major which begins immediately with a leap of a fourth, only the second species is usable in the lower counterpoint at the beginning:

**Example 204**

In minor, it is different (see below, Exercise 4).

**2.** In mixing the species one should try to avoid rhythmic monotony such as ♪♪♪|♪♪♪ for example, especially when it is associated with the simultaneous threat of motivic monotony:

**Example 205**

When such a danger arises, it is advisable to use if possible a rhythm such as this: ♩♩♩♩♩♩♩

The convenience of the rhythm ♩· ♩ (especially in mixtures of two counterpoints of the fifth species) may have induced the teachers of counterpoint to permit it; fundamentally, however, this rhythm contradicts the intent of strict counterpoint (*Cpt. I*, pp. 321–322).

In an environment of several quarter-notes, an isolated half-note on the downbeat is seldom of good effect; it is as though the second species were unable to make its presence felt convincingly enough through that one note (*Cpt. I*, p. 313); thus the following is undesirable: ♩♩♩♩♩♩ ♩♩♩♩♩♩.

3. Concerning the use of eighth-notes in mixed-species counterpoint, see *Counterpoint I*, pp. 326–329. It would contradict purity of style to use the eighth-notes partly in the service of decoration of dissonant syncopes or any other very simple type of embellishment of third- or fourth-leaps, but partly also for extensive melodic purposes. Even the following must be described as an excessive burdening of the space of a fourth:

**Example 206**

An idiom such as the following, however:

**Example 207**

is prohibited not only because the eighth-notes are improperly placed, but also because the rhythm ♩ ♩ or ♩♩♩ is hidden beneath, as is disclosed by the overall meaning; both, however, are inadmissible.

4. Already in *Counterpoint I*, p. 329, reference was made to a less natural—to be exact, a prolonged—manner of resolving dissonant syncopes with the aid of quarters and eighths, in which the dissonant syncope appears to be resolved already at the second quarter, so that the upbeat is released for a further continuation. Experience has shown that the application of this prolonged form causes the student considerable difficulty, even if he is completely aware of the difference in comparison to the natural form. The following comments may now provide a few aids. Idioms such as the following are still not too far removed from the naturally prescribed form:

**Example 208**

We gladly overlook the slight irregularity of these forms because of their clear origin in the following:

**Example 209**

whose all too colorful rhythm is eliminated by means of that prolongation. Much is contributed to the latter's good effect also by the fact that the eighth-notes in Example 209 are merely natural embellishments of a third-leap, and are perceived as such. Accordingly, idioms such as the following:

**Example 210**

can be described as more remote, because the embellishment of the third leap either is completely lacking, as in the first case, or is displaced, as in the second ($b\flat - g$). Still more remote is a case such as that shown by Fux in an exercise (*Cpt. I,* p. 342, no. 4, bars 1–2):

**Example 211**

Here the eighth-note acceleration clearly originates in the fact that in the second bar [of the underlying model] more eighth-notes are present than are permitted.

A neighboring-note motion finds acceptance in accordance with the remarks concerning Example 208:

**Example 212**

It should not, however, be so unclear as the following, for example:

**Example 213**

It is worth mentioning that *Albrechtsberger,* after concluding his treatment of the fifth species on pp. 119–120, presents (for the first time) two examples of the combined species—in particular, combinations of the second species with the third, and also of the third species with the fourth. *Cherubini,* who has already presented examples of the combined species in two previous places, completes his treatment of that genre after concluding with the fifth species (see his Example 115); he shows combinations of the second and fifth species and of two counterpoints of the fifth species.

## Exercises

**Example 214**
Fux XIII, 5

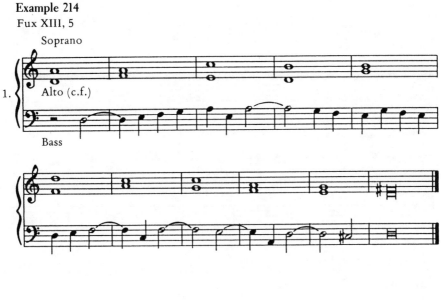

Fux XIII, 7

**Example 214** *continued*

Albrechtsberger, p. 110

Albrechtsberger, p. 113

**Example 214** *continued*

H. Schenker

## Comments on the Preceding Exercises

No. 2. In bar 1 the tie is omitted because of the difficulty that would have attended its use. Bars 2 and 5 show ♩·♩; see the commentary above in the text. The eighth-notes in bars 3 and 4 may be permitted as embellishments of third-leaps, but the monotony cannot be approved.

No. 3. In bar 4, embellishment of a fourth-leap. In bar 8 a "modulation," to "F major."

No. 4. Concerning the NB in bar 5, see *Counterpoint I,* p. 250.

# PART FOUR

## Four-Voice Counterpoint

Semper idem, sed non eodem modo.

## *Chapter 1*

# The First Species: Note Against Note

### General Aspects

#### §1. *About doublings*

In the sense of the overtone series, the original, natural ordering of intervals, including the octave, surely runs as follows (*Harmony,* p. 21):

$$\begin{matrix} 3 \\ 5 \\ 8 \end{matrix} \uparrow$$

Yet in strict counterpoint as in free composition, where an artistic-artificial voice leading regulates the course of events, any other ordering is also welcome, provided only that 8, 5, and 3 remain.

While a single doubling alone suffices to make the sound incomplete in three-voice counterpoint (for example, $\begin{smallmatrix} 8 \\ 3 \end{smallmatrix}$ | $\begin{smallmatrix} 8 \\ 6 \end{smallmatrix}$), in four-voice counterpoint, on the other hand, such a single doubling in no way prevents completeness of the triad; for example:

**Example 215**

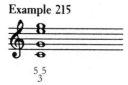

Rather, it is characteristic only of a twofold doubling to make the triad incomplete, as in $\frac{8}{33}$ or $\frac{8}{66}$ for example.

This much established, the following remains to be said about the [relative] value of the doublings: the best doubling is again that by means of the octave (Part 3, Chapter 1, §14), since it alone corresponds to the requirement of nature:

$$\frac{8}{\frac{5}{3}} \text{ and } \frac{8}{\frac{6}{3}}$$

Only after these may the doublings with 1 and 5 follow:

$$\frac{5}{\frac{3}{1}} \mid \frac{6}{\frac{3}{1}} \text{ and } \frac{55}{3}$$

In doublings of imperfect consonances, if the triad is complete, doubling of the third: $\frac{3}{3}$ is to be preferred to that of the sixth: $\frac{6}{6}$.

But if, in spite of the four-voice texture, the triad is nevertheless to remain incomplete, then in accord with the principle articulated in Part 2, Chapter 1, §22 the doubling must be of the imperfect consonances 3 and 6: $\frac{8}{33}$ | $\frac{8}{66}$, and not of the perfect ones: $\frac{8}{55}$ | $\frac{88}{1}$ .

*Fux* speaks about the necessity of doubling in general in four-voice settings (p. 106ff.):

[*Aloys*]: It has already been mentioned that the relationships of the harmonic triad are completely contained in a composition [of three voices]. Thus it is clear that the added fourth voice can have no place except as a doubling of a consonance that already appears among the three voices (leaving aside certain dissonant combinations that will be discussed elsewhere). Although there is a great difference between the unison and the octave with respect to interval and position, no such difference exists with respect to nomenclature. For both the unison and the octave are named C (for example), and the octave is regarded almost as a repeated unison. Thus a four-voice chord will consist usually of the third, the fifth, and the octave.

Concerning the "natural order" of intervals, we read in Fux on p. 108:

*Joseph:* What is the proper place of the consonances?

*Aloys:* It is the order that originated when the octave was harmonically divided. It is clear, then, that from this division the fifth originated first, and, further, that from the division of the fifth, the third appeared; this order should be retained in combining consonances, unless, as happens very often, this is precluded for some other reason—specifically, the progression to the following bars. Here is an example showing the natural order of the consonances:

**Example 216**
Fux XIV, 3

You see, first comes the fifth, which originated from the division of the octave; second the octave, which was given initially, and finally the third, or tenth, which originated in the division of the fifth.

*Joseph:* From the layout of the modern keyboard, it would appear that the third came first and ahead of the fifth, and that therefore the order of four voices should be regarded as the following:

**Example 217**

Fux XIV, 4

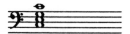

*Aloys:* That is merely appearance; in fact, it is not the case.

But Fux is also able to provide reasons this order cannot always be followed, and sometimes—for example, in constructing a beginning—should not even be attempted in the first place.

About doublings, he states on p. 107: "Where by reason of faulty progression the octave cannot be used (as often happens), the third is doubled, or, more rarely, the sixth."

In compliance with these rules, Fux adheres in his exercises first of all to completeness of triads and also doublings with 8 and 3, although other doublings—for example 1, 5, or 6—do occur.

*Albrechtsberger* definitively states his position on the doublings to be preferred in four-voice writing as early as the first species of two-voice counterpoint, as follows (pp. 26–27): "In four-voice counterpoint, exactly the same doublings [as in three-voice], but with addition of the fourth interval, which will usually be the perfect octave or the perfect fifth, or the doubled third, or the doubled sixth." In the section on four-voice counterpoint, he adds the following (p. 120):

> Here again, no chord is allowed except the perfect chord with the major and minor third, and the chord of the major or minor sixth with the diatonic third, and the perfect octave, $\frac{5}{3}$ and $\frac{6}{3}$. But in the latter, the placement should not be made in such a way that the sixth is minor and the third major, for this would be a false chord. One can and must often modify the perfect chord $\frac{8}{5}$, specifically as $\frac{5}{3}$ or $\frac{5}{3}$, when the fifths are perfect and the thirds are not the *semitonium modi*. The same holds true of the imperfect sixth-chords: $\frac{8}{6}$ if modified as $\frac{6}{3}$ or $\frac{3}{6}$. The two six-four chords $\frac{8}{6}\flat$ and $\frac{8}{6}\natural$ continue to be prohibited, as dissonant chords. Also prohibited is the *quarta fundata*, which indeed occurs in the second inversion of the essential seventh-chord, and which is used in the bass-scale on the second degree with the major sixth and minor third, for example $\natural\frac{6}{4}$. In free settings it is, like the other dissonant chords, allowed.

It goes without saying, however, that in Albrechtsberger's exercises incomplete triads (e.g., $\frac{6}{6}$, p. 125) can also be found. *Cherubini* writes (p. 42, first rule):

> Since the chords $\frac{5}{3}$ and $\frac{6}{3}$ consist of only three members, it is necessary to double one of these members in four-voice counterpoint. Thus in the chord $\frac{5}{3}$ all its members may be doubled in turn, according to the position of the parts, but

the octave and the third should be doubled more frequently than the unison or the fifth. If one or another of these chords is used in an incomplete form—which is permitted and often necessary—it is then requisite to double two of them, or triple one of them, an expedient to which recourse should be had only as a last resort.

Observation: The use of the unison should be avoided in this species as much as possible, although it is sometimes tolerated. It is allowed in the two low voices, but with many restrictions, and it can be used without reservation in all voices in the first and last bars.

One can even double all voices of the $\begin{smallmatrix}6\\4\end{smallmatrix}$ chord, especially the third, less often the others. In general, the doubling of intervals in each individual case depends on taste and experience.

Observation: No positive reason can be found why one or another voice of a chord is preferably to be doubled or not to be doubled. But it does appear to be true that the third deserves the advantage above the other intervals, and produces a fuller harmony; and that for the success of the composition in general, much depends on the felicitous choice of the intervals to be doubled.

The commitment to independence of voice leading, certainly laudable in itself, would have found a more reliable and more precise expression, however, had Cherubini been acquainted with the train of thought that I have developed in Chapter 1, §§4–14. He would then have had no need to deny differences of value among the doublings, and would have had only to explain how other voice leading reasons, which can already be perceived most accurately in any exercise of strict counterpoint (and especially in free composition), influence the process of doubling.

*Bellermann* (pp. 237–238), without mentioning Fux's name, follows the latter's teaching so exactly that he even reproduces his explanation of interval ordering (see above) almost verbatim.

## §2.  *Validity of the two-voice counterpoint of the outer voices as a foundation in four-voice counterpoint*

Because it cannot be emphasized often enough, let it be recalled here that in four-voice counterpoint as well, a good treatment of the counterpoint of the outer voices constitutes a principal requirement of good voice leading.

## §3.  *Open and close position*

If the open position is intrinsically more natural than the close (see Chapter 1, §21), its value is also corroborated in four-voice counterpoint by the registers and tessiturae of the four singing voices—again predetermined by nature—which lie at intervals of the fifth and fourth from one another. Nevertheless, it is true that the ultimate arbiter, beyond all such relationship with nature, is voice leading, which, in recognition of justifiable and higher needs of its own, often makes observation of the postulates of nature by no means desirable. It is only the voice leading which ultimately ensures, through effects of contrast, that close and open position are mutually placed in the correct light.

*Cherubini* presents in his Example 116 a table of all possible doublings, which I reproduce here only so that the student may have an opportunity to gain practice in discriminating among the externally open and close positions and also the internally open position:

**Example 218**

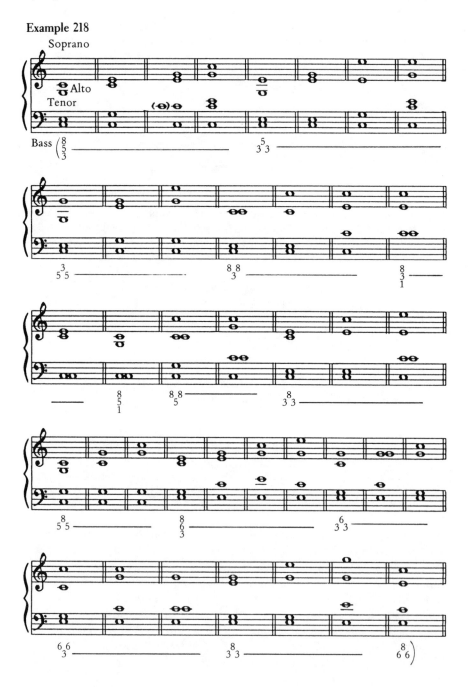

Observe, however, that Cherubini distinguishes between the two chords that follow:

**Example 219**

in the sense that he calls the first phenomenon (a) an "incomplete perfect triad with doubled third and first,"[1] while on the other hand he calls the second (b), strangely, an "incomplete imperfect chord with octave and doubled third." This claim of a difference, where obviously none is present for reasons of voice leading, can be explained only by the fact that in both cases he is thinking only of one and the same harmony on C (c – e – g), in accord with which he then assumes absence of the fifth g at a, and of the root C at b. In fact, however, the assumption of such a harmony is in agreement with reality only at a, since the assumption of roothood-tendency there speaks in favor of C. But by exactly the same principle, the root E, not C, must be assumed in case b. The assumption of the latter root at b thus betrays the fact that strict counterpoint has been directly and misleadingly adulterated by a manner of thinking borrowed from free composition and founded there on the instinct for scale degrees (see Chapter 1, §15).

## §4. *The effect of extended successions of thirds in the two lower voices*

If the third voice of the setting is led for some time in thirds with the fourth, lowest voice, the ear will not be able to overlook the poor effect of such a voice leading. On the one hand, specifically, it is the longer series of thirds in itself which produces the poor effect (*Cpt. I*, p. 160); on the other hand, the "moving-together-in-thirds" is made all the more noticeable by the contrast with the two higher voices; and finally, in view of the increased freedom of the voice leading, the particular unfree quality of an extended progression in thirds by the lower voices in this way must appear the more awkward the more it is unnecessary.

Also to be considered is the fact that thirds in the low register sound darker. But the ultimate, secret reason for this is that the third, as we know (*Harmony*, p. 21), celebrates its birth only in the third octave above the fundamental, and accordingly points to more distant elevations; it does not belong in most turgid adjacency to the fundamental, a region in which not even the fifth was yet born. And if, as might be objected, this directive of nature itself pertains only to the thirds of actual fundamentals, our ear nevertheless may, by extension, perceive a similarly undesirable, overly dark effect even in thirds that are merely thirds in the purely contrapuntal sense of an independent voice leading; that is, in a related sense, the ear does not gladly make a distinction in strict counterpoint between a and b of the following example:

**Example 220**

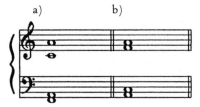

—least of all when several such thirds occur in direct succession.

The voice leading of four-voice counterpoint, therefore, will have to ensure that with respect to the spacing of voices in relation to one another, and especially the spacing of the third and fourth voices, variety shall always prevail. In the application of this principle, then, under certain circumstances—even precisely by virtue of contrast—a good effect will nevertheless be made by a close position of voices, in which the third voice freely moves to the distance of a third from the lower. Thus the spacing of voices is regulated still more according to the laws and circumstances of voice leading, in which variety and contrast can cause both the closer and the more open spacing of voices to be of good effect in equal measure.

> *Fux* (pp. 108ff.):
>
> . . . that the third in a low register close to the bass sounds muddy and indistinct, and that the larger the numerical proportion according to which an interval is defined, the more pungent the sound of the interval, and, therefore, the more it demands a higher register. The essential proportions of the fifth are 2:3, which equal 5, while those of the third are 4:5, which yield 9. Therefore, according to the natural order the fifth should be placed below, and the third above.

The foregoing remark, however, seems to contradict another one on pp. 109–110: "Incidentally, it should also be noted that the more the voices are brought into close proximity, the more perfect the resulting harmony will be, for as the saying goes, a force compressed is a force strengthened."

But Fux's translator, Mizler, has already thrown down the gauntlet before this sentence. In a footnote on p. 110, he states:

> I am not sure that this is correct. When the tones are occasionally spaced apart, they sound more pleasant than when they stand so close together. The harmonic triad *c, g, e¹, c²* sounds better than *c, e, g, c¹*, and in the latter the tones nevertheless stand closer together than in the former. By virtue of the natural order of the consonances, specifically as it originates in the harmonic division, too, the tones do not stand so very close together. One should be guided by the circumstances and try to maintain a middle course, which is always the safest.

We read the following, moreover, in Fux on p. 110:

> *Joseph:* In the first two examples I have, with some reservation, against your advice led the tenor so close to the bass that the thirds generally appear in the lower register; I did so because I could not find a different way to proceed in view of the constraint of the cantus firmus, which must be worked out in all four voices. Therefore, I submit it to your judgment and improvement.
>
> *Aloys:* It is true that this example, in which the cantus firmus must be maintained and which has only the purpose of an exercise, could not have been executed differently. It will be different when your invention is no longer constrained. In time, however, you will be amazed at how useful these exercises are to a student.

If we now draw the conclusion of all the thoughts that have been cited, we must acknowledge that Fux has probably touched upon all points of the question here under consideration—on the natural postulate of the open position, but no less on the good effect of the close, and finally on the effect of a good voice leading in successfully resolving all apparent contradictions. There is but one criticism he cannot be spared: if he invokes the prescription of nature for strict counterpoint as well, and indeed rightly so, he nevertheless overlooks that the decree of nature pertains only to the genuine thirds. But which third does he mean when he speaks of "the third placed in the low register and so close to the bass"? Does he mean the third of the actual root, or that of voice leading in general?

*Cherubini's* rule 2 on p. 44 reads as follows:

> The voices should not be too widely separated, and also, especially in the low register, should not be placed too close together; in particular, successions of thirds between tenor and bass should be avoided. The spacing of voices should always maintain in so far as possible the middle position, between excessively open and excessively close.

And the following "Observation" is appended: "When the voices lie too close together, especially in the low register, the effect is muddy; when they are too widely separated, it is unclear."

# Beginning

## §5. *Construction of the beginning*

Of primary importance are the principles of completeness and of the natural order of the triad. But the principles of voice leading must also be allowed to exercise their necessary influence on the formation of the beginning, to the extent that for the sake of some necessity, the beginning can occasionally also be constructed in a way that is different from just the most natural one. It is obvious, however, that, as before, $\frac{6}{4}$ is excluded.

We read in *Fux,* p. 108:

> . . . it is most important to determine in advance whether it would be possible to progress correctly from a first bar so organized to the second, third, or even

fourth bars; if not, the organization of the first bar must be changed, and a combination of consonances must be selected which can be led to the subsequent bars easily and without error.

Fux means by this to permit constructions of the first bar which deviate from the natural one ($\frac{8}{5}$—see above, §1) only in the free rearrangement of these intervals. The foregoing by no means intends to abjure completeness.

*Albrechtsberger* (p. 120): "It is very easy here to use $\frac{8}{5}$ or $\frac{5}{3}$ in the first bar."

*Cherubini* (p. 45, rule 6):

One should use the chord in its complete form in the first bar; but considerations of melody and voice leading, and the like, can also release one from this obligation. The unison can even be used in all parts, if it is suitable for the leading of the voices.[2] The preceding rule can be applied to the last bar of a piece as well, as can the examples just given.

We see how Cherubini in this matter goes beyond Fux, who conceives such beginnings neither in text nor in exercises.

*Bellermann* enunciates Fux's ideas on p. 238, almost in the latter's own words.

## Main Body

### §6.  *About voice-crossing*

Clearly, in four-voice counterpoint as well, one should not overlook the method of voice-crossing, which often enough ensures a good voice leading and protects against all manner of errors.

It may be mentioned in addition that not only adjacent voices may be crossed, but, under certain circumstances, also voices that lie farther apart, such as soprano and tenor, for example, or alto and bass.

*Fux* also occasionally crosses the bass, bearing the cantus firmus, with the tenor:

**Example 221**

Fux XIV, 7

Bass (c.f.)

(cf. also Table XX, Figure 3, bars 1–2, and Table XXI, Figure 2, bars 6–7).

*Albrechtsberger* (p. 147) crosses at one point not only soprano II and alto, but also soprano II and the tenor carrying the cantus firmus:

**Example 222**

(cf. p. 148, bar 5, and p. 150, bar 6).

Compare also *Cherubini,* third rule, p. 44.

## §7.  *About nonparallel similar motion*

It is first of all the increased number of voices in four-voice counterpoint, as compared to three-voice, that necessitates a further increase in freedom; for it often happens that a voice simply would have no other available path if it were forced to abide always by the rule just for the rule's sake.

Moreover, four-voice texture, because it is superior to three-voice in the purely sonic aspect, causes the inherently poor quality of the prohibited motions to recede into the background more than does three-voice texture. Finally, licenses are required in four-voice counterpoint also by the circumstance that here, in keeping with the design of the exercises, whole-notes must be used consistently. Because of this restriction, there is no possibility of improving the relationship of the voices by those many other means that are offered by free composition.

But with all of these licenses, whether they benefit the setting for this reason or that, one should above all observe this experience: any deviation from the principle of melodic fluency will be more noticeable in the upper voice than in an inner or the lower voice—an experience that applies even in situations that conform to the rule [concerning similar motion], but even more in the case of prohibited motions. By the same token, then, the bass, on the contrary—as though with prescience of true fundamentals (the scale degrees of free composition)—, is more suited for forceful motions than the upper voice, which, by virtue of its prominent high position, would always remain the domain of fluency, of melody.

*Fux* cautions as follows on p. 107: "For the rest, the rules of progressions and motion specified in the First Book must be observed insofar as possible, in respect to both the relationships of the [upper] voice to the bass and of the upper voices among themselves." (Similar remarks are found on p. 109.)

We thus find in his exercises progressions such as:

**Example 223**

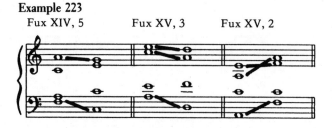

in which the upper voice participates in the faulty progressions only with steps of a second, while the bass voice involves fourths, fifths, and sixths. Other progressions, on the other hand, such as the following, for example:

**Example 224**

show leaps not only in the lower voice (as much as an octave-leap), but also even in the upper voice (leaps of a third or fifth).

It is obvious, then, that the inner voice may demand still greater liberty; Fux writes, for example:

**Example 225**

**Example 225** *continued*

Fux XXI, 2

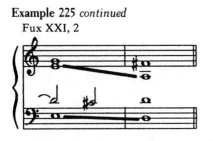

Fux comments on the following voice leading (pp. 112–113):

**Example 226**

Fux XVII, 1

"This progression, because of the necessity to use whole-notes,[3] could not have been written differently, and therefore must be tolerated. It could easily be improved if the whole-note in the tenor could be divided thus:"

**Example 227**

Fux XVII, 3

And then he adds, retrospectively, this comment: "This holds true also for the examples of the preceding species, in which much will be found that would have to be rejected as faulty if it were not for the necessity of using whole-notes." And, somewhat further on, he states: "I have already said, and repeat again, that because whole-note motion absolutely must be retained, such progressions sometimes must be tolerated, since even in free composition they cannot always be avoided; yet they are more tolerable in the inner voices than in the outer, as you have correctly remarked." It is clear, however, that Fux, with these last remarks, refers to a combination of the species (see below, Part 6).

As in Fux (pp. 112–113), in *Albrechtsberger* too we find on p. 127 (in the second species in four-voice counterpoint) the basic idea expressed as follows: "All of these errors, and also the licenses permitted earlier in the first species in which the highest voice makes a leap, can easily be avoided in free composition by the use of several notes and of contrary motion, which can be assigned to a filler-voice instead of having it sustain."

The licenses which, according to Albrechtsberger's point of view, must necessarily be granted strict counterpoint can be set forth approximately as follows (pp. 121–122):

> Hidden fifths, octaves, and unisons that do not sound offensive, and in which the upper of the two apparently faulty voices moves up or down by step, are all allowed; but such liberties can be tolerated most easily in inner voices. The licenses must, however, involve no leap greater than that of the perfect fifth in the uppermost voice; . . . But it should be noted well that if the highest voice uses such a license by means of one of the allowed leaps, at least one, if not two, of the other three voices should be set against it in contrary motion.

Examples are given on pp. 122–123:

**Example 228**

(cf. Ex. 224, after Fux)

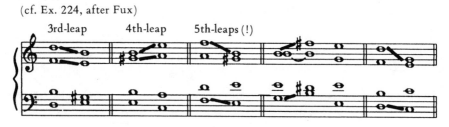

And from the exercises:

**Example 229**

p. 124

[etc.]

Page 122: ". . . in the lowest and inner voices, a sixth- or octave-leap may be used as well." Examples from pp. 122–123:

**Example 230**

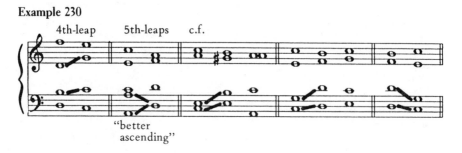

**Example 230** *continued*

octave leaps

And from the exercises:

**Example 231**

"license"

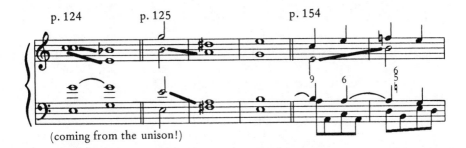

(coming from the unison!)

On the same page, finally, also this: "In the case of descending and ascending fourth-leaps in the bass, as well as in that of ascending sixth-leaps, hidden fifths and octaves in similar motion may always be used." Examples from pp. 121–122:

**Example 232**

Obviously in both of these cases[4] a part is played by the spirit of free composition, whose harmonic progressions by fifth and third are recalled here by the fourth- and sixth-leaps of the bass. On the other hand, we find on p. 123 the following examples explicitly designated as "poor":

**Example 233**

Compare also the two last bars of the exercise on p. 150:

**Example 234**

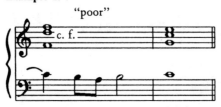

The remark quoted by Nottebohm on pp. 54–55,[5] obviously taken by Beethoven from Albrechtsberger's *Anweisung*, is, however, not sufficiently precise:

> The licenses are better in descending motion than in ascending. They may have at most a fifth-leap in the upper voice; in the bass and the inner voices they may also have a fourth-, sixth-, or octave-leap. In the ascending and descending fourth-leap, as in the ascending sixth-leap, hidden fifths and octaves in similar motion may be used.

Indeed, in spite of this remark, the exercise by Beethoven quoted by Nottebohm under No. 20 (p. 55) shows a license in the third bar in which the soprano (cantus firmus) makes a sixth-leap and the tenor merely a second-step, which Albrechtsberger nevertheless allowed to stand.

*Cherubini* directs the total force of the prohibition to the relationship of the two outer voices, which are to use a license only in cases of emergency.

In his fourth rule (p. 44), he speaks of the license of fifths by contrary motion (antiparallels): ". . . but two fifths in contrary motion between the [members of any pair of] the three upper voices, or [either of] the two inner voices and the bass, are tolerated. They are sometimes tolerated between the two outer voices, but this liberty should be used only seldom, when no other means is available."

In the fifth rule he speaks of nonparallel similar motions: "It is allowed to move to a perfect consonance by similar motion in the inner voices and also in [the relationship of] an inner voice to an outer; but it is an error, which can be justified for the avoidance of an even worse error, if this procedure is allowed between the outer voices."

Thus it by no means infringes against his point of view when he uses the following voice leading in his exercises:

**Example 235**

Ex. 118, 3     Ex. 118, 2     Ex. 118, 2     Ex. 118, 1     Ex. 118, 1     Ex. 118, 3

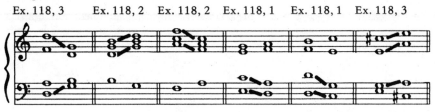

and likewise in exercises of the subsequent species, such as the following, for example:

**Example 236**

p. 50, 3rd ex.          p. 48, 1st ex.                    p. 48, 2nd ex.

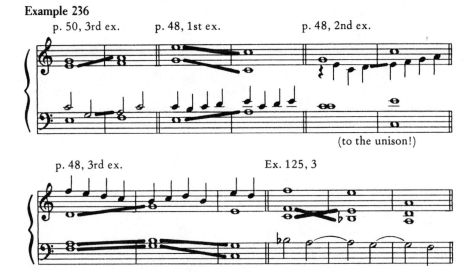

(to the unison!)

p. 48, 3rd ex.                              Ex. 125, 3

Cherubini provides no form of more precise justification for all of these rules, however. Such may perhaps be derived from these introductory words (p. 42):

> If the rules of three-voice counterpoint are already less strict than those of counterpoint of two voices, they are almost necessarily still less strict in the type of counterpoint now under discussion, and in this respect one finds even quite often in the works of the old classical masters—especially in *Palestrina*—examples that one could at first glance describe as errors, or at least as excessive liberties.

Yet the various difficult positions that these passages presented for the composer, and the usual custom of the masters to treat them in such a way, prove that these passages are only facilitating liberties of the strict rule—an easing of difficulties that is expanded as the number of voices increases; and thus, what first appeared faulty is [after all] acknowledged to be permissible.

After all of the reasoning provided in the text, I here spare myself the trouble of again revealing as such the errors contained in the last statements by Cherubini. It must suffice if I merely name them: just the reference to several passages in Palestrina by itself; the empty phrases "facilitating liberties of the strict rule" and "an easing of difficulties that is expanded as the number of voices increases"; and the most awkward expression of all at the end: ". . . and thus, what first appeared faulty is acknowledged to be permissible." Where so many convincing arguments are possible, turns of phrase and expressions that stand in their place are all the more embarrassing errors. But how these turns of phrase ensnare the young student, seeming to tell him and to give him something, and to help him, where in truth they only increase his confusion.

## Cadence

### §8.  *Construction of the cadence*

In view of the four-voice texture, one might at once acknowledge also the necessity of the third in the final four-note chord, although special circumstances of the voice leading or intentional archaisms are sometimes appropriate and may even compel one to avoid the third and to be content with other formulas, for example $\begin{smallmatrix}8\\8\end{smallmatrix}$.

In particular it should be mentioned in addition that when the bass carries the descending leading tone, the best procedure in the $\begin{smallmatrix}6\\3\end{smallmatrix}$-chord of the penultimate bar is to double the third, in which case the two thirds necessarily move by step in opposite directions:

**Example 237**

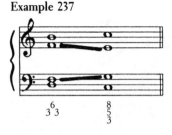

$\begin{smallmatrix}&6&\\3&&3\end{smallmatrix}$       $\begin{smallmatrix}8\\5\\3\end{smallmatrix}$

In view of the availability of such a solution, however, the other one, which would in itself be possible, must be rejected:

**Example 238**

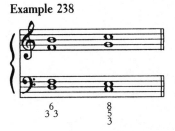

To desire the less valuable just because it is possible can never become the point of view of one who judges artistically.

Under certain circumstances, in the situation under discussion here the descending leading tone itself can, indeed, also be doubled (but see Example 66), in which case the connection to the final chord can be made in various ways:

**Example 239**

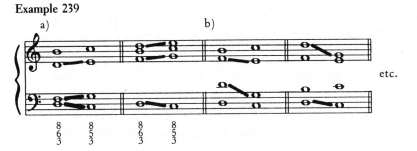

etc.

At a we see how the third of the penultimate chord is forced to rise to the fifth of the final one, because the third of the latter is already introduced by the octave of the [descending] leading tone; matters are reversed at b, where the octave of the leading tone must move to the fifth, because the third of the penultimate chord leads downward to the third of the final one.

The viewpoint of *Fux* in respect to the third (p. 92) was cited already in Chapter 1, §27, to which the reader is now referred.

*Albrechtsberger* presents various cadential formulas in a table (p. 121):

**Example 240**

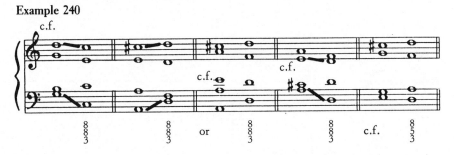

**Example 240** *continued*

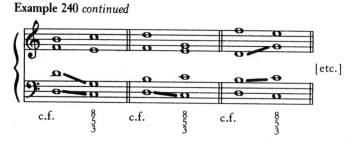

c.f.        $\begin{smallmatrix}8\\5\\3\end{smallmatrix}$   c.f.        $\begin{smallmatrix}8\\5\\3\end{smallmatrix}$   c.f.        $\begin{smallmatrix}8\\5\\3\end{smallmatrix}$

[etc.]

He accompanies this with the following remarks:

> The last bar, which should also be complete, can have those chords [$\begin{smallmatrix}8\\5\\3\end{smallmatrix}$ or $\begin{smallmatrix}5\\3\\1\end{smallmatrix}$] only when the cantus firmus stands in the lowest voice; for if it is in the uppermost voice, the last bar receives only $\begin{smallmatrix}8\\5\\3\end{smallmatrix}$ or $\begin{smallmatrix}8\\3\\1\end{smallmatrix}$, because the cantus firmus ends by descending to the tonic, and the major third that must be taken above the dominant in the penultimate chord along with the fifth and octave also moves to the tonic, as can be seen in the examples. When the cantus firmus stands in the lowest voice, the penultimate bar must be $\begin{smallmatrix}6\\\flat3\\\flat3\end{smallmatrix}$ or $\begin{smallmatrix}8\\6\\\flat3\end{smallmatrix}$.[6]

We read further on p. 126: The following cadences are constructed in a manner contrary to the ancient rule, because the *semitonium modi* does not ascend at the end; for example:"

**Example 241**

NB. "still worse in
the upper voice"

"poor"   NB.        "good"        c.f.

A cadential formation of Beethoven's, in one of his exercises (see Nottebohm p. 55, no. 20), which goes as follows:

**Example 242**

c.f.

is improved by Albrechtsberger thus:

**Example 243**

Nottebohm correctly comments as follows on this improvement:

> The cadence is not formed according to the rule. Albrechtsberger requires that when the cantus firmus lies in one of the upper voices, the bass must have the dominant of the key. (See the *Anweisung,* p. 120f.) Albrechtsberger also changes an occurrence shortly before the cadence of an interval leading away from the main key.

*Bellermann* expresses his opinion (from the historical standpoint) on the question of the major and minor third in cadences as follows in a comment on p. 239:

> The composers of the fifteenth and sixteenth centuries, and later ones up to the time of J.S. Bach, preferred cadences with perfect consonances—thus merely with the octave and fifth—to the full triad. But when they used the full triad in polyphonic settings, in any mode having the minor third (Dorian, Phrygian, and Aeolian) they raised that third to a major third, because the resulting major triad is a more consonant combination of tones than the minor triad. In the Phrygian mode this alteration has been retained without exception up to the present day. For the same reason they also avoided beginning a setting with a minor triad; such a triad can be well intoned in the main body of a setting, but is very difficult when the singer must begin with it. This should be observed even today in unaccompanied settings. The closing chord without fifth—with only octave and major or minor third—is found most rarely in the classical period of the sixteenth century. These comments may suffice concerning the raising of the third in closing and opening chords by the earlier composers.

I quote in addition what Bellermann has to say (with the same admirable thoroughness as in his treatment of three-voice counterpoint) about the cadence in four-voice counterpoint:

> Of these cadences, the ones that usually cause the most difficulty for beginners are those in which the bass has the descending leading tone, above which we must place the sixth-chord with minor third and major sixth (and in the Phrygian mode, that with the major third and major sixth). In this tonal combination or accompaniment of the descending leading tone, the best doubling is that of the third, as in the above examples. One can, however, also double the bass tone by its octave in one of the upper voices, which is then led upward to the third of the scale, while the third of the descending leading tone ascends to the fifth of the scale; for example: [examples follow of cadential construction in Dorian, Ionian, Aeolian, and Phrygian modes]. This type of cadence is indeed perfectly good, but is not found very often in the works of the older composers; the latter preferred, when the descending leading tone was

doubled, to have the third of this leading tone move downward to the third of the scale, and let the octave leap downward by a fifth to the dominant of the scale. It is true that hidden fifths thereby arise, which have so frequently been used by all better composers of older and more recent times, however, that they must be counted as a completely necessary and unproblematical exception to the strict rule. [Examples follows of cadential constructions in Dorian, Mixolydian, Aeolian, and Phrygian modes.]

Doubling of the descending leading tone in the Phrygian mode is automatically prohibited, since the doubling voice would have to make a leap from *f* to *g♯* (an augmented second) or from *f* to *b* (a diminished fifth). The augmented second in this position is completely bad and unusable; the other interval, however, from *f* to *b,* has been used without hesitation in the cadence by later masters, such as Bach, Handel, Graun, and their contemporaries. But in strict a capella setting it must be avoided as much as possible.

## Exercises

**Example 244**

Fux XIV, 5

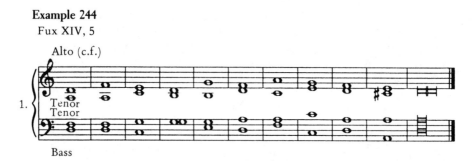

Fux XV, 4

Fux XV, 6

**Example 244** *continued*

Fux XVI, 1

Soprano

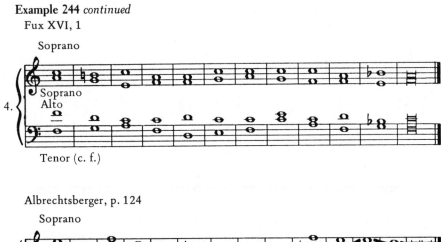

Soprano
Alto

4.

Tenor (c. f.)

Albrechtsberger, p. 124

Soprano

Soprano (c. f.)
Alto

5.

Bass

Cherubini, Ex. 118

Soprano

Alto
Tenor

6.

Bass (c.f.)

H. Schenker

Soprano

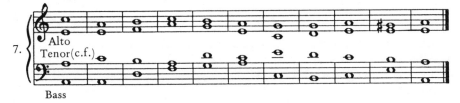

Alto
Tenor(c.f.)

7.

Bass

# Chapter 2

# The Second Species: Two Notes Against One

### §1.  *Recollection of several earlier principles*

1.   When and how completeness of triads is to be sought is decided by the same principles that were set forth for the second species of two- and three-voice counterpoint.

2.   Here as well, just as in the second species of two- and three-voice counterpoint, the neighboring note is better avoided than employed (it is found, for example, neither in Albrechtsberger's nor in Cherubini's exercises).

3.   To what extent one can speak of a change of harmony or a consonant passing tone (or consonant neighbor) in the case of 5 — 6 or 6 — 5 is to be judged according to the principles set down in Part 3, Chapter 2, §3. (Compare below, Exercise 1, bar 7; Exercise 4, bars 2, 5, 11, 13; also Albrechtsberger, p. 132, bars 1 and 5.) To be differentiated from such phenomena in all cases, however, is a succession in which the fifth (or sixth) represents a dissonant passing tone; for example:

**Example 245**

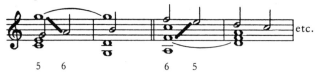

4.   Voice leadings such as the following, by Cherubini, are to be regarded as faulty in strict counterpoint:

**Example 246**

a) p. 47, 3rd ex.              b) p. 47, 4th ex.

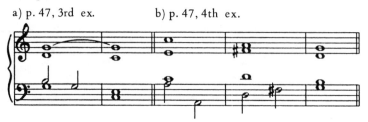

Here, at a the ascending leading tone is placed on the downbeat instead of on the upbeat, which is the only appropriate place for it; at b we see a doubling of the ascending leading tone, which could easily and well have been avoided.

5.   At the beginning, the $\frac{6}{4}$-chord must be avoided, even in cases in which the correct form would be recovered on the upbeat.[1]

Albrechtsberger mentions this explicitly on p. 129:

**Example 247**

"poor beginning"     " good beginning"

Compare also Albrechtsberger's remark on p. 148: "The $\frac{6}{4}$-chord is also prohibited at the beginning, both in major and minor modes."

## Exercises

**Example 248**

Fux XVI, 2

Alto (c.f.)

1.

Tenor
Tenor

Bass

**Example 248** *continued*

Fux XVI, 3

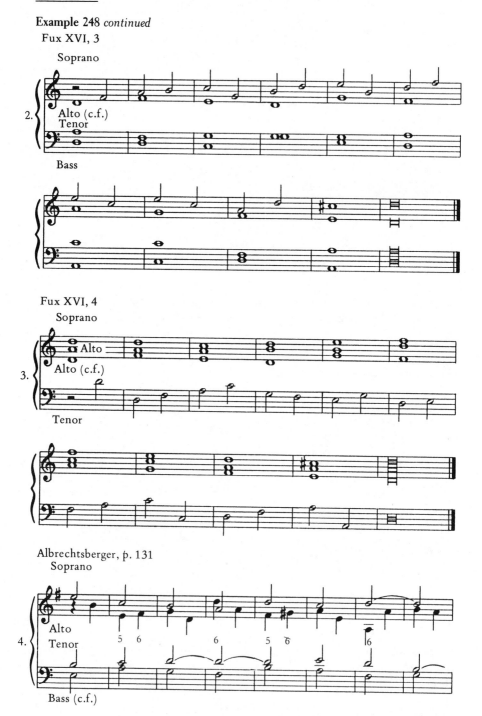

Fux XVI, 4

Albrechtsberger, p. 131

**Example 248** *continued*

# Chapter 3

# The Third Species: Four Notes Against One

### §1.  Recollection of certain earlier principles

1.  The quarter-notes here, as in the third species of three-voice counter-point, make the neighboring note occasionally more usable than in the second species.

*Fux* uses it chiefly in the penultimate bar for purposes of cadence; *Albrechtsberger* uses it more often, and indeed elsewhere than in the cadence (see below, Exercise 4, bar 2; Exercise 5, bars 2, 10); *Cherubini* (p. 48, third exercise, bars 5 - 6) even uses it at the end of the bar.

2.  The following fundamental observation by Fux (p. 112), which per-tains to bar 4 of the exercise quoted here as No. 1, also has to do with the matter of doubling:

*Joseph:* With your permission, dear master, why have you doubled the third in the fourth bar? Could one have used a unison instead of the third in the tenor, in this way:

**Example 249**

Fux XVII, 2

*Aloys:* Yes, it could indeed have been done in this way. But aside from the fact that the unison on the downbeat reduces fullness of texture not incon-siderably, the third, or tenth, that passes through in the upper voice would be deficient, because it could not be heard continuously.

Here, certainly, an inference back to the second species is in order.

## Exercises

**Example 250**

Fux XVII, 1

Fux XVII, 5

**Example 250** *continued*

Fux XVIII, 1

Albrechtsberger, p. 132

Albrechtsberger, p. 133

**Example 250** *continued*

H. Schenker

# Chapter 4

# The Fourth Species: Syncopes

### §1. Recollection of several earlier principles

1. The prohibition of doubling the tone of resolution remains in force also in four-voice counterpoint, although it would be easier for the latter to mitigate the poor effect, since it would already express [triadic] completeness with the other three parts. The doubling would call forth precisely the effect of a neighboring note, to which the same remarks would pertain as those set down in Part 3, Chapter 4, §3.

2. Despite the four-voice texture, it remains true here as well that the consonance which prepares any dissonant syncope is still completely unable to exert an influence on the coming harmony definite enough to make it appear that the paths of the voices had already been predetermined (as happens in free composition). Thus in four-voice counterpoint as well, the descending resolution of the dissonant syncope is required in all cases.

3. The open position of the outer voices is introduced by the syncope ⌒4 — 3 in the upper counterpoint, or ⌒2 — 3 in the lower, when these syncopes belong to the content of the outer-voice setting (cf. Part 3, Chapter 1, §21).

4. The proper place for the complete triad must be regarded as the downbeat in the case of consonant syncopes, and the upbeat in the case of dissonant ones. Yet in spite of the four-voice texture, triadic completeness can be relinquished any time the voice leading so requires.

5. For reasons of voice leading, the unison is often revealed to be necessary; for this reason, it may be used here with greater justification than in three-voice settings.

6. Assuming the compulsion of voice leading, under certain circumstances even a cadential formation such as the following can be approved:

Example 251

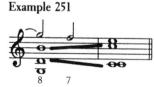

Here for the first time a passing tone $8-7$ (not a suspension!) becomes apparent.

## §2.  *Accompanying voices for the dissonant syncopes*

With $\frown 7-6$, $\frac{\frown 8}{3}-6$ and $\frac{\frown 7}{1}-6$ lead to complete triads; $-\frac{88}{5}-6$ yields an incomplete triad.

For $\frown 4-3$, complete triads arise with $\frac{8}{3}-3\Big|\frac{\frown 5}{-4}-3\Big|\frac{55}{-4}-3\Big|\frac{8}{-4}-3\Big|\frac{\frown 6}{-4}-3$ and even $-\frac{66}{4}-3$; only $-\frac{88}{4}-3$ makes the triad incomplete.

For $\frown 9-8$, triads become complete with $\frac{\frown 9}{3}-8\Big|\frac{\frown 9}{6}-8$, while $\frac{\frown 9}{33}-8\Big|\frac{\frown 9}{66}-8$ lead to incomplete triads.

For $\frown 2-3$, complete triads can be achieved with

$$\frac{\frown 4-5}{\frac{\frown 5}{-2}-3}\Bigg|\frac{\frown 5-6}{\frac{\frown 5}{-2}-3},\ \text{or}\ \frac{\frown 5-6}{\frac{\frown 5}{-2}-3}\ \text{or}\ \frac{\frown 4-5}{\frac{\frown 5}{-2}-3};$$

$\frac{8}{3}$ can never be achieved as a product of resolution, since $\frown 7-8$ is excluded from the outset. Moreover, since $\frac{5}{33}$ is an intrinsically better product than $\frac{55}{3}$, $\frac{\frown 4-5}{\frac{\frown 5}{-2}-3}$ accordingly is better than $\frac{\frown 4-5}{\frac{\frown 5}{-2}-3}$. Finally it should be remembered that with $\frown 2-3$, if it is accompanied by $\frown 4-5$, under certain circumstances there is also the danger of a diminished fifth on the upbeat; the comments in Part 3, Chapter 4, §6 apply to its use.

For $\frown 4-5$, a complete triad must be produced in all situations:

$$\frac{\frown 4-5}{\frac{\frown 5}{-2}-3}\ \text{or}\ \frac{\frown 4-5}{\frac{\frown 5}{-2}-3}$$

—but, to be sure, without the octave.

It is no more possible here than in three-voice counterpoint, however, to arrive at $\frac{\frown 7}{5}-6\Big|\frac{\frown 6}{-4}-3$ or $\frac{6}{5}$ if the completely strict principles are maintained (cf. Part 3, Chapter 4, §6, under e).

*Fux* (p. 115): ". . . they [the ligatures] call for those consonances that would accompany them if the tying were eliminated, for the reason cited in the same context [i.e., in three-voice counterpoint]: the ligature is nothing but a delay of the following note, which alters nothing in regard to the consonances." (Compare *Counterpoint I*, p. 269.) Here Fux presents as examples his Table XIX, Figures 2, 3, 4:

$$\frac{\frown 9-8}{\frac{5}{3}}\Bigg|\frac{\frown 4-3}{\frac{8}{5}}\Bigg|\frac{\frown 7-6}{\frac{8}{3}}$$

which, certainly, does not prevent him from investigating the necessity of voice leading with other combinations as well, as is provided by the exercises quoted below.

Decisive for Fux is the fact that already here, in four-voice strict counterpoint, he sometimes admits subdivision of another voice into half-notes (cf. also Example 227)—a procedure which, for a definite purpose and on the basis of my own principles, I reserve for a special combination-species (see below, Part 6). But just the fact that the early master already makes use of subdivision in the exercises that belong here (see below,

Exercises 2 and 3) necessitates that I introduce to the reader at this point rather than later the reason he cites for doing so. He states first of all, on p. 115:

[*Aloys:*] The examples will make the matter clear. (Table XIX, Figures 2, 3, 4.) These examples show clearly that the consonances are the same whether the notes are tied or not.

*Joseph:* Does this rule never fail, dear master?

*Aloys:* It fails in many settings of this species in which one is compelled to use the ligatures along with three whole-notes for a complete bar. This cannot happen, however, in a setting in which the seventh is used in combination with a fifth; for example:

**Example 252**

Fux XIX, 5

Here, the resolution of the tied note forms a forbidden dissonance with the tenor; this, to be sure, must be avoided.

*Joseph:* What can one do in this case?

*Aloys:* The whole-note in the tenor must then be subdivided:

**Example 253**

Fux XIX, 6

*Joseph:* But one is not supposed to subdivide any whole-note in this species.

*Aloys:* Quite right, insofar as possible. But various situations arise, as you will see from the examples, in which one is compelled to use subdivision, since necessity demands it. Thus the rule of this species that the harmony accompanying the tie must invariably consist of three whole-notes cannot be so accurately observed.

*Joseph:* The seventh accompanied by the octave requires no subdivision, as your previous example, Table XIX, figure 4, shows.

*Aloys:* But this is only in the particular case where no obstacle prevents use of the octave instead of the fifth; in settings in which, as often happens, the octave cannot be used because of the preceding notes and the continuation, the fifth must necessarily be used. Then, as in many other cases, the whole-note must be divided, as the following examples show.

We read further in Fux (p. 116):

> [*Aloys:*] Now to the remaining examples [i.e., those cited below (see Example 262) as exercise nos. 2–4], which reveal clearly that tying in four voices either cannot always be accompanied with three whole-notes, as this species requires, or, when it can be so accompanied, the harmony cannot always be made to comply fully with the rules.
>
> *Joseph:* I see why an occasional whole-note has been subdivided in these examples, but I cannot see that the harmony is, as you say, in any way lacking.
>
> *Aloys:* Do you not see that in the sixth bar of the first example the fifth is missing on the downbeat? The latter is nevertheless, necessary for complete harmony. Then, in the fifth bar of the last example, the second is doubled, while the sixth, which belongs to the complete harmony (see the following example) is lacking:

**Example 254**

Fux XX, 4

Finally, in the sixth bar of the same example the fourth is doubled, although according to the rule the second is doubled in preference to the fourth.

*Joseph:* Why should doubling of the second be preferable to that of the fourth?

*Aloys:* It is not only a matter of the second versus the fourth, but rather of completeness of harmony. For the complete harmony consists of the combination of third, fifth, and octave;[1] thus it is clear that the harmony lacks the full roster of its components. But here I am not speaking of the first part of the bar, which contains the second (an interval that in no way admits the octave into its company), but of the second part of the bar, which lacks the octave; for example:[2]

**Example 255**

Fux XX, 5

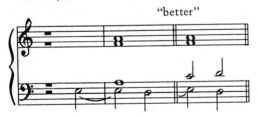

Defects of this kind, which are not too significant, are the result of the strictness of this exercise, which—as an exercise—is so useful to the student, not only by teaching the correct procedure in composition but also by showing the extent to which one may depart from the strict rules when necessity demands.

When we see, finally, how in bar 3 of Exercise 4 Fux uses a subdivision even when it is not absolutely necessary,[3] we must concede at once that the law he establishes for subdivision is by no means a precise and uniform one. In fact, it is the lack of a clearly defined insight alone which causes Fux to become bound up with such unfortunate contradictions or otherwise confused ideas as we have just been able to witness. It is, first of all, incontrovertible that a syncopated exercise, in spite of all the forces that come heavily to bear on it, can certainly be executed without subdivision as well; and it follows from this, in turn, that Fux shows subdivision at this point in his teaching not because it may not or cannot be otherwise, but only because Fux, having decided to introduce the subdivision process as well to students, prefers to introduce it here in the fourth species of four-voice counterpoint more by reason of [mere] opportunity than of inner consistency.

Fux's chief error, however, certainly lies in his effort to create more precise justification from the concept of a "complete harmony." Specifically, he is in the position of having characterized with one and the same concept two completely different chordal aggregates—both the triad (as the case of bar 6 of the second exercise and bar 6 of the fourth) and also the seventh-chord (as in bar 5 of the fourth exercise). Leaving aside the fact that such a characterization does not apply to the seventh-chord in exactly the same sense as it does to the triad—the statement on p. 103 quoted above in Part 3, Chapter 4, §6 would have to be called more accurate—, Fux would simply have had to make a decision to invoke already in strict counterpoint the concept of seventh-chords if he wanted to preserve its true purpose as a voice leading theory with laws of its own. And it was still less appropriate to make the first decisive approach to the difficult concept of seventh-chords with such a superficial comment, which, moreover, is marred by a false characterization. Thus, to state it precisely,. all of Fux's errors, including the incorrect construal of the topic of subdivision, the poor choice of placement, and finally the confusing treatment with its amalgamation of incommensurate concepts, may arise from his inadequate insight into the nature of the seventh-chord in general. The different way in which this prolongation is to be achieved and communicated, however, I myself shall show in Part 6.

At this point, then, all that remains is to devote a few words to the explanations offered by Fux of bar 6 of the second exercise and bar 6 of the fourth exercise (see above). In the first case, it might well occur to us that Fux possibly meant to enunciate the prohibition of doubling the tone of resolution when he refers to the fifth of the chord, which cannot be used here only because of $\frown 6 - 5$. But it is obvious in the second case that $\frown^4_2$ can lead to a resolution with the octave neither in three- nor in four-voice counterpoint; the precondition of such an octave, after all, would be the syncope $\frown 7 - 8$ in the lower counterpoint, which, however, is prohibited from the outset.

That *Albrechtsberger* (p. 136ff.), too, like Fux, sometimes "of necessity" takes the liberty even here of dividing a second voice into half-notes, and thus arrives at $\frown^7_3$ | $\frown^6_2$ (see below, Exercises 5 and 7) may deserve initially to be mentioned. That aside, he explicitly provides a table (pp. 137–139) of all possible combinations, which need not be reproduced here. Reference should be made only to the remark that he devotes to the syncope $\frown 2 - 3$ (p. 136):

With the second-ligature, which is the only tied dissonance for the lower voice, the doubled perfect fifth is appropriate, or a perfect fifth and the doubled second itself, especially when the bass tone resolves downward by only a half-step; in this resolution, then, an agreeable sixth-chord without a pungent octave arises, specifically: $\begin{smallmatrix} 6 \\ 3 \end{smallmatrix}$ or $\begin{smallmatrix} 6 \\ 3 \end{smallmatrix}$. But if it is desired to double the perfect fourth along with the ligature of the minor or major second (which is also permitted), then this ligature must be resolved downward by a whole step, so that in the resolution a major or minor third will result with two perfect—not false—fifths.

And the following examples are added on p. 139:

**Example 256**

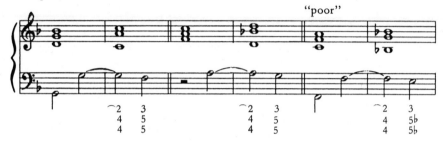

In Beethoven's exercise-notebook (see Nottebohm, p. 56), Albrechtsberger annotates:

In all species of four-voice counterpoint, even in the fourth and fifth species, when no dissonance-ligature is involved, the downbeats or strong parts of the bar must have full chords. Empty chords are allowed only in upbeats or weak parts of the bar. The empty chords are those in which three voices have the same tone, or also when they are related by octaves.

His correction thus reads as follows:

**Example 257**

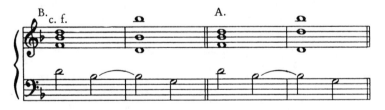

A gross transgression of the principles of strict counterpoint can be discovered on pp. 139-140, however:

For the rest, when no dissonant ligature is present, the consonances are combined with their complete or incomplete accompaniment; very often, for the sake of good and effortless melody, the third or sixth is doubled, if it is not the *semitonium modi*. It should only be observed that if the sixth is doubled, it must not be resolved to the perfect fifth; because in that case, at the upbeat, which must have only perfect chords or sixth-chords, the six-five chord $\begin{smallmatrix}6\\3\end{smallmatrix}$ would arise. But if the sixth resolves to a diminished fifth, it is acceptable, because this latter six-five chord $\begin{smallmatrix}6\\3\flat\end{smallmatrix}$ is not so sharply dissonant.

For example:

**Example 258**

It is clear that here we are really dealing with a true tied seventh in passing (see below, Part 6, Section 2), not with a genuine suspension or a syncope of strict counterpoint. But to permit or merely to tolerate a passing tone of this type already in strict counterpoint would be to confuse concepts to the detriment of both theory and student.

Albrechtsberger remarks (pp. 142–143) concerning this example:

**Example 259**

Albrechtsberger, p. 141

Sop. I

Sop. II
Alto

Tenor

as follows:

The NB above in the tenth bar over the note G in the alto means that, in order to have uninterrupted ligatures, in free composition this fourth in the lowest position may be set on the upbeat; it derives from the second inversion of the essential seventh-chord, which also, like the diminished fifth on the weak beat, can be approached freely:

**Example 260**

Albrechtsberger, p. 143

From this it is clear that Albrechtsberger was conscious of the concept of a passing seventh that uniformly governs in all of these cases, and when on p. 142 he expressly reserves such a voice leading for free composition, he himself admits the transgression that he committed with his remark on p. 139. From the outset, Albrechtsberger assigns the following setting to "free counterpoint":

**Example 261**
Albrechtsberger, p. 143

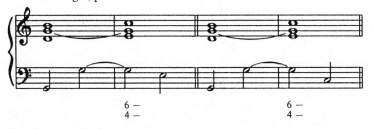

This, however, is obvious.

*Cherubini* not only takes over from Fux (see p. 50, Example 120) the division process with all of its novel effects, but moreover shows in examples 121–122 the setting of tied dissonances already presented in the fourth species of three-voice counterpoint now in various four-voice examples, which, however, will be discussed only later.

## Exercises

**Example 262**
Fux XIX, 7

**Example 262** *continued*

Fux XX, 1

2.

Fux XX, 2

3.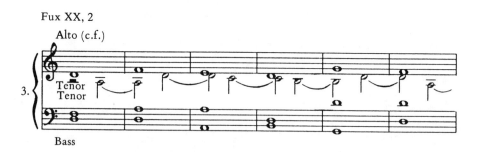

**Example 262** *continued*

Fux XX, 3

Albrechtsberger, p. 142

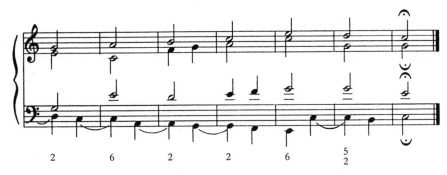

**Example 262** *continued*

Albrechtsberger, p. 144

Albrechtsberger, p. 142

**Example 262** *continued*

H. Schenker

# Chapter 5

# The Fifth Species: Mixed Counterpoint

## Exercises

**Example 263**

Fux XX, 5

Fux XXI, 2

**Example 263** *continued*

Albrechtsberger, p. 147

Soprano I

3.

S. II　"license"
T.

Bass　　　　　　6　　　　5　6

"license"

6　5　　　　　4　3

H. Schenker

Soprano

4.

Alto
Tenor (c. f.)

Bass

**Example 265** *continued*

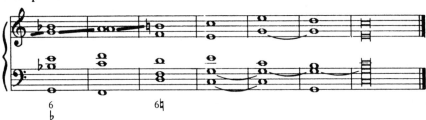

Cherubini, Ex. 133

H. Schenker

**Example 265** *continued*

Albrechtsberger, p. 372

Albrechtsberger, p. 373

**Example 265** *continued*

Albrechtsberger, p. 374

Albrechtsberger, p. 375

**Example 265** *continued*

Cherubini, Ex. 134

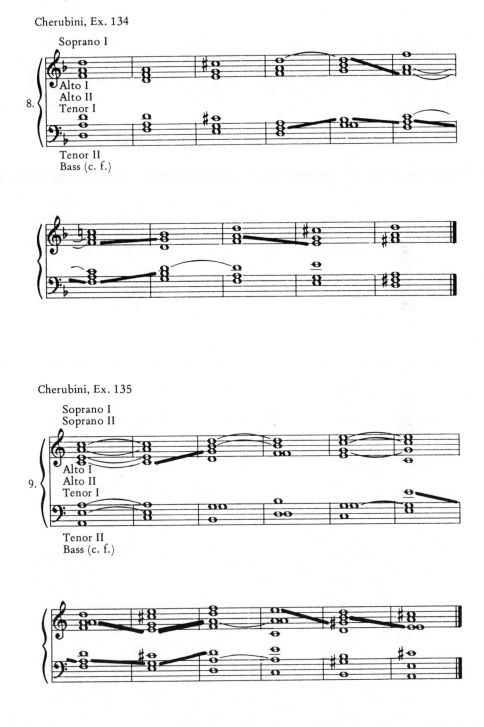

Cherubini, Ex. 135

**Example 265** *continued*

Cherubini, Ex. 136

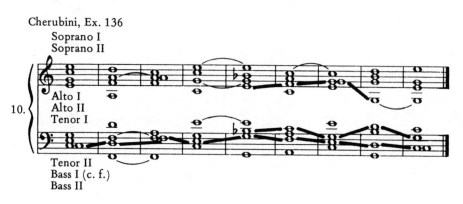

# PART SIX

# Bridges to Free Composition

## Introductory Remarks

Semper idem, sed non eodem modo.

In the treatises of Fux, Albrechtsberger, Cherubini, and Bellermann—the only ones I use here for purposes of citing literature—one finds interspersed here and there, along with the main subject-matter, also examples of exercises in which two, three, or several counterpoints move simultaneously in different species. They always include the cantus firmus, of course, and observe the principal laws of strict counterpoint, according to which the downbeat (except in the case of a dissonant syncope) always remains consonant, and the dissonant passing tone always appears on the weak beat, between two consonances. Reference can also be found there to a configuration $\frac{6}{4}+\frac{5}{3}$, or to a simultaneous subdivision of a second voice into half-notes in exercises of the fourth species, whereby the resolution of dissonant syncopes, in particular, takes a multitude of new forms. At the very first glance, however, one recognizes that these inserted remarks and precepts are located only very loosely in the general plan, and are merely ad-hoc instructions, which in no sense have their origin in precise observations stated in terms of a simple formula. In fact, these theorists were concerned only with doing justice under all circumstances to certain familiar phenomena and formulas of free composition; and since they otherwise had no artistically and intellectually valid bridges to the latter, they considered it completely sufficient just to blend the phenomena in question into their pedagogical edifice at any point and in any way, with or without explanation. They therefore would perhaps also have been the last to understand the extent to which they succeeded only in inflicting harm upon their own teaching of strict counterpoint, without, however, providing a foundation for free composition, which is certainly what they wished to do.

If I too now return in the following discussion to exactly the same phenomena, it could at first appear that I merely wanted to provide them with a more suitable place in the complete theory, and also the necessary

# Combinations of the Five Species with Continued Use of a Cantus Firmus as a Basis

*Chapter 1*

# The Combinations of Two or Three Counterpoints of the Second Species

### A. *Three-Voice Counterpoint:* Two Counterpoints of the Second Species:

### §1. *General characteristics of this combination*

If two counterpoints in half-notes are added to the cantus firmus, the opportunity arises, on the one hand, for new varieties of voice leading—particularly that of passing tones—such as could not yet be provided by three-voice strict counterpoint. That on the other hand the full range of possibilities must, as a result of the lack of rhythmic contrast of the two counterpoints, remain limited, can be shown only later, by comparison with combinations that do exhibit a variety of rhythm.

It is consistent with the manner of presentation observed so far that in treating these settings, too, I attempt in so far as possible to emphasize the difference between a strict and natural voice leading and one that is less strict. The purpose of this is not to say that preference must always be accorded only to the former, but rather to call attention to the difference per se, and to show that although one does remain closer to the basic principles with a strict voice leading, one nevertheless does not cancel those principles with a voice leading that is less strict, but only ventures forth into their prolongations.

### §2. *The strict construction of the setting*

If the setting is to be carried out in a fully strict manner, one must take care that the half-notes of the upbeat are either both consonant with the cantus firmus or both dissonant with it.[1]

1. In the first case, where the half-notes of the upbeat are both consonant with the cantus firmus, it is the law of consonance itself that justifies the setting. In particular, the following possibilities can arise in this case:

(a) If the downbeat has a complete triad, § or §, the upbeat can continue the harmony (see Example 283, Exercise 1, bar 9; Exercise 2, bar 6), or, under certain circumstances, also introduce a new harmony (see Exercise 2, bars 9, 10).

To be noted especially in connection with the *change of harmony* is the following: it can be produced here not only by means of 5 — 6 or 6 — 5, as in strict counterpoint (see Exercise 2, bars 9, 10), but also, above and beyond 5 — 6—exactly as would *not* have been possible in strict counterpoint—, in the following way, for example:

**Example 266**

(= A   —   E)

This is a type of change of harmony which shows the new feature that the two harmonies with the cantus firmus are a fifth apart, while the harmony-change of strict counterpoint (expressed by 5 — 6) shows harmonies only a third apart.[2]

It can be noticed here, as in strict counterpoint (see Part 3, Chapter 2, §3), that the interval-succession 5 — 6 (or 6 — 5) may more readily be interpreted, under certain circumstances, as producing the effect of a consonant passing tone or a neighboring note (see Exercise 1, bars 2, 5, and 6).

The effect of 5 — 6 or 6 — 5 can, moreover, be produced for the first time by means of an *exchange of voices:*

**Example 267**

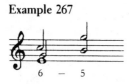

(cf. Exercise 1, bar 7); it must not be overlooked, however, that such an effect usually is produced by the voice leading itself, without any express intention of a voice-exchange; free composition often uses this technique consciously, in which case one may speak of a voice-exchange with more justification.

(b) If the triad of the downbeat is incomplete, the upbeat can complete it (see Exercise 1, bar 1; Exercise 2, bar 3) or leave it incomplete; or, finally, it can also introduce a change of harmony; for example:

**Example 268**

2.   If the half-notes of the upbeat should bring dissonant passing tones, they must always strictly obey the rule that strict counterpoint establishes for the passing tone; thus it is, primarily, exactly this strict adherence to the rule which shows the contrast between our combination of species and free composition, where the passing tone, in prolongation of the strict rule, also exhibits freer forms of occurrence. Thus it is not permissible in our combined-species setting to leap away from a dissonant passing tone, as here:

**Example 269**

But even on the foundation of voice leading that still adheres to the strict rule, it is revealed even here that the dissonant passing tones of the two counterpoints represent something comparable to an *obbligato two-voice setting* in which, as in two-voice settings of the first species, the voices must be consonant with each other:

**Example 270**

The reason that progressions in fourths are rejected in this combination:

**Example 271**

—from which, however, the following must be discriminated:

**Example 272**

—may be sought in the fact that the cantus firmus does not have the power to eliminate the effect of the fourth in the vertical direction, since, by sustaining, it merely represents a type of oblique motion. (Compare *Counterpoint I*, p. 112, and, in the present volume, Part 3, Chapter 1, §23.) It is as though in spite of the cantus firmus, only the setting of the passing tones were present, and thus the fourth would remain "uncovered" in the downward direction, and therefore have the effect of a dissonance.

It is equally obvious that a neighboring and a passing tone may be combined, or sometimes even two neighboring notes:[3]

**Example 273**

It is easily understandable, however, that under the strict preconditions required here, a fifth-relationship between the passing tones must be prohibited, because of the resulting 5 — 5 succession (imagine the half-notes of Example 271 in inversion).

### §3.  *The less strict construction*

A different characteristic effect arises, however, when a dissonant passing tone collides with a consonant leap (see Exercise 1, bars 4, 6, 8). Although the progression of both voices adheres most precisely to the principles of strict counterpoint, the difference between the two simultaneously operating laws nevertheless causes a conflict, which has the result that the dissonant nature of the passing tone cancels the consonant effect of the leaping interval. That it is precisely the dissonant passing tone which prevails in this situation probably rests on the fact that, as explained in Part 3, Chapter 2, §2, such a passing tone confirms and extends the harmony of the downbeat in far greater measure—that is, it preserves the harmonic unity of the bar much more decisively—than does a consonant half-note. Thus one might even say that by its superior influence, this dissonant passing tone in a way ensnares the consonant leap into the realm of its own dissonance, so that in such a situation it may appear by no means inappropriate to speak of *horizontalization of the leap*—that is, of the leap as, again, only a passing tone—and to speak even of a *"leaping passing tone."* (As will be shown in *Free Composition* [§172], similar causes result in "leaping passing tones" even in free composition; especially when they occur in the bass, they are frequently so confusing in effect that they can be recognized as passing tones only with great difficulty.)

One must accordingly distinguish from the voice leading just described a case such as that of Exercise 1, bars 2 and 10, in which a consonant passing tone joins with a consonant leap of the other counterpoint; there the two counterpoints, because they are consonant with the cantus firmus, require no further justification.

Yet even in the case of the dissonant passing tones first mentioned it can be seen that their setting, despite the inherently indisputable right of the counterpoint to leap to any chosen interval that is consonant with the cantus firmus, nevertheless cannot tolerate leaps that yield a second, fourth, or seventh, such as the following:

**Example 274**

Thus having excluded seconds, fourths, and sevenths, we again arrive at that *strict two-voice setting of passing tones* which has already been discussed in the preceding paragraph.

That a fifth can also be used here under certain circumstances stems from the fact that a leap can provide the requisite contrary motion (see Exercise 1, bar 4); yet similar motion is perhaps also admissible in a case such as:

**Example 275**

Accordingly, a voice leading like that at a of the following example:

**Example 276**

is excluded only because of the leap to the seventh, a fact that is best clarified by the contrasting situation under b, to which no objection can be raised.

Further, the combination of a dissonant passing tone with a change of harmony, as in the following example:

**Example 277**

must also be rejected, since it produces a contradictory, excessively opaque aggregation of effects: on the one hand, because of the dissonant passing tone, the harmony of the downbeat would have to be retained as that of the whole bar, while on the other hand the change of harmony in the same bar would demand recognition of a new harmony.[4] Even free composition can assert only one harmony in one place, and a voice leading like that of the first setting of Example 277 would therefore be easy to understand as a passing event within a *D* sound (a sixth-chord) only because *c* could be heard as a second passing tone (also coming directly from *d* or derived by substitution).

### §4. *More precise characterization of the setting of the passing tones*

1. In view of the fact that the intervals of the passing events follow their own laws, they could be regarded in general as a two-voice setting complete in itself, if occasional situations such as the following:

**Example 278**

did not necessarily make us conscious of the third voice and thus of the three-voice texture.

Special recognition is due the ⁶₄-chord that arises under certain circumstances on the upbeat:

**Example 279**

and which already here provides the first opportunity to observe how, assuming otherwise beneficial circumstances in the cantus firmus, a second §-chord connects felicitously to it on the following downbeat. If this tendency of voice leading is certainly understandable (since with three voices there is hardly any more convenient voice leading than to progress in similar motion with §-chords [*FrC.*, §173]), the only reason it is necessary to speak expressly of it here is to refer to a new possibility in the present combination—a possibility that favors §-progressions in a way of which the first species of three- or four-voice counterpoint still had no knowledge. For while there the succession from § to § involved whole-note values (indeed it could not be otherwise), here in the combined species it becomes possible also to employ the upbeat for this purpose, and this shows the particular suppleness of the §-chord, which, used on the upbeat, can mediate from downbeat to downbeat in such a happily fluid way. We see how precisely the *six-three chord,* endowed with such a characteristic, must rise to the status of *inner spirit of the setting of passing tones,* of which we are here able to identify the first trace.

Aside from such situations that naturally point to the three-voice texture, the setting of the passing tones, because of its otherwise self-contained two-voice structure, represents a nation within a nation, so to speak, and we can understand why it tolerates extended successions of thirds or sixths no more than any strict two-voice counterpoint.

2.    The setting of the passing tones, however, obviously by no means eliminates [the importance of] the two-voice setting of the outer voices. Already in combination with a third voice, and more still in combination with two other voices, it is revealed that the setting of the passing tones is more effective when it coincides with that of the outer voices—that is, when the outer voices themselves carry the passing tones: standing in the foreground by nature, the outer voices derive all the more strength and authority from the effect of the passing tones. The setting of the passing tones is already somewhat less effective when only one outer voice participates, and the effect is weakest when, as is possible in four-voice counterpoint, it lies only in the inner voices. It is especially true of these latter situations, then, that the better the two-part outer-voice structure, the more successful also the setting of the passing tones. And herein lies the root of that rule, so extraordinarily important for free composition, that one must above all pay attention to the bass as the low voice of the outer two-voice counterpoint, since with it, also the worth of the inner voices (and thus also the passing tones) stands or falls.

3.    The consonance in which the passing tones meet (including the leaping passing tones) provides a foundation for their setting not only in an external way; rather, it also enhances their inner meaning as passing tones. In pairs, the passing tones express their intent even more emphatically than singly, and they dissonate against the sustaining tone (or the tone that is only conceived as sustaining, such as is indigenous to free composition) as though in the manner of an even heavier weight because they are consonant with each other. The increment in voices thus intensifies the passing event as such,

with the result that its limited independence as a contrapuntal entity in itself at the same time appears in the correct light.

### §5. The absence of scale-degree significance of the chords in combined-species counterpoint as well

The sense in which one may speak even in the second species of the concept of composing out was already discussed in Part 3, Chapter 2, §2. It is clear that the further expansion of the half-note domain, as is here provided by the second contrapuntal voice (likewise in half-notes), must intensify the effect of composing out. In spite of this, it remains true here as well that any increase in composing out, however achieved, still cannot give the chords that final precision that they gain only in free composition by means of scale degrees. How easily one could yield to the illusion that the following case, for example, involved a sustaining root *F* with the interval-succession 6 — 5:

**Example 280**

(F. . . ?)

or that the next case involved a root *C* with the passing motion 8 — 7:

**Example 281**

(C. . . ?)

Or, consider the following case:

**Example 282**

( $B^7$?)

Doesn't the aggregate of a $B^7$ chord deceptively assert itself here in retrospect? But be that as it may, we must nevertheless strictly suppress even here any personal impression that tries to read into the voice leading various effects of free composition, and always evaluate what occurs on the upbeat purely according to principles of voice leading. For precisely because scale degrees are still lacking, it happens that in spite of the increased material substance, under all circumstances the setting of passing tones here first takes refuge in the law of consonance, since thereby it can attain comprehensibility in an unrestricted sense which, because of the lack of scale degrees, it would not be able to attain even with freer voice leading. But such effects that arise purely through independent voice leading may perhaps make it clear why free composition often charts similar courses, in order to fulfill *dissonant concepts by means of illusory consonances*—a technique whose great fecundity will be shown only later, in *Free Composition* [§§169, 170].

## Exercises

### Example 283

H. Schenker

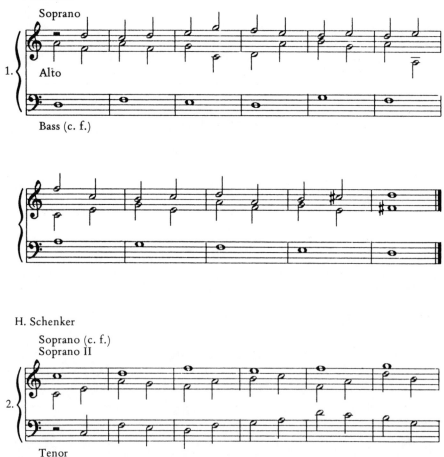

H. Schenker

**Example 283** *continued*

## B.   *Four-Voice Counterpoint:* One Counterpoint of the First Species, and Two Counterpoints of the Second:

**§6.   On the opportunity for richer §-formations in the setting of the passing tones, and on the change of harmony**

Such a combination fosters the tendency, introduced above in §4, toward §-formations all the more easily since here, besides the cantus firmus, another voice in whole-notes is included, which, along with the two other voices in half-notes, can make the execution of the §-chords more independent of the cantus firmus; for example:

**Example 284**

But with respect to the setting of the passing tones in itself, §-formations are not possible except, for example, in the following way (see for comparison Example 271):

**Example 285**

Here, certainly, because they are not in the lowest position, they do not come into question as true §- formations.

The more strongly consonance[5] appears to be expressed here by the downbeat, the more noticeable the contradiction, shown in Example 277, in the combination of a change of harmony with a dissonant passing tone. See a of Example 286; the form at b, on the contrary, is readily admissible.

**Example 286**

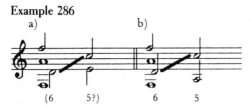

In the cadential formula of the exercise quoted in Example 288, an adumbration of the scale-degree progression II — V — I can be heard. This is a further contribution to a deepened understanding that the scale degrees have their origin in voice leading (cf. pp. 47–48). Yet other cadences are also possible—for example:

**Example 287**

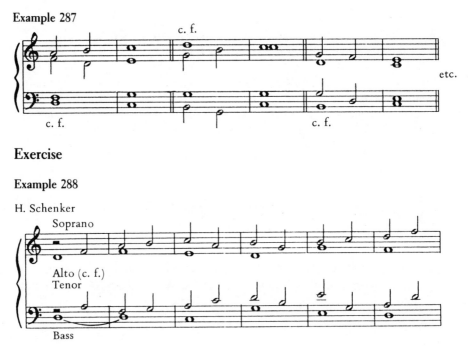

## Exercise

**Example 288**

H. Schenker

## C.  *Four-Voice Counterpoint:* Three Counterpoints of the Second Species:

### §7.  $^6_3$- *and* $^6_4$-*formations*

When three counterpoints move in half-notes, they find—as a three-voice setting *within* a setting, so to speak—still more favorable opportunities for $^6_3$-formations then in the preceding combination. Thus executed in three voices, the intent of passing-tone character appears, in a sense, as though in threefold commitment, and therefore its effect is also trebled; for example:

**Example 289**

The question whether the setting of the passing tones here might permit even $^6_4$ is to be answered as follows. In a stricter procedure a passing event such as the following, for example:

**Example 290**

really would have to be rejected, for the same reason that fourth-successions (see Example 271) were excluded from the combined species in three voices. But it cannot be denied that the completely self-contained three-voice texture of the $^6_4$-chord signifies an advantage, in comparison to those "naked" fourths, at least with respect to the cohesiveness of the involved voices among themselves; and in this sense, such a passing event, especially the one in close position under a of the above example, may be allowed to stand. (Such passing events in other combined-species settings and in free composition will be treated below in Chapter 2, §10, and in *Free Composition.*[6])

Here too, the cadential idiom that approaches II — V — I is attainable:

**Example 291**

It is obvious that for the rest, the achievements of the preceding combinations remain in effect; equally obvious, finally, is the fact that any more extensive unfolding [of effects] must falter above all on the equilibrium of rhythm of the half-notes, as was suggested only in a preliminary way in §1.

## Exercise

**Example 292**

H. Schenker

# Chapter 2

# Incorporation of the Third Species

## A. *Three-Voice Counterpoint:* One Counterpoint of the Second Species and One of the Third:

c. f.

### §1. *General characteristics of this combination*

In comparison to the combination-varieties of the first chapter, the one to be treated in this chapter already exhibits the new characteristic of a rhythmic contrast of the two counterpoints. Far from sacrificing the character of the half- and quarter-notes, this contrast rather leaves both in a state all the more true to their respective natures, and gives them additional force, so that unity is revealed only through the act of conquering the contrast. Thus the half-notes, in particular, here once again retain their quality as that decisive subdivision of the cantus-firmus tone (*Cpt. I*, p. 326) in comparison to which the quarters appear as the ultimate diminution admissible in strict counterpoint; and it is also the half-notes that decide matters of harmony, change of harmony, fourth-space, and the like. On the other hand, however, the opposition of rhythms makes it possible for the first time for the quarter-note at the upbeat to be dissonant against the half-note—a new phenomenon, upon which the difference between this type of combination and the former ones is most sharply imprinted.

### §2. *The strict construction*

The principles according to which a stricter construction of the combined-species setting is to be executed are the same as those of the three-voice combined species of Chapter 1, A, §2. Therefore, in brief, only the following need be said.

The upbeat can continue, with a consonance, the harmony of the downbeat (see below, Exercise 1, bars 1, 2, etc.).

A change of harmony can be brought about by the succession 5 — 6 (6 — 5).

191

(See, for example, Exercise 1, bars 8, 9, where the change of harmony is effected by means of an exchange of voices combined with a nota cambiata; also Exercise 2, bar 5; Exercise 3, bars 5, 7, etc.) It can, however, also be otherwise produced in various ways (see, for example, Exercise 4, bar 4, etc.). Under certain circumstances a change of harmony can appear even at the second quarter, as for example in Exercise 3, bar 7, which implies that the quarter-notes, for the purpose of a neighboring-note formation or something similar, make possible a twofold rhythmic grouping (see Part 3, Chapter 3, §2). The dividing line between a change of harmony and a consonant passing tone or neighboring note in the case of 5 — 6 (6 — 5) stands here as well under the criteria given in Chapter 1, A, §2 (cf. Exercise 3, bar 10, etc.). Concerning 5 — 6 in a fourth-space, however, see below, §4.

In the application of dissonant passing tones, the strict construction demands here as well (cf. Chapter 1, A, §2) that the passing tones be consonant with each other if they are both dissonant with the cantus firmus (see Exercise 1, bar 6; Exercise 4, bar 2). Accordingly, a voice leading such as the following:

**Example 293**

would overstep the rule—indeed, because here the second half-note of the first bar, which is dissonant with the cantus firmus, is impermissibly approached by leap. In free composition, however, such a voice leading could easily be explained either by according the second half-note the rank of an independent scale degree (in this example, I — IV⁷— V♯, perhaps) or by assuming a neighboring note (*g* before *a*).

### §3. The less strict construction

A less strict construction of the combination adds for the first time to the setting of the passing tones (see Chapter 1, A, §§2 and 3), as mentioned already in §1 of this chapter, the prolongation according to which even a dissonant collision can be used at the upbeat. If we begin with a very simple example:

**Example 294**

we perhaps recognize in the following circumstances the reasons such a prolongation can be defended.

Above all, the half-note of the upbeat, because of its leap—or, which comes to the same thing, because of its interval that is consonant with the cantus firmus—, ensures that we must perceive the harmony of the downbeat as remaining in effect for the upbeat as well.

Added to this is the fact that the harmony of the downbeat finds confirmation no less in the domain of the quarter-notes as well, and, moreover, already at the second quarter, so that the abutment of consonance is as though doubly strong.

Next, it is the contrast of rhythmic values between the counterpointing voices—one in quarters and one in halves—that accentuates the passing event incomparably more strongly than was possible with half-note against half-note.

And if the quarter-notes (to take up this matter as well)—here executing a passing tone from the second to the fourth quarter—make use only of a strict rule that applies to them in any case, what possible objection could be raised against such a dissonant collision in view of so much preservation of clarity and unification? Observe, incidentally, how the dissonant passing tone, because of the attacking second half-note, at the same time also provides new nourishment for the concept of *accented passing tone* (whose seed was encountered already in two-voice counterpoint—see *Cpt. I*, p. 228) in that it emphasizes above all the passing effect, so that the effect in the vertical direction (nothing less than that of an appoggiatura) completely recedes or dissipates.

The extent to which the good effect in Example 294 is made possible by the consonant leap of the second half-note can best be understood if I show, by contrast, the attendant increase in difficulty of voice leading in another example in which the second half-note passes through in a dissonant state:

**Example 295**

If I first of all remind the reader that a dissonant passing tone underscores the harmony of the downbeat more unequivocally than a consonant one, and if it is thereby already decided that, accordingly, here as well the quarter-notes have no choice but to remain within the harmonic unit, then the following comments are relevant to the various configurations shown in our example. The dissonant collision at a (the stricter procedure—see above, §2—requires a consonant relationship between the two passing tones) is defensible only if, for unavoidable reasons, ⁵₃ must be used at the following downbeat; but if ⁶₃ is possible at the following downbeat, the voice leading at b takes first priority;

by simultaneously complying with the strictest rule, it leads to the same goal with a better effect than the solution at c, which shows a dissonant collision at the upbeat. But it is not only the availability of a better procedure, as at b, that causes the latter to be sensed as poor: the poorer effect derives, moreover, from the offense against the law of the passing tone, in that the third quarter, ensnared by the dissonant half-note into the passing function (see Chapter 1, A, §3), has now relinquished the right to leap (which may serve as additional proof of the sensitivity of the fundamental rule of the dissonant passing tone).

Yet the possibility of a dissonant collision at the upbeat is not restricted only to the more natural cases in which the whole bar preserves the harmonic unit; this liberty can be permitted with a change of harmony as well, by means of which, to be sure, a more artificial voice leading results—for example:

**Example 296**

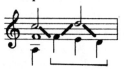

The justification of such a contrapuntal formation, naturally, is provided by the passing-tone configuration that extends from the second to the fourth quarter-note. One can tell exactly from this construction which tone must necessarily appear as the fourth quarter-note, and therefore the second half-note also can easily be heard as relating to that tone even before the fact. Thus the collision on the third quarter is more readily tolerated the more effortlessly one can recognize its cause in the passing-tone structure alone. (The relationship

just described is often particularly effective and useful in deciphering many difficult voice-leading structures in free composition.)

### §4. *Passing tones in the space of a fourth*

It goes without saying that here, by means of the quarter-notes, a fourth-space can be expressed, exactly as in the third species of three- and four-voice counterpoint. Here a consonant upbeat, such as the following examples show:

**Example 297**

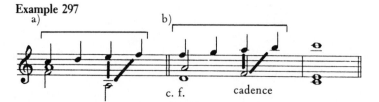

requires no further justification. The only matter of significance is the question of whether the upbeat may also be dissonant. According to the points of view set forth in §3, there is no objection to voice leadings such as:

**Example 298**

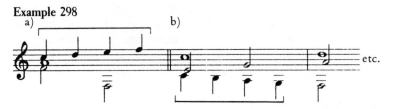

In both cases, the half-notes consonant with the cantus firmus adequately secure the unity of the overall harmony; this in turn confirms the fourth-space as such (cf. also Exercise 4, bar 5).

The extent to which the fourth-space contributes to the clarification of effect in other situations can be seen in the fact that a voice leading such as that of Example 299a will certainly satisfy nobody:

**Example 299**

If we merely fulfill the law of passing tones in the space of a fourth:

**Example 300**

we immediately recognize, by the better effect, the true cause of the error committed in Example 299. At b in Example 299, on the other hand, we see, with a similar sonority, a passing tone in a third-space, which permits a continuation by leap.

With a voice leading such as the following:

**Example 301**

we touch upon the composing out of a seventh-chord, in that the sum of the quarter-notes is heard also as the fourth *f—b* (an augmented fourth, to be sure, but nonetheless strictly diatonic). But it is only as a result of the unequivocally perceived consonance of the downbeat (which, in keeping with the remarks in Chapter 1, A, §5, is to be interpreted only as what it actually is: $\frac{8}{3}$, and not as what it could perhaps appear in retrospect: $\frac{7}{3}$) that we must ultimately regard such a voice leading as admissible in our contrapuntal settings. Strictly speaking, a similar effect is produced also by the voice leading that Bellermann uses at the cadence of his exercise (see below, Exercise 3), and which I here quote once again for the sake of clarity:

**Example 302**

Here the fourth quarter, after arriving at a state of agreement with the second half-note and the cantus firmus in the sonority $\frac{6}{3}$ (cf. Example 296), is obviously perceived in retrospect as belonging to the fourth-space $b-f$, as though the initial tone $b$ were already represented on the downbeat: $(b)-a-g-f.$[1]

In contrast to the fourth-spaces of Examples 297a, 298a and b, and 300 (cf. Example 117), in which both beginning and end remain in the same harmony, the fourth-spaces in Examples 297b, 301, and 302 show, along with all their differences of effect, the common characteristic that their harmonies are different at the end than at the beginning (they even approximate II — V — I here). Therein we can glimpse a prolongation of the *nodal-point concept* (see Example 90, and also Examples 123 and 125): just as the concept of a third-space is not canceled merely because its beginning and end belong to two different harmonies, a fourth-space, similarly, is no more affected by such a phenemenon.

*Fux* takes up this type of combination at the conclusion of the third species of three-voice counterpoint, on p. 98ff: "It can scarcely be expressed how much appeal and excellence the composition gains through this threefold differentiation of note-values. Therefore I particularly recommend to you this exercise, with each of the three (or four) different placements of the cantus firmus such as we have used up to now." That is all that Fux has to say about the matter; I already took the opportunity earlier to refer to several details in his exercise (Example 305, no. 1), so that any further comment here would be superfluous.

*Albrechtsberger* too, who mentions this combination—and combinations in general—at the conclusion of three-voice counterpoint, thus after completion of the fifth species (p. 119), neglects to provide any more detailed explanations, and states only that "if two of the first five species are used simultaneously above a cantus firmus, such an artificial example likewise belongs to the fifth species, and is a foretaste of free composition, where different note-values may be used in each voice." It should be mentioned that from a correction of a Beethoven exercise quoted by Nottebohm on p. 53:

**Example 303**

it can be inferred that Albrechtsberger under certain circumstances considered it better to avoid, by means of a neighboring note, a nonparallel similar motion, whenever (as here) it is, at the very least, unnecessary. My opinion concerning the leap to a seventh in bar 10 of his exercise (Example 305, no. 2), however, can be read in *Counterpoint I*, p. 245.

*Cherubini* devotes the following words, on p. 35, to the combination here under consideration: "One must take care that the voice that has the half-notes begins after that which has the quarters:"

**Example 304**

I need not even mention that such an opening configuration also conforms to the strict rule. Cherubini adds: "In this combination of the two species, it is almost impossible to prevent one of the voices from moving in leaps. One must therefore sacrifice the rule that prescribes a preference for melodic fluency."

In *Bellermann*, who takes up combined-species settings for the first time in the fourth species of three-voice counterpoint, we read on p. 210:

> In working out three-voice settings in this manner, we may use no passing dissonance in the voice that sings half-notes; otherwise, because of the added quarter-notes, unpleasant harshness will arise. The exercise thereby causes very much inconvenience, and it is difficult to give the half-notes (which thus must all be consonant with the cantus firmus) a fluent stepwise motion. It is, however, very easy to write the quarter-notes in a fluent manner. But we must take care that the third quarter always be consonant not only with the cantus firmus but also with the counterpoint that sings the half-notes. Only the fourth may constitute an exception, when, as in bar 11 of the last example [Exercise 3 below], it is accompanied by the sixth.

Set forth so clearly and emphatically, Bellermann's commitment to strict adherence to consonance on the upbeat as well really represents an unnecessary severity. Above all, he should not have ignored the fact that the opportunity for dissonant passing tones is open to both counterpoints even according to the strictest point of view; this recognition would have spared him the necessity of making an "exception" of the ⁶₄-formation (see above, Example 302), and he also would have found no need to criticize the two dissonant passing tones (consonant with each other) in Fux's exercise (see Exercise 1, bar 6) as a "very poor-sounding simultaneity." This shows where self-deception can lead a theorist: he hears a simultaneity that is perfectly good-sounding and also in compliance with the rule as "poor-sounding," and fails to notice that the only dissonance here is that between this theory and the truth.[2]

## Exercises

**Example 305**

Fux X, 5

Albrechtsberger, p. 119

**Example 305** *continued*

Bellermann, p. 210

3.

Alto

Tenor

Bass (c. f.)

H. Schenker

Soprano

4.

Alto (c. f.)

Bass

**Example 308** *continued*

H. Schenker

## Comments on the Preceding Exercises

No. 1. In bar 3 a voice leading such as the following would be inadmissible:

**Example 309**

because the dissonant relationship of the two half-notes to the cantus firmus forbids an approach by leap. Free composition, on the other hand, can immediately justify such a voice leading with the scale-degree progression $II - V^7$ in C major, for example.

In bar 4, idioms such as these:

**Example 310**

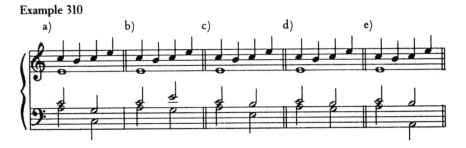

would cause various effects to predominate: at a, the upbeat is completely consonant; at b, c, and d the half-notes are indeed consonant with each other, but their setting is dissonant with the third quarter; sometimes the dissonance involves only one half-note, as at b and c; sometimes, as at d, it involves both half-notes; and at e the half-notes are dissonant with each other. If we discount altogether the completely legitimate voice leading at a, among all of the others only that at b would be approved as admissible. In bar 6 the following, for example:

**Example 311**

would have to be rejected because of its gratuitous harshness, especially as the parallel sixths have an empty effect.

No. 2. In bars 2 and 3, dissonant settings of the half-notes, such as:

**Example 312**

may illustrate why they are still to be excluded in such exercises.

## D. *Three-Voice Counterpoint:* Two Counterpoints of the Third Species:

### §7. *Consonant setting of the quarter-notes*

The comments in Chapter 1, A, §§2 and 3 concerning the setting of the half-notes applies in this combination also to the setting of the quarters—that is, under all circumstances, because of the lack of rhythmic contrast, they must be consonant with each other if they are dissonant with the cantus firmus, and this holds true regardless of whether they are both dissonant or whether, as may happen more often with quarter-notes, only one is dissonant, while the other forms an interval (either by step or by leap) that is consonant with the cantus firmus.

The danger of extended successions of thirds and sixths is still greater here than with the half-notes of the combination-type described under C (§6). These must be countered by the most extreme attentiveness.

Since in this combination two counterpoints use quarter-notes, one has the opportunity to observe even better than in the earlier combination-types how easily passing tones and neighboring notes tend to operate in pairs rather than singly [*FrC.* §§221–229]; but this by no means excludes the possibility that quarter-notes even of different description (passing tone, neighboring note, harmonic tone) meet in a consonant relationship—this not only promotes variety of intervals, but also often helps the voice leading to avoid embarrassments.

## Exercise

**Example 313**

**H. Schenker**

## Comments on the Preceding Exercise

In bar 2, voice leadings such as the following would have to be criticized:

**Example 314**

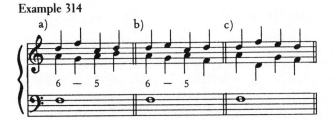

At a the voice leading is too heavily burdened by the dissonant collision at the second quarter, and by the change of harmony that follows immediately at the third quarter. (Observe on the other hand the better execution of a similar intent in bar 9, where the quarter-notes in the second position are at least consonant.) To use a consonance at the third quarter in the manner at b, however, belongs only to free composition, which may employ a neighboring note that is left by leap. At c, in violation of the strict rule, the dissonant third quarter of the inner voice is approached by leap.

In bar 4, the following voice leadings, for example, would be inappropriate:

**Example 315**

At a the quarter-notes in the second position form a dissonance; at b a dissonance at the second quarter is approached by leap; at c a dissonant passing tone in the inner voice at the second quarter is followed so quickly by a dissonant neighboring note in the upper voice at the third quarter that the ear is literally overrun by these phenomena, and is able only too late to form an evaluation of them. It is therefore advisable here still to avoid such a voice leading, although it otherwise conforms to the rules.

In bar 6, a setting of the quarter-notes in fourths, as for example:

**Example 316**

would obviously be faulty—indeed, for the reasons stated in connection with Example 271. To write in bars 7 and 8 as at a in the next example would be faulty because of the leap away from the neighboring note:

**Example 317**

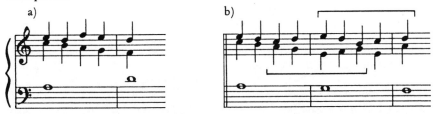

The dovetailing of two nota-cambiata formations however, as at b, on the other hand, is quite possible.

### E. *Four-Voice Counterpoint:* One Counterpoint of the First Species, Two Counterpoints of the Third:

### §8. *Continuing applicability of the principles of setting quarter-notes*

What was said in §7 concerning the setting of quarter-notes in the preceding combination-type naturally applies to their setting in the present one as well.

### Exercise

**Example 318**
**H. Schenker**

### F. *Four-Voice Counterpoint:* One Counterpoint of the Second Species, Two Counterpoints of the Third:

### §9. *The quarter-notes, consonant with each other, assert themselves as a setting against the half-notes as well*

This combination represents a kind of counterpart to the one presented in §6—that is, just as the passing half-notes there maintained to some extent a contrapuntal structure of their own opposite the quarter-notes, here, conversely, the quarters maintain their own structure opposite the halves.

## Exercise

**Example 319**

H. Schenker

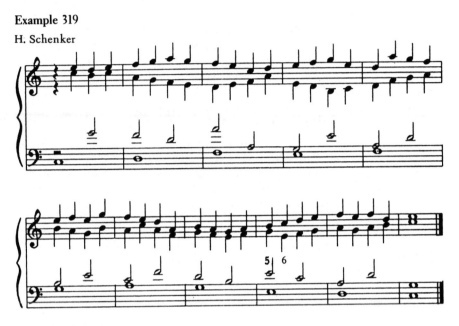

## G. *Four Voice Counterpoint:* Three Counterpoints in Quarter-Notes:

§10. *How in the setting of the passing tones the quarter-notes in particular tend toward ⁶₃- and ⁶₄-formations*

A three-voice setting of the quarter-notes provides opportunities in greater measure for ⁶₃- and ⁶₄-successions. And just here one can find the most emphatic confirmation of the fact that for the concept of the dissonant passing events, it is completely immaterial whether the chain consists of ⁶₃- or of ⁶₄-formations (cf. Part 3, Chapter 2, p. 58). The decision concerning whether ⁶₃ or ⁶₄ should be used in a given case depends only upon the nature of the point of departure—that is, if at the point of departure the three voices form a ⁶₃- or a ⁶₄-chord, the continuation will automatically yield ⁶₃- or ⁶₄-chords respectively. Compare examples 289 and 290. (This discovery will be of very special value, admittedly, only in free composition.)

### §11. *Passing- and neighboring-note harmonies*

It is also possible already here for the three-voice setting of quarters shown by this combination-type, because of its greater rhythmic fluidity, to show more easily than another combination-type how a passing tone or a neighboring note can exert its effect on the quarters in consonant combination as well, and thereby this type of setting can elevate the consonant sound as a whole to the status of a *passing-* or *neighboring-note harmony*, which promotes all the more strongly the passing- or neighboring-note effect that has been sought (see, for example, Exercise 1, bar 1, third quarter; bar 2, second quarter; bar 5, second quarter).

Yet this fact alone does not permit the description of a case such as the consonant harmony of Exercise 1, bar 7, fourth quarter, as such a passing-tone harmony; here, because of the absence of scale degrees, we are required always to interpret the sounds only as what they actually are from the standpoint of voice leading. The situation concerning such chords, to be sure, is different in free composition, which very often strives to achieve dissonant effects by means of detours through consonant sounds [*FrC.*, §170]. (Compare p. 186.)

## Exercises

**Example 320**

H. Schenker

**Example 320** *continued*

H. Schenker

# Chapter 3

# Incorporation of the Syncopated Species into the Combination

### A. *Three-Voice Counterpoint:* One Counterpoint of the Second Species and One of the Fourth:

## §1. *General aspects*

Because in addition to the syncopes a second voice also moves in half-notes, advantages develop for the former that are in many respects of the highest significance; indeed, not only does this provide new possibilities for resolution of all syncopes taken over from strict counterpoint, but moreover, completely new settings of syncopes find the first opportunity to arise.

## §2. *New resolution-possibilities for the syncopes taken over from strict counterpoint*

As the following examples show, the forward motion of the second voice in half-notes leads to sounds that were formerly unattainable for three- and four-voice counterpoint:[1]

**Example 321**

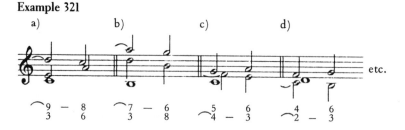

At the same time, it is clear from these few examples that a conceptual compilation of all resolution-possibilities is unthinkable.

210

Because of the special importance of the case, however, it should perhaps be expressly emphasized here that for the syncope ⌒9—8, the progression of the lower voice in half-notes makes it possible to avoid the succession 8⌒9—8, which is still completely faulty in strict three- and four-voice counterpoint, so that here ⌒9—8 may also be tied to an octave:

**Example 322**

§3.   *New syncope-settings:* ⌒⁷₅ |–⁶₂ |–⁶₄ *and* |–⁶₃

To this group of new syncope-settings belong both a few new combinations involving the syncopes ⌒7, ⌒2, and ⌒4, and also the completely new –⁶₃-setting.

Thus the motion of a second voice in half-notes provides for ⌒7 also the possibility of ⌒⁷₃, since the fifth, as a consonance, can move ahead to a consonant interval (either a third or a sixth) at the upbeat:

**Example 323**

Similarly, in the case of ⌒2, –⁶₂ can be used as well, since the sixth likewise may move to a consonant interval:

**Example 324**

In the case of ⌒4, the same holds true of –⁶₄:

**Example 325**

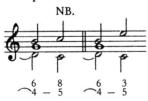

⌐4 — 3; it is rather to be understood as a temporal succession: first, fulfillment of the fundamental concept; afterward, the new harmony.

### §6.   (b) Influence of the combination on ⌐7, ⌐2, and ⌐4

Such an abbreviation, a temporal succession, is, however, unthinkable for the group of syncope-settings ⌐$\frac{7}{5}$ |–$\frac{6}{2}$ |–$\frac{6}{4}$. The path to the new upbeat harmony does not lead, as it does with ⌐9 — 8 and ⌐4 — 3, over the bridge of fundamental-concept fulfillment in the sense of a suspension-resolution: if the second voice did not move ahead, we would by no means arrive at consonant suspension-resolutions, but rather at new dissonant combinations: ⌐$\frac{7-6}{5-5}$|–$\frac{6-7}{2-3}$ | –$\frac{6}{4}$–$\frac{7}{5}$, which would run counter to the fundamental concepts of ⌐7, ⌐2, ⌐ 4—in other words, would cancel them. If the suspension-resolution in the earlier group of syncopes signifies the unity of the harmony, here the non-appearance of a suspension-resolution signifies a contrast of two harmonies.

The adjoinment of a 5 to ⌐7, a 6 to ⌐2, and again a 6 to ⌐4, thus has the effect that the dissonant harmonies which thereby arise place themselves in contrast to the ones that follow on the upbeat—that is, they make themselves more independent in comparison to the latter than is at all possible in strict counterpoint when the same syncopes occur in other combinations of intervals.

In all of these cases, it is as though within the group of time-units associated with a dissonant syncope: ♩ ♩ ♩ ♩ the first two were to separate themselves from the last in the following way: ♩♩♩ ♩ (cf. p. 86).

### §7.   (c) Influence of the combination on –$\frac{6}{5}$

The act of making the harmony of the downbeat independent is most forceful in its effect in the case of–$\frac{6}{5}$, but here again for completely different reasons than for the syncopes of the preceding paragraph. We know that this sound is not attainable in strict counterpoint, neither in the first species of three-voice counterpoint (see Part 3, Chapter 1, §3) nor in the syncopated species of two-, three-, or four-voice counterpoint, where the resolution of a dissonant fifth would have to lead to the prohibited $\frac{4}{2}$-sound. For this reason alone it is clear that –$\frac{6}{5}$ obviously has nothing to do with a fundamental concept, and that the tied fifth of this setting is no more to be counted as a true suspension (or one clouded by a state of uncertainty) than as the fifth of some triad. (It also should not be overlooked in this connection that all of the other syncope-concepts with which we have become acquainted do admit various combinations; only in the case of–$\frac{6}{5}$ is just one combination possible.)

## §8.   *The budding seventh-chord*

If we now place the syncopes described in §§6 and 7 in a row: $\overline{7}$₅ $\vdash$₂⁶$\vdash$₄⁶ and
$-$₈, we easily recognize chords therein which sound the same as the seventh-chord of free composition or its inversions. Now we understand the effect described in §§6 and 7 in which the downbeat-harmony becomes more
independent: wouldn't the suspension-effect of $\overline{7}-6$, $\overline{2}-3$, $\overline{4}-5$ in the
settings $\overline{7}$₅ $\mid$ $-$₈ and $-$₄ have to be thwarted by the 5 or 6 if these intervals
coincide with the fifth of the seventh-chord—which, however, is completely
distinct from a suspension-formation?[2] [At least] as seen from the standpoint
of free composition. The latter discloses, however, that the so-called seventh-
chord (see *FrC.* [§§176, 178]) in turn represents nothing but a triad in which,
by means of abbreviation, the passing tone of the seventh appears to be
incorporated as a chord member. (The passing tone, however, relinquishes
nothing of its independence through the fact that it moves forward to another,
no less independent, sound.) Nevertheless, there is certainly still a considerable
difference between the seventh-chord of free composition and the syncope-
settings named above. Consider above all that the combination-types, which
promote those settings for the first time, can produce them in no other way
than by tying to a preparing consonant harmony, so that, strictly speaking,
only the procedure of strict counterpoint returns here. The reason for this is
that in the absence of scale degrees—the cantus firmus is, of course, present—as
in the absence of a preordained compelling force for the paths of the voices,
it is independent voice leading alone which rules, and this has as a consequence that here, exactly as in strict counterpoint, we are unable to adjoin
conceptually to the passing tone of the seventh that consonant point of
departure presupposed by it (as by any passing tone whatever). Therefore, as
a substitute, we must at least provide the dissonance in question with a
preparation by means of a consonant harmony on the preceding upbeat. But
since the latter consonance (as in strict counterpoint, see p. 85ff.) has the effect
of preventing us, in the case of the dissonant syncope, from even inferring the
elision of the consonant point of departure, in the combination-types the
phenomenon of three time-units likewise prevails; it remains the same for both
the authentic suspensions $\overline{9}-8$ and $\overline{4}-3$ as for the other syncope-settings,
and, indeed, regardless of the different effects of the two groups. Thus it is
precisely this sharing of external appearance ($\flat\mathsf{T}\flat\ \flat$) which disguises those
seventh-chord settings in our [present] combination type.

On the other hand, in spite of that effect of three time-units, it is equally
impossible to suppress the other effects that are attendant on 5 with $\overline{7}$, on
6 with $\overline{2}$, on 6 with $\overline{4}$, and on $-$₈ in general, and which, as I have already
mentioned above, emphasize a form of independence of the dissonant sonority
on the downbeat, as though the syncope contained, in all these cases, only
two time-units. And in precisely this new accompanying effect the darkly

embryonic idea of the seventh-chord is concealed! It derives its first nourishment, to be sure, from the condition of uncertainty that arises with ⌒7 — 6, ⌒2 — 3, and ⌒4 — 5 (but not with ⌒⁶₃). This condition is all the less possible to remove in view of the fact that (exactly as in strict counterpoint) it is perfectly possible to have the syncopes mentioned conform also to the rule of strict counterpoint if need be: ⌒⁷₃⁻⁶ | ₋⁴₂₋₃ or ⌒⁴₂₌₃ₓ. But further: if it is often difficult in free composition to ferret out the true significance of a seventh—a definite decision undoubtedly can always be made there in view of the many aids that are present—how much less definitely must the seventh be expressed in our combination-type, where we do without such aids, and therefore the setting, clouded by its lack of scale degrees, can never develop to the precision attainable in free composition! Because of just this last residue of uncertainty, therefore, the syncope-settings mentioned on the one hand still belong to strict counterpoint, while on the other hand, since they proclaim their independence more sharply than in strict counterpoint, at the same time they already point ahead to the realm of the seventh-chords of free composition. (Compare the effect of apparent seventh-chords, such as are sometimes produced indirectly by means of consonant sonorities in the combination-types treated in Chapters 1 and 2 of this part, see pp. 185 and 195.)

Among the syncope-settings mentioned at the beginning of these paragraphs, it is certainly the –⁶₃-setting which distances itself the farthest from strict counterpoint. In fact, the tied fifth of this chord represents that authentic seventh which free composition has learned to derive by means of abbreviation of an 8 — 7 passing motion and to incorporate into the triad. Thus this fifth, born as a seventh, falls under the concept of passing tone, in spite of the fact that just in this combination-type it creates, by means of tying, the impression of a suspension, so that now, finally, from the contrast between the fundamental concepts of strict counterpoint on the one hand and –⁶₃ on the other, it can be discovered even here that triadic consonance alone—limited in strict counterpoint to ⁵₃ and ⁶₃—governs the fundamental concept of the syncope. Thus I repeat once more: In the beginning is consonance! It is consonance alone that carries within itself the fundamental laws of suspensions! That which does *not* belong to these fundamental laws, therefore, clearly points beyond the boundaries of 5 and 6 into a realm in which new laws comparable to and coordinated with the [fundamental] law of consonance are not to be found, but rather only prolongations of that law, in which—to take the case of –⁶₃, for example—it is not a suspension that is involved, but, rather, a passing seventh, for which, however, we once again presuppose only consonance as point of departure. The fifth and sixth cannot be overstepped in strict counterpoint! All phenomena, regardless of the traits they exhibit, either come from them or return once again to them.

All that remains to be explained, then, is why the second inversion of the seventh-chord, ⁴₃, is not to be found in this combination along with ⁶₅ and ⁶₂. This has to do with the fourth, which, since in a true inversion of a seventh-chord it coincides with the chord's root, does not represent a dissonance; here in the combined-species, on the other hand, it can enter the picture only as a tied dissonance, in which form it cannot tolerate the simultaneous presence of the third (see pp. 90–91):

**Example 330**

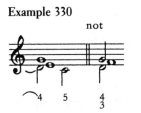

It will be shown later, however, in §15, that when quarter-notes are incorporated in the setting of the combined species, the possibility often arises to use even the $\frac{4}{3}$-setting at least in passing on the second quarter.

### §9.   *On the inadmissibility of a passing tone dissonant with the tone of resolution*

A passing tone that would be dissonant with the tone of resolution is better avoided in the exercises of this combination-type. The determining reasons are the following.

First, here again it is only half-note against half-note, a setting which, in accord with the principles already articulated in the first and second chapters, does not tolerate a dissonant collision at the upbeat.

Second, since our exercise is burdened by the demand of the syncope and therefore of consonant preparation at the upbeat, the strict postulate is fulfilled best of all if the second half-note at the upbeat avoids a passing tone dissonant with the tone of resolution.

But there is little objection to a passing tone that is dissonant with the cantus firmus but consonant with the tone of resolution. Examples of this type can be found below in Example 342, Exercise 1, bar 8, and Exercise 2, bar 7. For the first example, the concept of abbreviation can also be used as an explanatory aid (cf. above, §5); it is as though the passing tone here were to occur only after the completion of the resolution ⌒6 — 5. In the second example, the passing tone dissonates with the cantus firmus in the relationship of a diminished fifth, which, even in the syncopated species of strict counterpoint, not only could, but under certain circumstances even had to, be tolerated. In any case, this combination-type by its very nature offers little opportunity for passing tones, and therefore the second voice moving in half-notes is usually restricted to leaps unless it is the lowest voice; in that case, to be sure, it has the opportunity also to progress by steps of a second.

## §10.   *The possibility of a change of harmony*

It is sufficiently clear from the preceding discussion that this combination-type also admits change of harmony.

It was explained in Part 4, Chapter 4, §2 that *Fux* uses the subdivision of a second voice into half-notes already in the fourth species of four-voice counterpoint. It is obvious, therefore, that that combined-species setting[3] is worked out in four voices. Fux shows a three-voice combined-species setting only in the context of three-voice fugal exercises on p. 131ff.; thus the setting (as a constituent part of a fugue) includes no cantus firmus, and therefore deserves even far less to be called a combined-species setting in my sense than the four-voice exercise mentioned above. Fux writes:

The perfect cadence can be avoided also by keeping the major third in the upper voice but giving the lower voice a different consonance instead of the octave:

**Example 331**

Fux XXIV, 5

This can be done in a more refined fashion with a large number of voices:

**Example 332**

Fux XXV, 1

Just in the example à 3 we again find our combination, and we see that in the case of a syncope that would originally have been $^-{}^4_2{-}^5_3$, Fux achieves the continuation $^-{}^4_2{-}^6_3$, which is the only thing that makes possible the deceptive cadence at the downbeat of the next bar (cf. also Example 321).

And it is likewise only for the sake of a matter pertaining to fugue when Fux immediately continues (p. 132ff.): "Using the following subject, let us see how a perfect cadence can occur even at an unusual interval with the aid of a thematic entrance":

**Example 333**

Here, for the first time, he establishes the setting $-^6_5$.

The following instructions by Fux already present a more orderly appearance (p. 133):

> You may do so[4] as soon as I have shown you how one can add the lowest voice to two voices wherein the seventh descends to the sixth and the second to the third—a technique which considerably facilitates the leading of the voices:

**Example 334**
**Fux XXVI, 1**

and:

**Example 335**
**Fux XXVI, 2**

leap. (Concerning $\frac{6}{4}$ in Bellermann, incidentally, compare also an earlier passage, pp. 216–217.) He then writes (p. 226):

> In this manner the most varied combinations can be achieved, which, however, cannot all be enumerated; just for the sake of example, I provide here the following small setting of them:

**Example 340**

By this process, however, otherwise prohibited motions can also be made correct; for example, the ninth can be prepared by the octave, and the hidden octaves can then be avoided by giving the bass a new tone at the resolution, as the two following examples show:

**Example 341**

The composers of the fifteenth and sixteenth centuries, however, did not favor such idioms; thus they are prohibited in strict a capella vocal settings.

Now follows a quotation from Handel's *Joshua* which shows the use of this "liberty," and a legitimation by word and example from Kirnberger, about which Bellermann pronounces the following judgment: "It is my opinion, however, that to use the ninth in this way even in the freer style must be viewed as a liberty that should be taken only in the rarest instances."

With all of its merit, Bellermann's account nevertheless loses in clarity, since, instead of developing the fundamental concepts gradually with examples, he begins with a general chapter that meanders about among all of the combination-types and also touches on free composition—a chapter which, abruptly situated with its generality in the syncopated species of three-voice strict counterpoint, can only disturb the flow of the presentation and the logical continuity of its disposition. The transition to the exercises of our combination, therefore, can only be viewed as inadequate (p. 227): "Here we introduce the exercise of setting against a cantus firmus in whole-notes two voices, of which one sings syncopated half-notes and the other ordinary half-notes." And of these exercises themselves Bellermann states (p. 228):

> This exercise is not entirely without difficulty; its great importance derives from the fact that the voices in free composition very often [!] move in similar ways,

and the resolution of dissonances along with moving voices finds frequent application, producing a great variety of harmony. However, we find that the voice which moves in ordinary half-notes has little freedom of movement, and thus is often forced to make ungraceful leaps.

To point to just the similarity of the motion in free composition as the reason the exercise must be introduced exactly here and in no other place—is that not all too childish? Is it not rather the case that this exercise, like any other, must first of all point out only effects in themselves, which effects then, in a correspondingly varied manner, are subject to some form of continuation in free composition? Regarding bar 7 of his first exercise (here Exercise 2), to which I already devoted some words of explanation in the preceding text, Bellermann comments in a footnote: "The half-note *c♯* is here to be interpreted as a passing dissonance against the *g* of the cantus firmus."

## Exercises

### Example 342

Cherubini, Ex. 114, p. 40

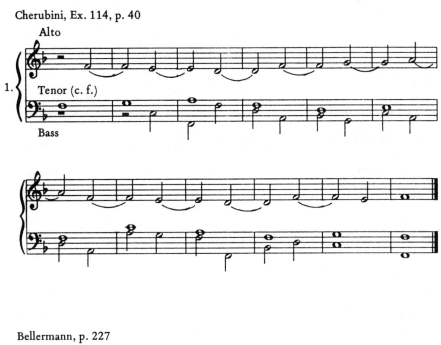

Bellermann, p. 227

**Example 342** *continued*

Bellermann, p. 228

Alto

Tenor

3.

Bass

H. Schenker

Soprano

4.

Alto

Tenor

**Example 342** *continued*

H. Schenker

H. Schenker

# B.  *Four-Voice Counterpoint:* One Counterpoint Each of the First, Second, and Fourth Species:

### §11.  *The influence of four-voice texture on the further elaboration of individual syncopes*

The four-voice texture of this exercise now makes it possible for many syncopes to achieve their complete form, such as $\overset{-9}{\underset{3}{5}} \mid \overset{-7}{\underset{3}{5}}$ or $\overset{6}{\underset{2}{4}}$. The complete setting $\overset{6}{\underset{3}{5}}$, however, is possible only under the assumption of a crossing:

**Example 343**

in which the third makes a leap. It goes without saying that in the case of $\overset{-7}{\underset{3}{5}} \mid \overset{6}{\underset{2}{4}}$ and $\overset{-6}{\underset{3}{5}}$ the completeness of the harmonies now also elevates their degree of independence in comparison to the harmony that follows on the upbeat ( $\mathbb{P}\top\mathbb{P}\ \mathbb{P}$ ; see above, §8).

It is appropriate to recall that *Fux* achieves and uses these settings as well already in the exercises of strict four-voice counterpoint through the process of subdivision; a true combined-species exercise of this type, however, is not found in his work. It has already been stated that *Albrechtsberger* and *Cherubini* follow Fux in this respect.

### Exercises

**Example 344**

H. Schenker

c. f.

**Example 344** *continued*

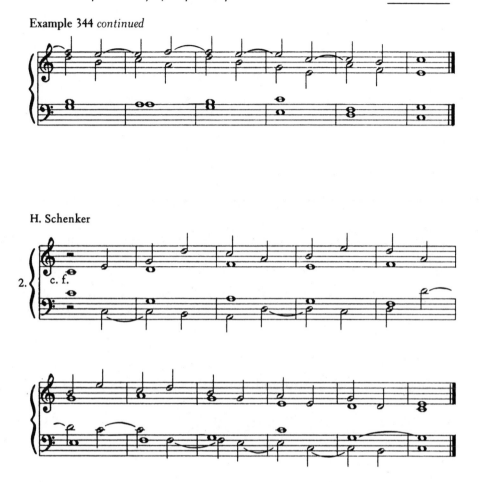

H. Schenker

## C.  *Four-Voice Counterpoint:* Two Counterpoints of the Second Species and One of the Fourth:

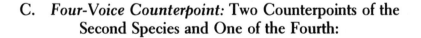

c. f.

### §12.  *The unrestricted possibility of* $-\frac{6}{3}$

The circumstance that in this combination-type a second voice moves in half-notes makes it possible for $-\frac{6}{3}$ to be completed by the third in all situations.

## Exercise

**Example 345**
H. Schenker

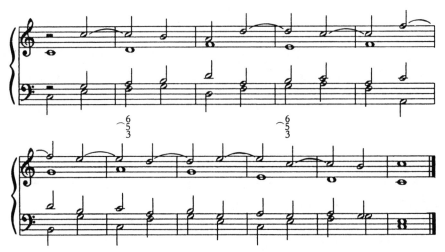

## D.  *Three-Voice Counterpoint:* One Counterpoint Each of the Third and Fourth Species:

### §13.  *General aspects*

The principles of Chapter 2 are now adjoined to those treated here under a, b, and c. The syncopes now gain the potential of expressing themselves in other, novel prolongations.

These extensions, however, are all bound and governed first and foremost by the highest principle of the syncopated species of strict counterpoint, according to which only the rhythm of the half-notes remains definitive for the resolution of the syncope. Especially it is the leaping passing tone which here, under the protection of the resolution-rhythm, already arrives at forms such as are manifested (to be sure, yet more sumptuously) by free composition.

### §14.  *The laws of the second and fourth quarter-notes: (a) When they move by step*

The second or fourth quarter-note can arrive by step:

1.  As a passing tone, and, indeed, irrespective of the consonant or dissonant nature of the syncope:

**Example 346**

⌢4

2. As a neighboring note (upper or lower), as, for example:

**Example 347**

But it should be explicitly mentioned that in the case of a ⌢7 — 6 suspension, even the lower octave of the dissonant suspension-tone may be used as a neighboring note; for example:

**Example 348**

⌢7 ——— 6

So long as both the organization of the neighboring note and half-note rhythm of the resolution are unerringly preserved in such a case, it is not even necessary to assume any kind of relationship between the seventh and the neighboring note—therefore not even the presence of an interval 8—, to say nothing of a consonant effect that would altogether cancel the dissonant nature of the seventh: the concept of syncope here achieves total victory over the neighboring note of the second quarter (see above, §13).

3. As a component of a nota cambiata. But here several possibilities with varying effect would have to be observed. In this example:

**Example 349**
Bellermann, p. 228

if one is perhaps willing to overlook 8 — 8 on the downbeats (Part 3, Chapter 3, §3), the requirements of the nota cambiata coincide most fittingly from the outset with those of the syncope, while in the following case:

**Example 350**
Bellermann, p. 233

the concluding tone of the nota cambiata (on the downbeat of the second bar) is embedded in the setting of a dissonant syncope ⌢4 — 3 (cf. also example 370, Exercise 3, bars 7 – 8); and the situation is also similar here, for example:

**Example 351**

except that the last tone of the nota cambiata flows into the setting $\overset{4}{\underset{2}{}}$—thus into a sound which, under certain circumstances (exactly such as those present here), may also have the effect of a seventh-chord.[7]

Conversely, the *initial* tone of the nota cambiata can be incorporated into dissonant syncope-settings; for example:

**Example 352**
Bellermann, p. 220                     p. 230

Or even in the following:

**Example 353**

where the nota cambiata has its origin in a $\overset{6}{\underset{5}{}}$-setting (of a seventh-chord).

Especially from the last three examples it can be inferred that both voice-leading phenomena—the dissonant syncope and the nota cambiata—, while following their own laws, can also very easily appear in conjunction with one another. At the downbeat, to be sure, we are conscious only of the situation of the dissonant syncope, but this alone suffices to elicit simultaneously an awareness of its expected resolution—an awareness, therefore, of the consonant chord; the resolution then occurs as the nota cambiata is still in progress. In conclusion it should be recalled that here as elsewhere, a nota cambiata extending from upbeat to upbeat is also quite possible (see, for example, Bellermann, p. 233).

### §15. (b) When they leap

It is clear that the second quarter-note cannot leap to a suspended tone; if it were to do so, since the dissonance cannot be led upward as here:

**Example 354**

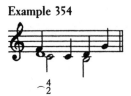

parallel motion, either 1 — 1 or 8 — 8, would be inevitable. Equally inappropriate is a leap to the tone of resolution; this is implied by the prohibition of doubling that tone.

It is also inadmissible to leap at the second quarter to a tone that would produce a new dissonance with the significance of a change of harmony, as, for example:

**Example 355**

for, as in strict counterpoint, the law of the fundamental rhythm of half-notes (see above, §13) demands here as well that preparation and establishment of such a dissonance always run its course from upbeat to downbeat.

If Fux and Albrechtsberger nevertheless use such a technique in their exercises (see above, Example 335, bars 2 and 5, and below, Example 370, Exercise 1, bar 3)—but only at the fourth quarter, to be sure—, they may have done so either with a view toward free composition or because at the fourth quarter the resolution of the dissonant syncope has already been negotiated, so that the latter is protected from any obfuscation that would result from the new dissonance. Finally, it is in fact the rhythm of the resolution that reduces a dissonance so approached by leap at the fourth quarter to the concept of merely a leaping passing tone instead of an independent syncope.

If all tones are avoided which are subject to a prohibition for the above reasons, then, only a limited group of tones can come into consideration for a leap at the second quarter; they all share the common characteristic of belonging conceptually to the same triad, or to $\overline{\phantom{7}}^7_5 \mid -^4_2 \mid -^6_5$ as representatives—for now, the only possible ones—of the seventh-chords.

1. To take up first of all the syncopes that lead to triads, the second quarter-note will have to restate the tone of the cantus firmus or supply any missing interval of the delayed triad, depending upon the situation; for example:

**Example 356**

Such an approach by leap to the tone demanded by the triadic concept is permitted even when the quarter-notes are in the lower voice, and regardless of which new intervals with the two upper voices (either consonant or dissonant) arise as a result of the second quarter; for example:

**Example 357**

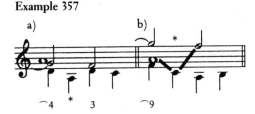

Thus neither the $^8_7$- nor the $^6_5$-setting, as they occur at the second quarter of the first and second examples, respectively, presents an obstacle to the way of writing; this shows how completely, for both effect and interpretation of the phenomenon, the only definitive element is the course of the dissonant syncope, which places the second quarter-note in the position of a passing tone in the service of the rhythm created by the half-notes, and thus reduces its value as an independent voice-leading component.

A voice leading such as the following, on the other hand:

**Example 358**

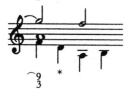

must be rejected, because the $\overset{\frown}{\underset{3}{9}}$ that appears at the first quarter would probably imply $\overset{\frown}{\underset{3}{9}}$ (in keeping with the roothood-tendency of the lowest voice)—an assumption which, however, would be contradicted with the establishment of a new harmony at the second quarter.

If one examines Examples 356 and 357 more closely, incidentally, one finds that the tones approached by leap are the same ones that the syncopating voice might incorporate as decoration even according to the strictest principles (but using a second-step rather than a seventh-leap),[8] so that here, in respect to just these tones, all that is present is only a type of *substitution* by the voice in quarter-notes for the voice in halves.

One could, if one wished, go further still and say that in these patterns, to some extent even the principles of four-voice counterpoint indirectly take effect as well, since the second quarter moves to just that interval which can be used simultaneously with the other three tones in a true four-voice setting (although, in the case of Example 357, only in the higher octave). Thus this setting of the combined species establishes convincingly that an increment in the types of movement (such as the simultaneous effect here of whole-notes, syncopes, and quarters) of itself necessarily presses toward an ever more distinct *composing out* of independent harmonic concepts: under such increasingly complicated circumstances, there is almost no other path—especially for a voice moving in quarter-notes—than that of a more comprehensive composing out of the one sound.

2. In the case of $\overset{\frown}{3} \mid \overset{-4}{-2}$, a leap makes it possible to add 5 or 6 [respectively] after the fact, for example:

**Example 359**

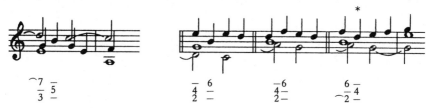

It is clear that a leap to the third below can be made in the case of $-\overset{6}{5}$:

**Example 360**

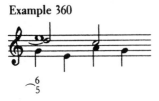

Yet even an ascending third-leap, which retrieves the interval still lacking from the seventh chord, may be no less admissible:

**Example 361**

since the-$\frac{4}{3}$-setting at the second quarter (such as the sound marked with an asterisk in Example 359) has an effect completely different from that of the same setting on the downbeat (see above, Example 330). The difference between such a technique, which merely retrieves the missing interval in $\widehat{\phantom{7}}\frac{7}{5}$ | $\overset{\frown}{\phantom{4}}\frac{4}{2}$ | $\frac{6}{5}$, and those mentioned above by Fux and Albrechtsberger (Example 335 [bars 2 and 5] and Example 370 [bar 3]), however, is clear: in the first case it is a matter of supplying a missing interval, but in the second, of the addition of a superfluous interval, which is rendered harmless only by virtue of the passing character. The tone approached by leap in Examples 359–361 could just as well be used on the downbeat itself as a fourth voice.

### §16.   *The law of the third quarter-note*

Concerning the consonant or dissonant character of the interval between the second half-note and the third quarter, the principles of the second chapter are decisive. Accordingly, here too, both possibilities are admissible; for example:

**Example 362**
Bellermann, p. 233

a)

b)

It follows that even this, for example:

**Example 363**

would not be objectionable. In the last example, it is only a result of the passing motion, which encompasses the second through fourth quarters, that the resolution of the dissonant syncope appears to enter too early; in truth, its rhythm remains the same as in every regular case. The difference in comparison to Example 355, however, can easily be understood.

### §17.  *More exact definition of the concept of leaping passing tone*

We recall from Chapter 1, A, §3, how the nature of a leaping passing tone was there determined by the predominant effect of a simultaneously entering dissonant passing tone. And likewise here, where a syncope is incorporated into the combination, a stronger law—the law of the syncope-rhythm—becomes definitive for the interpretation of a leaping quarter-note as merely a passing tone. So long as the dissonant syncope has not yet been resolved, an independent interpretation of the relationship of the second quarter to the syncope is irrelevant (as was already said in §15), and it is rather as though even the leaping interval were nothing but a true passing tone or a true neighboring note (by second). Therefore at a in the following example:

**Example 364**

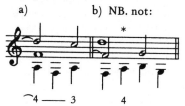

the second quarter, in spite of the fact that it is consonant with the other two voices, by no means cancels the dissonant character of ⌒4—3, just as the leap to the second quarter in Examples 360 and 361 effects no further modification in principle of the syncope established by the downbeat, so that despite the third-leap, even at the second quarter the setting remains only a $-\frac{6}{3}$ [or $-\frac{6}{4}$] syncope-setting. Such an interpretation of the leaping tone carries with it also the fact that at the second quarter, in passing, not only the setting $-\frac{4}{3}$ (see Examples 359 and 361[9]) must be considered admissible, but also, for example:

**Example 365**

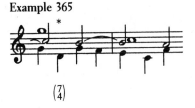

$\left(\dfrac{7}{4}\right)$

since here as well, the dissonant relationship of the second quarter is no more a matter of any consequences at all than in examples such as 356 and 357.

It is clear: under the influence of a stronger law which establishes the passing event with absolute precision—the influence, that is, of the dissonant passing half-notes in Chapter 1 and of a dissonant syncope in this chapter—even a leap, whether to a consonant or a dissonant tone, is assimilated into the primary effect as a passing event.

In comparison to the phenomena of the first chapter, here the leaping passing tones with $^-\begin{smallmatrix}7\\5\end{smallmatrix}$ | $-\begin{smallmatrix}4\\2\end{smallmatrix}$ | $-\begin{smallmatrix}6\\5\end{smallmatrix}$ in particular count as a significant extension of the concept. Specifically, by adding a fourth interval to these sonorities, in spite of the given tying they not only promote the independent value of these settings as seventh-chords more emphatically than was heretofore possible, but they show also how composing out takes on ever broader dimensions, and how, from a purely voice-leading standpoint, that which the theory of harmony calls an "arpeggiation" of the chord must, even despite the leap ("arpeggiation"), be counted only as a mere passing tone when a stronger law so decrees.

It can be judged only according to the particular circumstances, however, whether the neighboring note (see above, Examples 347 and 348), because of the greater pliability of its motion by second, can serve better than a leaping passing tone.

The appropriate example by *Fux* (Table XXVI, Figure 2), which, however, does not represent a true combined-species exercise, was already cited above under A., §10, Example 335. The leaping passing tones in bars 2 and 5 [of that example] also have already been discussed in the preceding text, in §15.

Similarly, the leaping passing tone in *Albrechtsberger's* exercise (see below, Example 370), which is found at the conclusion of the fifth species of three-voice counterpoint (pp. 119–120), was discussed as well in the same context.

*Bellermann* is the only one among the teachers who makes an effort also to approach the issues of the current combination in an explanatory way where possible (p. 229ff.). But his account is set forth in such a circuitous manner that it seems to digress into completely different issues, and one runs the risk of overlooking the heart of the matter—which can indeed be found in his explanations. Thus first of all he is correct to approve under 1 as a possibility the use at the second quarter of a regular passing dissonance or a nota cambiata. But it already sounds misleading when he states, immediately afterward under 2:

It is a different matter, however, when a note other than a passing tone is used from the first to the second quarter; in most—if not all—such cases, this involves a leap to the second quarter. Then this second quarter must either be consonant with the other two voices (that is, with both the cantus firmus and the tied dissonance), as here:[10]

**Example 366**

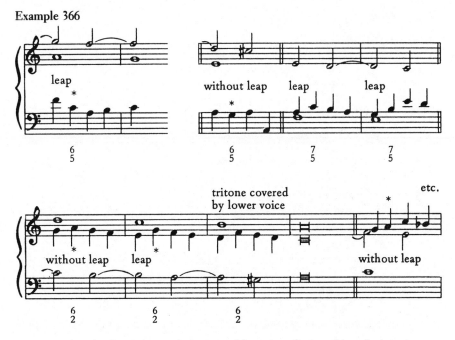

**tritone covered by lower voice**

or it must take the unison or the octave of the cantus firmus, although the voice in question thereby leaps to an interval that forms a dissonance with the tied half-note, as here:

**Example 367**

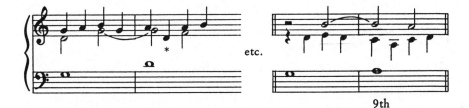

9th

Example E [i.e., the last], on the other hand, cannot be recommended as a model. In the case of a ninth, it is better to avoid the octave or unison of the cantus firmus at the second quarter, because the interval of the ninth, according to the stricter rule, may be dissonant only in relation to the bass.

And on p. 231, Bellermann writes:

Along with these rules that require strict observation, however, a liberty is permitted of which I can, to be sure, cite no example in Palestrina, but which occurs very early, and is freely used later by the composers of the seventeenth century, and subsequently by Bach and Handel, among others. This liberty consists in the following: when the fourth stands on the strong beat in one of the upper voices and is accompanied only by the octave of the lower voice, as in the second bars of two following examples a and b:

**Example 368**

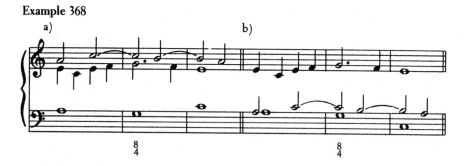

the voice that sings the quarter-notes can make a descending fourth-leap—that is, it can leap at the second quarter of the bar to the seventh (a) or the second (b) of the tied dissonance, at the same time arriving at the fifth of the bass, as here:

**Example 369**

When the quarter-notes lie in the bass, the fourth-leap obviously is not permitted, because through it we would reach the lower fourth of the cantus firmus, and thus a new dissonance.

How much more simply and at the same time more comprehensibly all of this could have been said if Bellermann had merely set forth the requirements (as I have done in the above text) that he imposes on the second quarter as what they really are—in particular, if he had represented the leap [at the second quarter] as a leap to one of the tones belonging to a triad or seventh-chord. He would thereby have been spared so many a contradiction—for example, describing the nota cambiata sometimes, as on p. 229, as covered by the "familiar rules," but other times, as on p. 230 (see Example 366 here), failing to recognize it as such, and instead suddenly placing it under a completely different, false concept ("a note other than a passing tone"—see the above quotation); or, to take another example, allowing on the one hand that the leap may also be to a note that is dissonant with the tied half-note (see the part of the quotation preceding Example 367), but on the other hand, as can be seen from the concluding portion of the excerpt quoted here—which involves precisely the setting $\frac{4}{3}$ $^{11}$—, rejecting a dissonance against the cantus firmus.

Finally, mention should be made once again of a cadential formula used by Bellermann in an exercise on p. 234 (*Cpt. I*, p. 319).

## Exercises

**Example 370**

Albrechtsberger, p. 119-120

Cherubini, Ex. 114

**Example 370** *continued*

Bellermann, p. 232

Bellermann, p. 232-233

**Example 370** *continued*

H. Schenker

5.

H. Schenker

6.

H. Schenker

7.

**Example 370** *continued*

## E. *Four-Voice Counterpoint:* One Counterpoint Each of the First, Third, and Fourth Species:

### §18. *The inaccessibility of $\frac{6}{3}$ in this combination-type*

All that need be recalled here is that, because of the counterpoint in whole-notes, the complete setting $-\frac{6}{3}$ (see above, §12) is found to be inaccessible; this does not, however, exclude the possibility of using that syncope with a sixth-doubling: $-\frac{66}{5}$.

### Exercises

**Example 371**

H. Schenker

**Example 371** *continued*

H. Schenker

## F.  *Four-Voice Counterpoint:* **One Counterpoint Each of the Second, Third, and Fourth Species:**

§19.  $-\frac{6}{3}$ *is accessible*

In the present combination, on the other hand, because of the half-notes, $-\frac{6}{3}$ is again possible.

*Fux* shows such a combination-type on p. 138 of his (Latin) original edition (see below, Example 375, Exercise 1).

*Albrechtsberger* offers (after the conclusion of the fifth species of four-voice counterpoint, as said earlier) two exercises of this type, which he follows up in Chapter 33 (entitled "Examples with Cantus Firmi in Strict Counterpoint," devoted, like the chapter preceding, to five-voice counterpoint) with a similar five-voice exercise. These three exercises are included below in Example 375 as exercises 2–4.

*Cherubini* cites in Example 126, p. 53, the example by Fux (this time naming the latter explicitly), but changes the cadence as follows:[12]

**Example 372**
Cherubini

That is, at the third quarter, instead of Fux's consonance, he places a passing dissonance, and without regard to the cross-relation (here certainly inadmissible) between *f* of the third quarter and *f♯* at the downbeat of the closing bar. He comments, moreover, that "the voice that has the quarter-notes cannot begin otherwise than with a quarter-rest, for example:

**Example 373**
Ex. 127

Alto

and the voice that has the half-notes can begin only after a rest of one and one-half bars, to give the entrance of that voice more elegance:"

**Example 374**
Ex. 128

Soprano

*Bellermann* concludes the syncopated species of four-voice counterpoint with the present combination-type, and gives three examples of it on p. 263ff.; the first of these repeats Fux's example (used already by Cherubini). Bellermann comments in general: "This is indeed a very difficult, but altogether necessary and useful exercise," and in particular, concerning the final exercise:

> The circumstance that the bass has the syncopes makes the exercise still more difficult, because the use of the dissonances in this voice is more restricted than in the upper voice. For example, the inversion of the ninth—that is, the seventh [in the bass] that resolves to an octave (see above, p. 197[13])—is prohibited, and the second that resolves to a third must, where possible, be accompanied by the sixth and fourth if the setting is not to sound all too sparse. In view of the difficulties, in the next two examples the steady course of the half-notes in the alto voice is interrupted in two places by syncopes.

# Exercises

### Example 375

Fux

1.

Albrechtsberger, p. 153

2.

**Example 375** *continued*

Albrechtsberger, p. 154

"license"

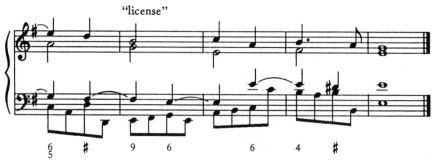

**Example 375** *continued*

Albrechtsberger, p. 376

4.

c. f.

"license"

Bellermann, p. 264

5.

**Example 375** *continued*

$$\begin{smallmatrix}9\\3\ 3\end{smallmatrix}$$

Bellermann, p. 265

6.

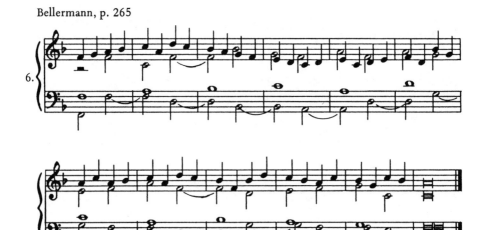

## G.   *Four-Voice Counterpoint:* Two Counterpoints of the Third Species and One of the Fourth:

c. f.

### §20.   *Renewed application of the principles of setting quarter-notes*

Since in this combination-type two counterpoints use quarter-notes, the principles set forth in chapter 2, D–G, again govern their setting.

## Exercise

**Example 376**
H. Schenker

## H.  *Three-Voice Counterpoint:* Two Counterpoints of the Fourth Species:

### §21.  *Impossibility of working out such a problem*

The working out of such an exercise founders on the double constraint of the cantus firmus on the one hand and the syncopes on the other; for even if it were possible now and again somehow to coordinate the syncopes in thirds or sixths, equally often a continuation of the syncopes would nevertheless be made suddenly impossible by the movement of the cantus firmus. As easy as it is to convince oneself of this by a hasty attempt, it is equally important to derive from this effort a deepened understanding of the principle, set down at the beginning of this chapter, that in any syncopation-exercise, the matter of concern above all is the two-voice setting of the syncopated voice and the low voice, while this setting does not therefore always have to be at the same time the fundamental one of the outer voices. Accordingly, one understands that two syncopating voices would have to form a contradiction to that two-voice setting [between the lowest voice and a single syncopating voice], and that their continuing competition can only cripple the motion of both; one recognizes that a coupling of two syncopes presupposes above all the disappearance of any *requirement* of simultaneous syncopation; the only opportunity at all for such a thing would be presented by an exercise like that of the mixed (fifth) species in two voices (see below, Chapter 4), or by the omission of the cantus firmus altogether.

# Chapter 4

# Incorporation of the Fifth Species into the Combinations

§1. *On the stylistic limitations in general of an incorporation of the fifth species*

The mixed species, as we already know from three- and four-voice counterpoint, admits several counterpoints of the first species in whole-notes, in which case the extra voices signify what might be called mere chordal extensions of the cantus-firmus tone, whose rhythm in whole-notes is exactly the one that they share; on the other hand, it may be described as a stylistic contradiction to add to a counterpoint of mixed species other counterpoints of different species—for example, the second, third, or fourth species. Such combinations—such as that of the second and fifth species, or the third and fifth species (in three-voice counterpoint)—are indeed possible, but the possibility of their execution, of which anyone can most easily become convinced, offers no proof against the contradiction, which is chiefly to be found in the fact that the mixed species, by including and mixing within itself all other species, from the outset expresses a degree of freedom and variety that cannot fail to cause the monotonous constraint of half-notes, quarter-notes, or syncopes in the remaining counterpoints to appear only as an inconvenient and pointless opposition. Where a voice already moves with such freedom as is bestowed by the fifth species even in the company of a cantus firmus, the remaining counterpoints, if they do not set out simply to support the rhythm of the cantus firmus in whole-notes, may well use exactly the same kinds of liberties. In the following discussion, then, let us consider only demonstrations of combined-species exercises in which the mixed species appears in at least two voices.

§2. *The combination of two or three counterpoints of the fifth species, and the first possibility of simultaneous syncopes*

A four-voice exercise with, for example, one counterpoint of the first species and two counterpoints of the fifth already shows the possibility of the simultaneous occurrence of two syncopes.

Observe how already the execution of two counterpoints of the mixed species imposes the need for a constant alternation and completion in the rhythms of the counterpoints, and thus achieves a colorfully animated propulsion (see below, Example 378, Exercise 1).

But especially in a four-voice exercise with three counterpoints of the mixed species, all constraint already appears to have vanished, and if it were not for the tones of the cantus firmus, one could imagine that one were already in the domain of free composition (see Example 378, Exercise 2).

On the other hand the polyphonic examples by Cherubini just cited disclose no rational ground for the author's having restricted himself to a cantus firmus at all.

In *Albrechtsberger* (p. 143), we find among others the following example:

**Example 377**

This could, if one wished, be regarded as a fragment of an exercise with two counterpoints of the mixed species.

## Exercises

**Example 378**

Cherubini, p. 54, Ex. 130

**Example 378** *continued*

Cherubini, p. 54, Ex. 131

2.

c. f.

Cherubini, p. 57, Ex. 134

3.

**Example 378** *continued*

Cherubini, p. 57, Ex. 134

Cherubini, p. 58, Ex. 135

**Example 378** *continued*

Cherubini, p. 59, Ex. 136

# An Instance of Tying from a Dissonance

## §1.  General aspects

While two-voice counterpoint still had no authority whatever to permit a voice leading such as, for example:

**Example 380**

for the specific reason that the cantus firmus was not allowed to remain in the same place for two bars (see Part 1, Chapter 2, §3), three-voice counterpoint, to the extent that one decides to allow a dissonance at the upbeat under certain circumstances to count as preparation for the following dissonance, makes at least possible a voice leading such as the following:

**Example 381**

## §2.  The prerequisites of such a phenomenon

The special prerequisites of this new phenomenon are the following:
1.  it requires two full bars;
2.  the low voice in these two bars must sustain, which by itself suggests that it is not this voice that carries the cantus firmus;
3.  the cantus firmus must therefore be in the one other voice (whether the upper or the lower [of the remaining two]) that moves in whole-notes;
4.  the progression  is unconditionally requisite, which also suggests that, by virtue of its tying along with a cantus firmus, this case would in a certain sense be classified in the fourth (syncopated) species.

258

### §3.  *Explanation of the individual characteristics of the concept*

The following may serve as explanation of the individual characteristics of this concept.

It is a violation of the rule of strict counterpoint here that the $\frac{6}{4}$-dissonance of the upbeat also serves as preparation of the next dissonance on the downbeat. This, then, is also the reason I neglected to introduce the above phenomenon, in spite of the syncope-constraint, already in the syncopated species of three-voice strict counterpoint. It by no means belongs to strict counterpoint (far less even than the ottava battuta and nota cambiata); rather, if—for the sake of tradition—it is even to be considered in the theory of counterpoint, it belongs conceptually among the transitional forms to free composition; decisive in this above all is the fact that among its prerequisites must be included the appearance on the downbeat of the $-\frac{6}{4}$-setting, which, however, we have learned to produce only in the combined species (Part 6, first section, Chapter 3, §3). (It is not unimportant to keep in mind here that any other opening, such as one with $\overset{\frown}{\phantom{}}\frac{7}{3}$ or $\overset{\frown}{\phantom{}}\frac{7}{3}$, cannot possibly lead to our figure, so long as the cantus firmus and whole-notes in the third voice are to be retained.)

But it should not be overlooked that for the rest, both the entrance into and the exit from this two-bar entity otherwise run their course completely in keeping with the principles of strict counterpoint, in that only consonances are used both for the preparation of $-\frac{6}{4}$ and for the resolution of $-\frac{5}{4}$. Thus at least beginning and end of the figure appear as regularly constructed pillars, which can the more easily bear the burden of the voice leading that runs an irregular course between them.

Further, the constraint of using syncopes must be taken into account here as well, since it can be attributed to their urgency that on the upbeat, as an exception—just because it cannot be otherwise—, even the dissonant $\frac{6}{4}$-syncope is admitted. (In free composition, too, the compulsion of a previously introduced rhythm sometimes imposes demands on the continuation which, in the absence of such compulsion, could not make their effect with such conviction.)

If we recall that the syncope $-\frac{6}{4}$ would have had to cause the bass to move ahead at the upbeat (see Part 6, Chapter 3, §3), we understand that just by sustaining, the bass places itself in conflict with the principles governing $-\frac{6}{4}$, so that sustaining here takes on a significance completely different from that of the tone-repetition otherwise freely permitted for counterpoints in whole-notes. Thus understood, it is really the bass alone that truly bears the responsibility for the irregularity of our figure, and not, as might be assumed on first reflection, the resolution of the fifth to the fourth and the tying of the latter, which is, rather, merely a consequence of the bass's act of sustaining. (Our intuition is privy to the fact that a voice counterpointing in whole-notes may under certain circumstances also sustain; it is only for this reason that the bass, the truly responsible party,—although strictly speaking it should not sustain—succeeds in shifting the blame to the syncopated voice.) Consistent

## §6.   The dissonant nature of ⁶₄ nevertheless remains unchanged

One should not be deceived by the use of ⁶₄ on the upbeat under the prerequisites described, however, into believing, as so many pedagogues assume, that this setting would have the power to make an exception and alter or cancel the dissonant nature of the fourth—that is, to transform the fourth back into a consonance for these cases; rather, it remains true that even this fourth is to be regarded as a dissonance. For if ⁶₄ were truly consonant in this context, then any other desired path could be taken in departing from it; this is not at all the case, however, since the subsequent path is under all circumstances restricted only to ⁵₄‾₃. From this, therefore, we clearly infer that we are dealing here with a phenomenon still completely alien to strict counterpoint—specifically, the realization of a single intent within the space of two bars, which, exactly for that reason, presupposes the participation of the fourth on the upbeat as a driving, motivating dissonance, but which does not, on the contrary, certify it as a consonance. It is as though the very inner nature of the dissonance refused to tolerate the lie of a transformation into a consonance, and as though the dissonance-content of the fourth had to be continued in a new dissonance at the downbeat and prolong its effectiveness in that dissonance before finding ultimate liberation in the consonance of the next upbeat.

Free composition in fact interprets Example 382 (and also 381) as an accented-passing-tone phenomenon—approximately as follows:

**Example 386**

—and, accordingly, we grasp the weight that burdens this voice leading.

## §7.   The decisive, fundamental significance of the above voice-leading settings

By far the most important result to which we are led by the above phenomena, however, remains, in a fundamental respect, the following: they show us for the first time—and, indeed, still in the presence of a cantus firmus—the possibility (1) that in spite of dissonance, a tie can be applied to a passing tone; (2) that the weight emanating from a passing tone naturally establishes from the outset the path to achievement of the ultimate goal; and (3) that in view of the cohesiveness so strongly expressed between passing tone and the long path ahead, the significance of tying as such recedes behind that of the passing tone. From the opposition inherent in a tied dissonance, one learns to understand all the more easily why strict counterpoint must adhere exclusively to a consonant preparation of the dissonant syncope as a precondition which, at least in itself (that is, considered as a consonance), is still unable to exert any kind of pressure on the subsequent voice leading (see Part 3, Chapter 4, §3).

And if the tying of a dissonance here, with the cantus firmus, is at first, to be sure, bound to stricter prerequisites (such as the origin of $-\frac{6}{5}$, the sustaining of the bass tone, and the duration of two bars), it is nevertheless possible to gain from this vantage point a view even of the increased freedom of free composition, according to which any dissonance chosen can be similarly tied, and even several such ties can occur in direct succession, and the like—especially as free composition has access to the scale degree as an entity that can guarantee the most comprehensive protection even for the most extended successions of this kind.

Still to be considered, finally, is the difference between the $\frac{6}{4}$-sound in our present configuration and a $\frac{6}{4}$-phenomenon used only in a passing manner in a combined-species setting (see Examples 285, 291,[1] etc.). While the latter is completely accounted for as a regular passing tone, the former is not *only* a passing tone, but at the same time has the meaning of the syncope-preparation of a subsequent dissonance, so that its effect is definitively concluded only with the resolution on the upbeat of the following bar.

As early as the syncopated species of three-voice counterpoint, *Fux* abruptly applies the following voice leading in the exercise of Table XI, Figure 7:

**Example 387**

[etc.]

He explains it in the text (p. 103) as follows:

> *Joseph:* I have not forgotten that the first part of the ligature would have to be a consonance; I have nevertheless used a dissonance there, partly because I see that it cannot be otherwise (since two half-beats necessarily had to be used), and partly because I recall having seen the same kind of example in the works of good masters.
>
> *Aloys:* Your doubt is laudable, since it is a witness to your attentiveness. But it does not matter if not every bar corresponds to the strictest form of the rule. For the principle you have mentioned, that the first part of the ligature would have to be a consonance, is to be understood as applying to settings in which the lowest voice moves ahead in each bar; not to those in which the lowest voice (or bass) sustains, in which latter case a ligature consisting of all dissonances not only is not faulty, but is quite beautiful, as the following example shows:

In example b, we no longer even have a fourth with the bass, but a seventh which prepares itself.

But how easy it should have been for Bellermann to derive, precisely from these examples, a conclusion pertaining to the whole issue, and an insight into the true nature of the allegedly "consonant fourth." How easy it would have been from this vantage point to grasp that the fourth used in such a manner is by no means one which "prepares itself," but is merely a simple neighboring note, which, as such, can under certain circumstances also be a seventh. There follow in Bellermann a citation from Kirnberger's *Die Kunst des reinen Satzes in der Musik* and a historical overview of the use of similar idioms by Palestrina, Orlandus Lassus, and Heinrich Isaac (with examples).

# On the Elision of a Voice as Bridge to Free Composition

### §1. *The result of elision for combination-types involving syncopes in particular*

To place the thought to be presented here in the clearest light, I shall first demonstrate it with examples of combination-types with syncopes, since they are the most suitable for this purpose. Recall, for example, the illustrations by Fux quoted in Examples 334 and 335, and delete from them the voice moving in whole notes. (That this voice does not represent a true cantus firmus and is only a more or less close approximation to one is unimportant for the present result). The elision now produces the following voice-leading pictures:

**Example 395**

It is clear that such a voice leading exceeds the limits imposed by the strict form of the rules as we know them from Parts 2 through 5; for under no circumstances can the unsyncopated voice in an exercise of the syncopated species—whether in two or in more voices—move ahead before the resolution has occurred. The correctness of the setting here is guaranteed not only by the fact that in this case we know the origin, but far more by the circumstance that we are also able—indeed compelled—to add conceptually a third voice moving in whole notes: for the treatment of the syncopes alone forces us to conclude that the setting in this form obviously is not adjusted in a completely strict way to the original concepts. In particular, our setting could not be confused with one in which it was assumed only that the values had been reduced—that is, that the half-notes basically stood for whole-notes. For even if one were to substitute larger values for the smaller ones, the course of the dissonant syncopes still would not satisfy the requirement of strict counterpoint. The course of the above setting thus points from the outset to a combination of two species, such as we encountered in Part 6, but there—note well—under the actual sponsorship of a cantus firmus (that is, a voice in whole-notes). According to the principles set forth in that context, it must therefore be clear that, just as in the original settings, the cases shown in our examples also involve the effect of an abbreviation of two processes: the complete fulfillment of the syncopation-concept and the forward movement of the bass. But of far greater importance is the inevitable conclusion that to voices moving in such a way according to the principles of two or more species, it is possible to add conceptually, without any doubt, another voice which by itself provides the first explanation of the voice leading and the foundational concepts, and which completes, clarifies, and supports the harmonies.

### §2.  How a bridge to free composition is thereby opened

The same experiment can also be made with combined-species settings without syncopes; in spite of the absence of abbreviation, which provides so much clarification, in such voice leadings as well the voice in whole-notes (the cantus firmus) can be deleted, which produces a setting for which, even without knowledge of its origin, one can nevertheless infer additional voices in whole-notes.

According to the above experiments, it is possible in some way to find a unifying tone of longer value that interprets the movement and voice leading of voices led in various rhythms; with this discovery a bridge to free composition is opened, and at the same time it is established that free composition, despite its so extensively altered appearances, is mysteriously bound by this elision, as though by an umbilical cord, to strict counterpoint. Even in free composition, a setting executed in such a way can always be supplemented by an additional voice, which, as though it were actually written down, accompanies the voices, in one position or another, only in longer values. Usually it will be supplied there by our perception, precisely in keeping with the nature of free composition, in the low register, where it provides a substructure for the upper voices and, especially, confers altered meanings upon the dissonances. Our guess is that it is the scale degrees that complete the setting in this way. The kinds of modifications that the scale degrees effect by providing such a substructure, however, can again be illustrated best of all by syncopes—for example:

**Example 396**

### §3. *Admonition against false inferences*

Even though all voice leading is founded in fundamental concepts, it is not permissible to describe a setting such as that in Example 396 as one that is directly based only on the fundamental concepts. Purity of understanding does not tolerate a view of fundamental concept and prolongation as of equal significance; rather, the fundamental concept must be understood first of all in the unconditional sense of strict counterpoint (with cantus firmus), so that its prolongation, too, can be understood in its special sense in each case.

Yet on the other hand one would commit an error also with the assumption that the elision were the "modern" way to teach and confirm the principles of counterpoint, so that exercises should be based only on scale degrees from the outset, and that accordingly, for example, a two-voice setting could be produced by appropriate abbreviation of a four-voice—that is, by the elision of two voices.[1] For the doctrine developed in my work takes as its first point of departure the fundamental concepts of voice leading, and if, after enumerating those fundamental concepts, I then proceed to teach how they are preserved even in free composition, always and everywhere—even where run-of-the-mill theory speaks only of "exceptions" and the like—my procedure is diametrically opposed to that which sets out from the beginning with the most advanced transformations of concepts, with the most extensive elisions, and precisely for that reason fails to arrive at an exact and orderly definition of the fundamental concepts in general, so that in the end a murky darkness falls over all the phenomena under consideration.

As early as the conclusion of the fifth species of four-voice counterpoint, *Fux* writes as follows:

Later, after we have in time discarded the cantus firmus, I will introduce you to imitation and to the fugue. But first it must be noted that a few dissonances, once out of the control of the cantus firmus, can also be resolved in a different way—for example, the ninth to the sixth, and the seventh to the third; and the fourth to the sixth and to the third:

**Example 397**
Fux XXI, 3

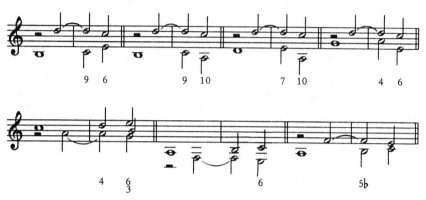

*Joseph:* Why are those resolutions used outside the cantus firmus, and not also with it?

*Aloys:* Do you not see that both parts move at the resolution? that this could not, however, occur with the cantus firmus, which remains fixed? Thus there is a difference, and it must be clearly observed that these resolutions cannot take place where oblique motion is unavoidable.

Thus Fux fails to provide any hint as to how all of the above progressions, which must without doubt be approved by all composers and teachers, are to be understood. Just to say that only the omission of the cantus firmus has made them possible is no explanation at all. Fux is not at all conscious that in all of these and similar cases, nothing more nor less than mere prolongations—arrived at by the path of abbreviations or elisions of the cantus firmus—of fundamental laws are to be found, or that, in a word, even in such phenomena of free composition the principles of strict counterpoint therefore continue to apply; this finally explains the certainly inadequate position of the master with respect to the ultimate goal of clarity and utility of his teaching, in spite of his admittedly immortal contributions, which posterity can never diminish nor erase.

*Albrechtsberger* (like Fux, within the theory of imitation[2]), p. 162ff.: "In strict counterpoint, therefore, the four dissonance-ligatures treated above can be resolved here, and also in fugues, to other consonances, when the other voice with which they are formed moves by leap and the resolution by oblique motion is not obligatory":

**Example 398**
e. g.

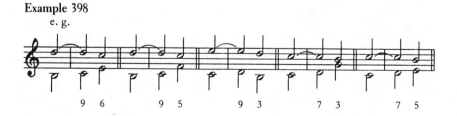

**Example 398** *continued*

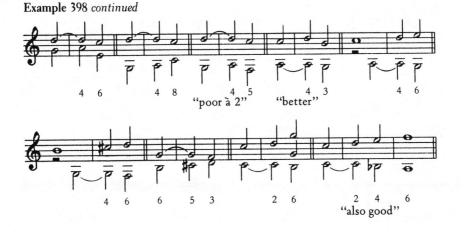

It would have been better, however, if Albrechtsberger, instead of speaking merely of a resolution with a moving lower voice, had undertaken to show how even in such settings, which may be compared to segments of combined-species exercises, voices may be conceptually added (be they upper, inner, or lower voices), by which procedure the complete unity with strict counterpoint in respect to fundamental concepts would have to appear as demonstrated. How Albrechtsberger moreover (or better: nevertheless) employed a cantus firmus even for contrapuntal exercises of free composition will be shown later, in part 7.[3]

Concerning *Bellermann*'s instruction about "resolution of dissonance with moving voices," see above, Part 6, first section, Chapter 3, §10. But for our purpose of finding a bridge to free composition and of revealing the unity of all fundamental concepts, it may be far more instructive to demonstrate, for example, the addition of a third voice to the small setting quoted in that section as Example 336:

**Example 399**

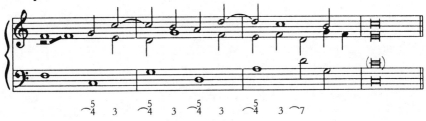

# Notes

The editor's notes and additions are enclosed in square brackets. All others are from Schenker's original text.

## Author's Preface

[1. See Appendix A, "Works of Heinrich Schenker." All citations of *Harmony, Harmonielehre, Counterpoint,* and *Free Composition* without further specification refer to Schenker's own works. Al citations of the theorists Fux, Albrechtsberger, Cherubini, and Bellermann refer to the works identified in *Counterpoint I,* Introduction, notes 1, 3, 2, and 7 respectively. See also Appendix B, "Bibliography of Works Cited."]

[2. See Appendix A, "Works of Heinrich Schenker."]

3. Compare "Von der Sendung des deutschen Genies," *Tw. I.*

[4. From "Selige Sehnsucht."]

[5. Decapitation.]

[6. "... der Menschheit 'ewig Weh und Ach, so tausendfach'...."]

[7. "Give me a place to stand...," from Archimedes' famous testimonial concerning the power of the lever.]

[8. Draft materials from this unfinished work are included in the Oster Collection at the New York Public Library for the Performing Arts.]

## Part Three, Chapter 1

[1. *Prolongiert* (see *Cpt. I,* Introduction, note 9). This term and its derivatives are encountered frequently from now on.]

[2. See especially below, p. 16.]

[3. That is, the tones that form the diminished fifth or augmented fourth now enter into relationships as thirds and sixths with the bass, and the latter relationships take priority.]

[4. This is the first of dozens of references to "II³"—that is, vol. III of *Counterpoint,* as Schenker had originally planned to designate the work we know as *Free Composition.* Since the plan of the latter work changed between 1922 and its publication in 1935, several of the titles Schenker refers to here—including the present one, "Musical Causality"—were not included in the finished work. Henceforth, where *Free Composition* does contain material relevant to the topic under discussion (even if under a different title), a specific citation has been provided; otherwise, the reference to *Free Composition* is retained, but without specific page-number or section-title citation.]

[5. The last part of this remark applies to free composition. In strict counterpoint, the only triads to be treated as consonant are those that actually are consonant; in free composition, the diminished triad, though literally dissonant, is sometimes "to be treated as consonant"—that is, to be exempted from the resolution-requirement.]

[6. *Erfordernis.* "Demand" or "requirement" would be the primary equivalents, but the actual significance here is closer to "tendency," since, as will become clear in §5, the demand is one that need not be fulfilled.]

7. In everyday life, too, a situation is not simply accepted as it is presented to us; it is also judged, and judged precisely in terms of the other possible resolutions of the situation. For example: a frail elderly person enters a streetcar and finds no seat; young, healthy passengers observe this, but pay it no heed. Indeed, this very callousness certainly provides a resolution of the situation, but we judge this resolution in the light of other possible resolutions and therefore decide against the behavior of the young passengers. It is clear, then: even in the world of social behavior there is something akin to the nature of voice leading, in which the solution actually applied is judged with reference to possible better solutions.

8. The latter type of figuring will denote, throughout this work, the doubling of the interval in question.

[9. That is, because the sixth is derived by inversion.]

[10. That is, the use of the $\frac{6}{4}$-spacing at the beginning.]

[11. The quotation relates directly to Example 9; see §14.]

[12. That is, the two complete bars of Example 14.]

[13. Or, of course, 1, in the first or last bar of an exercise. There is a potential confusion in Schenker's language concerning doubling in this section. Obviously, doubling in any polyphonic texture can be effected only through use of the unison or octave. When Schenker speaks, in the next paragraph, of "not only doubling of the octave, but also doubling of other intervals," he means "not only doubling of the lowest tone itself (by the [unison or] octave), but also doubling of tones of the upper voices."]

[14. The final version of *Free Composition* did not treat this topic.]

15. See *Counterpoint I,* p. 171, and below, §27.

[16. "Der siebente grosse Ton"—that is, the one that lies a "large" (major) seventh above the tonic.]

[17. Bars 5 and 11, respectively, of Exercise 5 (see Example 81); Schenker's quotation does not reproduce the NBs and other rubrics.]

18. Concerning the priority of perfect consonances, see part 2, Chapter 1, §21.

19. In this light, we gain a new reason for the prohibition of nonparallel similar motion—a reason that can be added to those set forth in *Counterpoint I,* p. 129ff and especially pp. 130–132. From the above account it can be understood why, in treating the matter in two-voice counterpoint, I omitted any mention of the reason based only on our inner sense of other voice-leading possibilities: such a reason become more easily identifiable only in three-voice counterpoint!

And finally, to preclude the danger that a possibility of voice leading sensed as though internally might be confused with that internally perceived interval which, as I said in *Counterpoint I,* p. 131ff., the earlier theorists invoked to justify the prohibition of so-called hidden progressions, let the distinction be formulated as follows: while the interval I designate as internally sensed appears causally determined by voice leading and harmony at the same time, the fifth (or octave) as posited by those theorists remains only a product of [their] embarassment. This may be inferred best of all from the fact that whatever the sound of the passage in question, thus even in cases like Examples 32 and 34, it is only the fifth or the octave, and no other interval, that is assumed to be hidden:

tion of the concept two different tones are required, which are also to be defined in terms of two different intervals; thus the syncope must rather be described as a phenomenon in which—to remain with the above example—the dissonant second is followed by a consonant third. For a similar linguistic reason, incidentally, so many beginners have difficulty also in understanding the concept of interval in general, in which again only one name or figure stands for the relationship of two tones. But exactly that is the profound sense, the happy fate of language: it reflects with only one word the relationship of two things to one another. How well it expresses the ultimate mystery of the syncope (to return to that phenomenon) with a usage which at first seems to contradict its nature. If we consider that the dissonant syncope really reflects a passing tone, and if we recall that the latter (see Example 90) foreshadows the concept of nodal point, acccording to which both beginning and end belong to the same horizontal harmony, then we understand that it is just this unity from which flows the effect that beginning and endpoint of the passing motion appear to merge completely, in such a way that to speak of the one is at the same time to speak of the other. Granted, in the final analysis, unity in the passing tone originates in the unity of whole triadic concept; how the triad, in spite of its tripartite nature (first, third, and fifth partials), signifies a unity unfolding in a tone remains an ineffable secret of Nature, whose trace, as we see, reverberates softly in human language as well.

[7. Schenker here again refers the reader to a "Section on the Seventh" in *Free Composition;* the relevant section of the finished work (§176), however, includes no discussion of the diminished fifth.]

[8. That is, the latter 8 would have to lie an octave below the former.]

[9. The bracketed interpolations are by the editor.]

[10. Bellermann's emphasis, not retained by Schenker.]

[11. See Example 190.]

[12. *Urlinie,* to be understood here only in a general sense.]


## Part Four, Chapter 1

[1. I.e., bass.]

[2. Cherubini's Example 117 follows here. The examples he provides show that it is not literally the unison that is meant, but rather, different registral representatives of the same pitch class.]

[3. *Viertel,* by mistake, in Mizler's German.]

[4. That is, the fourth-leap and the sixth-leap.]

[5. *Beethovens Studien.*]

[6. The alterations to 6 and 3 mean simply major sixth and minor third, not raised sixth and lowered third as would be the case in literal figured-bass terms.]


## Part Four, Chapter 2

[1. *Niederstreich* in the original, an error.]

## Part Four, Chapter 4

[1. Schenker here omits the words "while in the example under discussion, instead of the octave, the fifth is doubled."]

[2. This still does not answer the question of why doubling of the second is preferable to that of the fourth, since doubling of the second does not yield an octave at the resolution either.]

[3. The soprano's $c^2$ could equally well have been a whole-note.]

# Bridges to Free Composition

## Introductory Remarks

[1. Compare also in *Harmonielehre* the diagram on p. 204, which was not retained in *Harmony*.]

## Part Six, First Section, Chapter 1

[1. The examples given here in §2 do not always abide by this restriction, however. Example 272, which is correct and fully strict voice leading, shows a dissonant inner voice at the second half-note together with a consonant upper voice (a sixth). The same applies to the fourth illustration in Example 270, which is also legitimate voice leading. The real distinction between the strict construction and the less strict (see §3) is that in the former, if the upbeat is dissonant, then *both* half-note voices must move by step in a single direction, while in the latter, one of them may, under certain circumstances, proceed by leap.]

[2. Certain possibilities of a related kind do exist even in strict counterpoint—for example:

C – F     G  –

Since we cannot and do not assume a dissonant ♮ at the downbeat of the first bar, a change of harmony at the upbeat is clearly indicated.]

[3. That is, such a voice leading would be quite understandable. Elsewhere (Part 2, Chapter 2, §4) Schenker excluded the neighboring note from the second species. (See also Part 3, Chapter 3, §2.)]

[4. The same might appear to hold of Example 276b, which Schenker approves; but there we can far more easily assume in retrospect a D harmony (incomplete at the downbeat) for the entire bar. This is supported especially by the fact that it is the bass whose second half-note is consonant, while in the second setting of

Example 277—which also begins with an incomplete chord—the bass is dissonant, and only the inner voice would be assigned the responsibility of completing a harmony merely implicit at the downbeat. It is clear that Example 276b is more transparent in effect than either setting of Example 277, and such transparency is the governing criterion for judging the virtual infinitude of possible situations that arise in the combined species.]

[5. Or, more exactly, harmony.]

[6. This is not discussed in detail in *Free Composition*. Relevant examples there include Fig. 50, 2, 3.]

## Part Six, First Section, Chapter 2

[1. The setting is better interpreted as expressing 5 — 6 (divided between two voices) above the bass tone *D* in half-notes. Compare Schenker's statement at the beginning of the next paragraph, which appears to contradict his preceding remark on Example 302.]

[2. Schenker's discussion of this same setting in *Harmony*, pp. 159–160 ("satisfactory voice leading would require a full consonance at the upstroke") indicates that he changed his own position with respect to this particular combination-type between 1906 and 1922.]

## Part Six, First Section, Chapter 3

[1. Schenker's meaning is not entirely clear; all of the vertical sonorities in Example 321—on both upbeats and downbeats—have been available in three-voice strict counterpoint. His remark does, however, apply to Examples 323, 324, and 326, which are indeed the new phenomena of very special interest.]

[2. This properly applies to the first two sonorities, and not to $\frac{6}{4}$, which really does not belong in this context, and which, in any case, was already available in strict counterpoint, in the fourth species of three-voice counterpoint.]

3. I call it by that name for the sake of brevity, although the subdivision occurs only occasionally in the exercise, and therefore it does not represent a true combined-species setting.

[4. That is, advance to the study of fugue in three voices.]

[5. The situation Fux has in mind is that shown in Example 321, c; the fourth resolves to the third, while the fifth moves on to the sixth.]

[6. But see note 2 in Part 2, Chapter 2.]

[7. The effect of the seventh-chord derives from the relative harmonic independence of downbeat and upbeat in this case; Example 350, on the contrary, shows an "authentic suspension" (see p. 85), and therefore a uniformity of harmony throughout the bar.]

[8. That is, in a fifth-species elaboration of a suspension-resolution.]

[9. Only Example 361 shows the $\frac{4}{3}$ setting. The second quarters in the various settings of Example 359 do, however, exhibit the same "leaping passing tone" quality.]

10. Both here and in the continuation, I quote only excerpts from the examples.

[11. In this case the second quarter would yield $\frac{4}{3}$ only if the configuration at the first quarter were $\frac{8}{7}$.]

[12. In our copy of Fux's Latin text, the quarter-note voice appears as in Cherubini's quotation (Example 372) rather than as in Schenker's Example 375.]

[13. Bellermann's reference to his own text, although apparently incorrect; the appropriate reference would be p. 216.]

[14. The topic is not treated in *Free Composition*.]

## Part Six, Second Section

[1. These example numbers are apparently incorrect: Example 291 contains no ♮, and Example 285 only a ♮ among the upper voices. It is not clear whether Schenker means to refer to patterns like that of Example 272, which show a passing ♮ in relation to the bass, or that of Example 290, in which the upper voices move in parallel ♮-sounds.]

## Part Six, Third Section

[1. By "elision" here, Schenker probably means the amalgamation of pairs of voices into a single voice rather than simply the omission of two voices.]

[2. Fux's discussion actually occurs just before his chapter on imitation.]

[3. Schenker does not actually pursue this in *Free Composition*.]

# Appendix A

# Works of Heinrich Schenker

The following is a list of Schenker's major publications, both in the original German as well as in English editions and translations.[1] The German publications marked with an asterisk are in print.

*Ein Beitrag zur Ornamentik.* Vienna: Universal Edition, 1904.
   *New and enlarged edition, 1908. (See also under English translations.)
*Neue musikalische Theorien und Phantasien.*
   Vol. I: *Harmonielehre.* Stuttgart: Cotta, 1906. (See also under English translations.)
   Vol. II, Part I: *Kontrapunkt I.* Vienna: Universal Edition, 1910.
         Part II: *Kontrapunkt II.* Vienna: Universal Edition, 1922.
   Vol. III: *Der freie Satz.* Vienna: Universal Edition, 1935. *Second edition, edited and revised by Oswald Jonas. Vienna: Universal Edition, 1956. (See also under English translations.)
J.S. Bach. *Chromatische Phantasie und Fuge, Erläuterungsausgabe.* Vienna: Universal Edition, 1909. *Newly revised edition by Oswald Jonas. Vienna: Universal Edition, 1970. (See also under English translations.)
*Beethovens neunte Sinfonie.* Vienna: Universal Edition, 1912.
*Erläuterungsausgabe der letzten fünf Sonaten Beethovens.* Vienna: Universal Edition.
   Op. 109, published 1913.
   Op. 110, published 1914.
   Op. 111, published 1915.
   Op. 101, published 1920.
   (Op. 106 was never published.)
   *New edition of Op. 101, 109, 110, 111, revised by Oswald Jonas. Vienna: Universal Edition, 1970–71.
*Der Tonwille,* 10 issues. Vienna: A. Gutmann Verlag, 1921–24.
*Beethovens fünfte Sinfonie* (reprinted from *Der Tonwille*). Vienna: Universal Edition. (See also under English translations.)
*Das Meisterwerk in der Musik.* Munich: Drei Masken Verlag.
   *Jahrbuch I,* published 1925.
   *Jahrbuch II,* published 1926.
   *Jahrbuch III,* published 1930.
   *Photographic reprint in one volume. Hildesheim: Georg Olms Verlag, 1974. (See also under English translations.)

[1] A complete, comprehensive, carefully annotated list of Schenker's writings is to be found in David Beach, "A Schenker Bibliography" (*Journal of Music Theory* 3, no. 1 [1969]: 2–26; a revised edition has been published in *Readings in Schenker Analysis,* ed. Maury Yeston [New Haven: Yale University Press, 1977]). This bibliography also includes the most important books, monographs, and articles by other authors.

*Fünf Urlinie-Tafeln.* New York: David Mannes School, and Vienna: Universal Edition, 1932. (See also under English editions.)

*\*Brahms, Oktaven und Quinten.* Vienna: Universal Edition, 1934. (See also under English editions.)

## Editions of Music

*\*Ph. Em. Bach, Klavierwerke* (selections). Vienna: Universal Edition, 1902.

*Beethoven, Klaviersonaten: Nach den Autographen und Erstdrucken rekonstruiert von Heinrich Schenker.* Vienna: Universal Edition, 1921–23.

\*New edition, revised by Erwin Ratz. Vienna: Universal Edition, 1947. (See also under English editions.)

*Beethoven, Sonata op. 27 no. 2.* Facsimile, with an introduction by Schenker. Vienna: Universal Edition, 1921.

## English Editions and Translations

"J.S. Bach, The Largo from Sonata No. 3 for Unaccompanied Violin" (from *Das Meisterwerk in der Musik,* vol. 1). Translated by John Rothgeb. In *The Music Forum,* vol. 4. New York: Columbia University Press, 1976.

"J.S. Bach, The Sarabande of Suite No. 3 for Unaccompanied Violoncello" (from *Das Meisterwerk in der Musik,* vol. 2). Translated by Hedi Siegel. In *The Music Forum,* vol. 2. New York: Columbia University Press, 1970.

*J.S. Bach's Chromatic Fantasy and Fugue: Critical Edition with Commentary.* Translated and edited by Hedi Siegal. New York: Schirmer Books, 1984.

*Beethoven, Complete Piano Sonatas.* Reprint of the edition of 1921–23, with an introduction by Carl Schachter. New York: Dover, 1975.

"Beethoven, Fifth Symphony, First Movement." Translated by Elliott Forbes. In *Beethoven, Fifth Symphony* (Norton Critical Scores). New York: Norton, 1971.

"Brahms, Octaves and Fifths." Translated and annotated by Paul Mast. In *The Music Forum,* vol. 5. New York: Columbia University Press, 1980.

"A Contribution to the Study of Ornamentation." Translated by Hedi Siegel. In *The Music Forum,* vol. 4. New York: Columbia University Press, 1976.

*Five Graphic Music Analyses.* Photographic reprint of *Fünf Urlinie-Tafeln,* with an introduction by Felix Salzer. New York: Dover, 1969.

*Free Composition.* Translated and edited by Ernst Oster. New York: Schirmer Books, 1979.

*Harmony.* Edited and annotated by Oswald Jonas. Translated by Elisabeth Mann Borgese. Chicago: University of Chicago Press, 1954; (paperback edition) Boston: M.I.T. Press, 1973.

"Organic Structure in Sonata Form" (from *Das Meisterwerk in der Musik,* vol. 2). Translated by Orin Grossman. *Journal of Music Theory* (1968). Reprinted in *Readings in Schenker Analysis,* ed. Maury Yeston, New Haven: Yale University Press, 1977.